The Establishment of Manufacturing in Nigeria

The Establishment of Manufacturing in Nigeria

ALAN SOKOLSKI

FREDERICK A. PRAEGER, Publishers
New York · Washington · London

The purpose of the Praeger Special Studies is to make specialized research monographs in international economics and politics available to the academic, business, and government communities. For further information, write to the Special Projects Division, Frederick A. Praeger, Publishers, 111 Fourth Avenue, New York, N.Y. 10003.

FREDERICK A. PRAEGER, *Publishers*
111 Fourth Avenue, New York 3, N.Y., U.S.A.
77-79 Charlotte Street, London W. 1, England

Published in the United States of America in 1965
by Frederick A. Praeger, Inc., Publishers

Library of Congress Catalog Number: 65-18324

Printed in the United States of America

For My Mother

Pearl Herzig Sokolski

In Memoriam

ACKNOWLEDGMENTS

I am immensely grateful to all those who assisted me in every conceivable way during the conduct of the library work for this study in New York, Washington, D.C., and London, and of the field work in Nigeria.

Dean C. C. Walton of the Graduate School of Business at Columbia University, Professor William A. Hance, Chairman of the Department of Geography at Columbia and the sponsor of my research, and Professor Michael T. Florinsky of the Department of Economics at Columbia were sources of constant encouragement.

Generous financial assistance was proffered by the Eastman Kodak Business Foundation; and by the Carnegie Corporation of New York through the aegis of the Maxwell School at Syracuse University. Additional financial help in the form of accommodation was supplied by the West Africa Program of the Rockefeller Brothers Fund in Lagos. Robert I. Fleming and Ernest E. ("Monty") Montgomery of RBF untiringly offered advice, materials, and hospitality. The personnel of USAID/Nigeria, the Shell-BP Petroleum Development Company, Pfizer Products Ltd., Union Trading Company Ltd., and the United Africa Company Ltd. were of particular help in Ibadan, Port Harcourt, Aba, Enugu, and Kaduna, respectively.

Felix A. Ede, Vice-Consul of the Nigerian Consulate General in New York, was instrumental in the establishment of introductions to the Nigerian federal government. J. B. Dada of the Federal Ministry of Commerce and Industry was only the first of countless civil servants in four Nigerian governments who welcomed me, and patiently answered an endless series of questions.

I wish to acknowledge the invaluable assistance I received from Dr. and Mrs. Saul Krugman, Paul Dawson,

George David, J. Constant Mertens, Anthony H. M. Kirk-Greene, Dr. Gerard Mangone, Dr. and Mrs. Edward Marcus, Dr. Yves Maroni, Dr. R. Frodin, Dr. Richard Sklar, B. E. E. Adam, S. E. Idemudia, C. O. Chukwuaini, A. E. Igere, P. C. U. Ogugua, Mr. and Mrs. M. Brampton, E. R. Carr, Heinrich Jaggi, P. Jerome Bennett, Mr. and Mrs. Donald Marshall, Ralph Hirschtritt, Mr. and Mrs. Jack Galinas, Mr. and Mrs. Earl Stitt, and Mr. and Mrs. Irving Sokolski.

Also too numerous to cite, but individually not forgotten, are the managers of many of the modern manufacturing establishments in Nigeria, the officers of the statutory corporations, the American AID, USIS, and Embassy/Consulate officials, the staff of the *Economist* library in London, members of the business community in Nigeria and the U.S., and many, many others.

With respect to the writing stage, I note my great appreciation for the helpful suggestions of Thomas R. Goethals, Professor Arthur R. Burns, and Professor Charles F. Stewart. I wish also to extend my thanks to Professors Eli Ginzberg, Herman F. Otte, and Ian M. Matley, all also of Columbia University, and to Dr. Schuyler D. Hoslett of the University of Hawaii. Mrs. Shirley Lerman prepared the different drafts of the manuscript. I wish, once again, to acknowledge my special indebtedness to Dr. Hance.

My wife, Carol, has more than earned a line of her own. Her contributions were vital to the success of this venture.

CONTENTS

Page

LIST OF TABLES

Table		Page

Table		Page

LIST OF MAPS

PREFACE

This work focuses upon one aspect of the economic growth of a new nation-state in West Africa, the Federal Republic of Nigeria.

Manufacturing has been an interest of the writer since his days as an undergraduate mechanical-engineering student. It developed into an especial interest during the period 1956-60, when he practiced this profession. His doctoral research year at Columbia University (1961-62) presented him with the opportunity to examine the establishment of modern industry in Nigeria, the most populous country on the African continent.

During the field trip, the writer gathered extensive material, much of which is of a statistical nature. For the large part these consist of official reports of the various ministries, statutory corporations, development corporations, marketing boards, statistical offices, and other agencies of government. In addition, use is made of the national income study (1950-57) by E. F. Jackson of Oxford and Dr. P. N. C. Okigbo, Economic Adviser to the Prime Minister of Nigeria. Their estimates, based on both production and expenditure, were extrapolated through 1960 by Drs. W. Stolper, L. Hansen, and E. O. Iwuagwu of the Federal Ministry of Economic Development. The first two named, it might be added, were Ford Foundation economists who occupied advisory positions in the Ministry during the years 1960-62. Stolper *et al.* estimated gross capital formation by type of capital as well as evaluating subsistence activities. Of course, at this stage, they could be calculated only indirectly and roughly. Yet, the U.S. Economic Mission to Nigeria in its report of June 17, 1961, to H. R. Labouisse, Director of the President's Task Force on Foreign Economic Assistance, stated, "There is little doubt that their [Stolper *et al.*] estimates rank among the best for underdeveloped countries with similar economic structure."

The writer realizes that many of these figures should be used with caution. There are gaps in the available statistics. For example, the Eastern and Northern Regions have no departments of statistics, and the one for the Western Region is of recent date. Moreover, some of what is presented may be of questionable accuracy. What is used herein, however, is the best available information. Furthermore, because modern manufacturing industry contributes so little to the GNP, the figures quoted, even if they are not completely accurate, are relevant since they place the industrial sector in its proper position vis-a-vis the rest of the economy. The conclusions arrived at are not directly dependent on specific statistics. Therefore, throughout, they should be considered primarily as qualitative and descriptive in nature, representing relative magnitudes and trends rather than quantitative absolutes.

The World Bank, in a comprehensive study of the Nigerian economy in 1954, put the contribution of industry (in 1952-53) at 10.5 per cent of the gross domestic product. The Bank, however, used the term industry very broadly to include not only manufacturing but handicraft production, construction, and power production. Alternatively, Professor Stolper, using a narrower definition, calculated a figure of 1.5 per cent for 1960. This, then, is a matter of definition that should be resolved.

Many towns in Nigeria, proud of their handicrafts, "the embodiment of African traditional skill,"[1] cater to a larger-than-local market. Benin City, capital of the new Mid-West Region, specializes in wood carving, brass,[2] and silver working; Kano in the Northern Region is noted for leather working, metal working, and hand-colored prints; and Ikot Ekpene in the Eastern Region pursues rope and mat-making. This list could be extended manyfold. Weaving, for instance, is an occupation in many sections, notably the North. In 1851 the German explorer Heinrich Barth visited Kano, and was quite impressed by the homemade cloth, as well as by the manufacture of sandals. Today, even with the advent of large integrated textile mills, weavers continue to be important suppliers for the textile market.

This book, however, being limited to modern manufacturing, will not treat craft production. The researcher who deals with traditional handicrafts would find that statistics are either lacking or particularly inadequate, that these crafts are often primitive, and so, from a statistical standpoint, are usually associated with national income data for agriculture.

Related to the traditional crafts are the simple, individual operations of a manufacturing nature carried on in urban centers. For example, there are the "tailors" with their Singer sewing machines who are omnipresent in the markets and side streets of every town and city in the country. Still, relatively few of these have grouped together to form the cottage industries so common to Japan. As an observer of the West African scene, J. I. Roper, has remarked, "[urban] handicraft production shows no marked tendency towards the division of labor in larger workshops and factories. The individual handicraftsman remains dominant. This is true even in shoemaking and garment making, for example, which are suitable for team working."[3] So, as with traditional crafts, numerous problems face the researcher who would discuss these "modern" crafts.

In this study, manufacturing will be taken as synonymous with the term modern manufacturing industry. It will exclude mining (but not ore processing or smelting); handicrafts; construction; power production; and plantation cultivation, cattle raising, fishing, and forestry (but not any process associated with them on a factory scale, e.g., slaughtering and meat-packing). In conformity with the definition of the United Nations Statistical Office, repair work, the manufacture of carbonated mineral waters, baking, printing, and assembly operations will be considered to fall within the limits of manufacturing.[4]

With respect to terminology, the old West African pound (£), the Nigerian £, and the £ Sterling each equals $2.80; the references to annual periods or to overlapping periods, e.g., 1952-53, other than calendar years, are to fiscal years commencing on April 1; and tons and gallons, unless otherwise noted, are respectively long tons (2,240 lb.) and imperial gallons (277.42 cu. in., or slightly less than 1.25 U.S. standard gallons).

In the years since my field trip, I have been able to continue gathering data. The present text is, basically, an updated version of the manuscript submitted to Columbia University in partial fulfillment of the requirements for the degree of Doctor of Philosophy. It was cleared for publication by the Board of Governors of the Federal Reserve System for whom I worked in 1962 and 1963. I have since been employed by another agency of the U.S. Government and have once more had the opportunity to visit Nigeria. In no case, however, do the views expressed herein necessarily represent the views of the Board of Governors of the Federal Reserve System or any other department or agency of the U.S. Government.

Footnotes to Preface

1. United Nations, Department of Economic and Social Affairs, Economic Survey of Africa Since 1950 (New York, 1959), p. 69.

2. "Benin is well known throughout the world for its bronze castings of obas [kings], leopards, horsemen, birds, serpents and Portuguese soldiers. Unfortunately, most of those bronzes now lie in museums outside Nigeria. The craft is still carried on in the brass-workers' quarter and in a co-operative workshop." (James Grant, A Geography of Western Nigeria [Cambridge: Cambridge University Press, 1960], p. 59.)

3. J. I. Roper, Labour Problems in West Africa (London: Penguin Books Ltd., 1958), p. 7. The Asian lesson has not been lost on the Nigerian leaders. Premier S. L. Akintola of the Western Region has

expressed the hope that India would be able to help Western Nigeria in the establishment of village industries, and the Eastern Nigerian Government has decided on the Oji River area as a test area for the pilot establishment of cottage industries.

4. "Manufacturing is defined as the mechanical or chemical transformation of inorganic or organic substances into new products whether the work is performed by power-driven machines or by hand, . . . whether the products are sold at wholesale or retail. The assembly of component parts of manufactured products is considered manufacturing except in cases where the activity is appropriately classified in group 400 [construction]." (United Nations, Statistical Office, Indexes to the International Standard Industrial Classification of All Economic Activities [Statistical Papers, Series M, No. 4, Rev. 1, Add. 1; New York, 1959], p. 22.)

PART I

BACKGROUND OF A NEW NATION

CHAPTER 1 THE SUBJECT AND ITS SETTING

In 1961 the United States pledged $225 million to the 1962-68 development program of a new nation in sub-Sahara Africa. An American Trade Mission returned with glowing reports. Said one Mission member, "Some participation by Americans and others in know-how and capital could produce an industrial belt . . . similar to that of Pittsburgh, Cleveland, Detroit, and Chicago in the United States."[1] The Director of the West African Program of the Rockefeller Brothers Fund said he was "privileged to live in what I believe to be the happiest corner of Africa."[2] A former Chairman of the Tennessee Valley Authority and the U.S. Atomic Energy Commission wrote that this country is "different."[3] This country is the Federal Republic of Nigeria.

A relatively short time ago, on October 1, 1960, while the Lagos skies were brilliantly illuminated by scores of dancing fireworks, large, populous, agrarian, tropical Nigeria assumed the mantle of freedom. Only one year later, the United States promised large sums of money to her; and many businessmen, foundation executives, and development consultants saw in her a great new vista. What Great Britain hath wrought will be answered indirectly, as this book focuses on Nigeria's modern manufacturing industry.

Has Nigeria untapped natural and human resources that can be utilized in forging an industrial society? Or is Nigeria, by virtue of the present structure of her economy and the numerous political, social, and economic difficulties being encountered, not so malleable? An American or European often looks at Nigeria in terms of his own country's growth, and he may see in Nigeria a frontier because he believes there are none left in his own land. In turn, the Nigerian leader may view Nigeria through the eyes of the foreigner, thus visualizing a blueprint for rapid industrial development. An appraisal of Nigerian industry should separate the realistic from the visionary.

This work will attempt to ascertain the role, nature, and extent of modern manufacturing industry in Nigeria and assess its prospects in terms of the obstacles and opportunities that are indigenous to Nigeria. In order to meet these objectives, we shall study her resources, infrastructure, markets, and finances. We shall also examine the rationality of current industrial development, the position of modern manufacturing in the present Nigerian economy, and the influence of the five Nigerian governments as they attempt to promote industry.

So, this book not only will examine those sectors of the economy, and those factors that relate to the establishment of modern manufacturing, but also will consider, in some detail, eight industries that epitomize many of the opportunities and limitations faced by Nigerian modern industry in the early 1960's.

The writer hopes that this study will reveal, to some extent, the potentials for the growth of manufacturing in Nigeria. And in a broader framework, the author believes that, by studying the endeavor to transmute the possible into the actual, a lesson of value may be learned that is relevant to other newly independent African countries.

NIGERIA'S STAKE IN INDUSTRIALIZATION

Manufacturing facilities, during the past two decades, have been erected in Nigeria at an ever increasing pace. Yet, it is felt by many in Nigeria that the limited status of manufacturing in the overall economy typifies Nigeria's backwardness and dependence on others, Britain in particular. Thus, of many problems facing the Republic--specifically, the

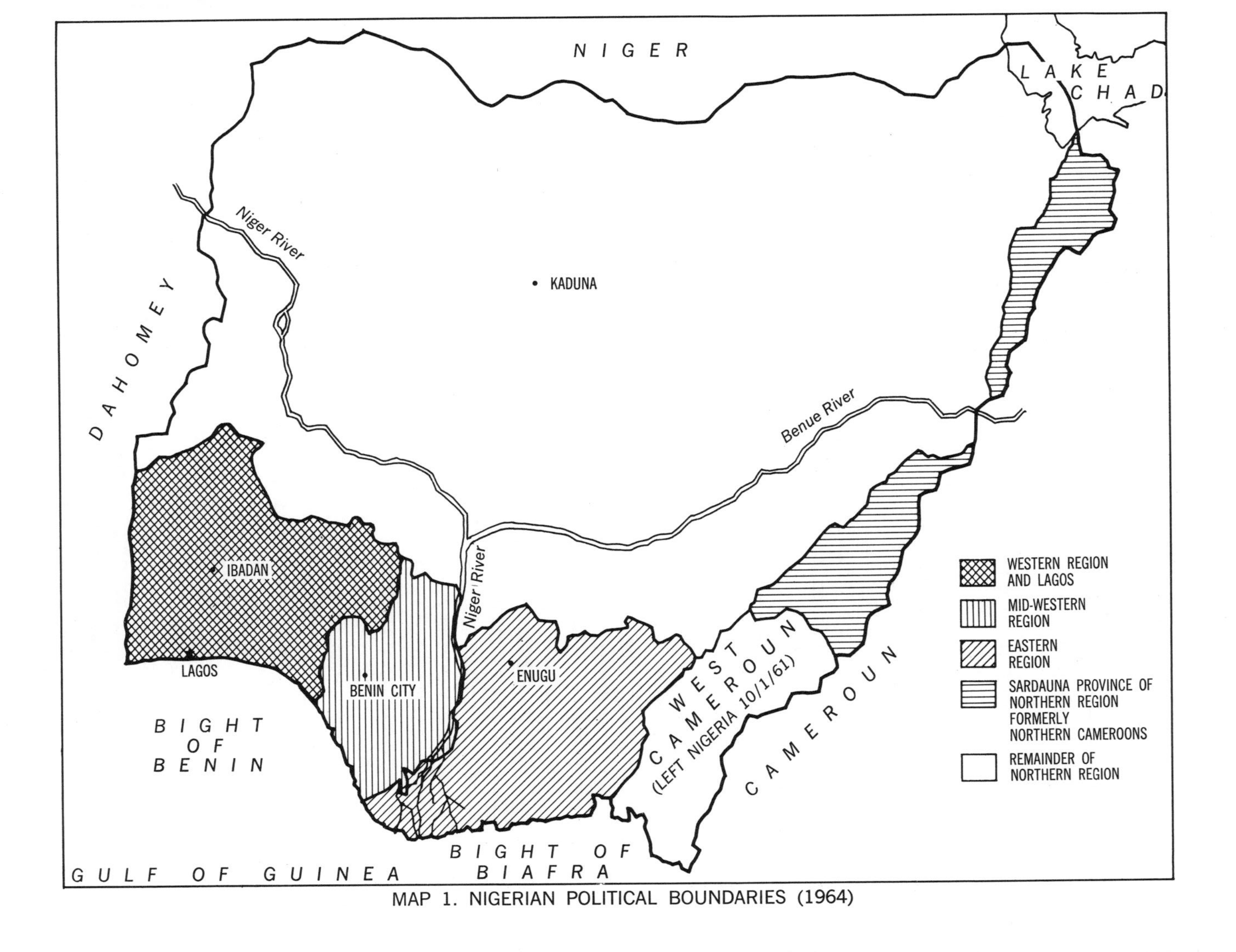

MAP 1. NIGERIAN POLITICAL BOUNDARIES (1964)

maintenance of internal stability, the achievement of national unity, and the modification of traditional social systems--"the problem of how to put an end to centuries of poverty and ensure decent living standards is one of key importance."[4]

A change from the status quo is what the Nigerian has in mind when he talks of economic independence. To the Nigerian, economic independence also means that political independence will be worthwhile, that his country will no longer be dependent on the export of primary products, agricultural and mineral. This state of affairs, rightly or wrongly, he equates with the old colonial system. Therefore, this new nation-state, like so many others, is striving to increase her national wealth rapidly. The process of industrialization is viewed as one means to this end.

It is eminently understandable for Nigerians to postulate that their manufacturing industry should be broadened. They believe that many benefits to the economy will be realized: additional employment, especially for the urban dwellers; acceleration of the growth of national income, particularly since industry appears to be more amenable to an increase in productivity than agriculture; earning, and in some cases saving, foreign exchange; and diversification of the economy, enabling Nigeria to avoid the full force of price fluctuations in world raw-material markets. Furthermore, as a corollary, they hope that if Nigeria acquires modern, large-scale industry--the hall-mark of the major world powers[5]--there will arrogate to Nigeria a large measure of prestige, particularly on the African continent.

But, it should not be forgotten, the endeavor to acquire a sizeable industrial base will provide challenges for Nigeria's incipient democracy, her federal form of government, and her moderate stance on the international scene. How Nigeria meets these challenges will determine her success in establishing economic well-being while maintaining political independence.

A GEOGRAPHICAL INTRODUCTION

Nigeria is large. Her area of 356,669 square miles[6] is slightly less than that of Pakistan and more than one-ninth of the size of the continental United States (Texas plus Washington). The greatest distance from east to west exceeds 700 miles; from north to south, 650 miles; and the coastline approaches 500 miles in length.

Nigeria is populous. With a population greater than 40 million,[7] Nigeria has more people than any other African country, containing approximately 16 per cent of Africa's and 22 per cent of tropical[8] Africa's population. By the same token, she can also claim the position of being the most populous Negro land in the world.

Nigeria is agrarian. The farmers raise both subsistence and cash crops. The manufacturing sector of the economy as yet contributes little (less than 2 per cent) to the gross national product.[9] Now that political independence has been achieved, this imbalance has drawn the attention of national and regional leaders as they turn to the quest for economic freedom and increased well-being.

Nigeria lies wholly within the tropics, between the fourth and fourteenth parallels north of the Equator, and between the second and fifteenth meridians east of Greenwich. On three sides, the west, the north, and the east, this land, looking somewhat like a transplanted Iberian Peninsula, is bounded by French-speaking Africa.

The terms tropical rain forest, savannah, and steppe will be used. These are vegetation zones closely related to the quantity and distribution of rainfall. Heavy rains pelt the whole country during the wet season (April through October), turning the parched area of the north into shades of green and washing out southern roads, even in the main cities.[10] In much of the south, two rainy seasons exist, for the rainbelt moves northward in the spring and

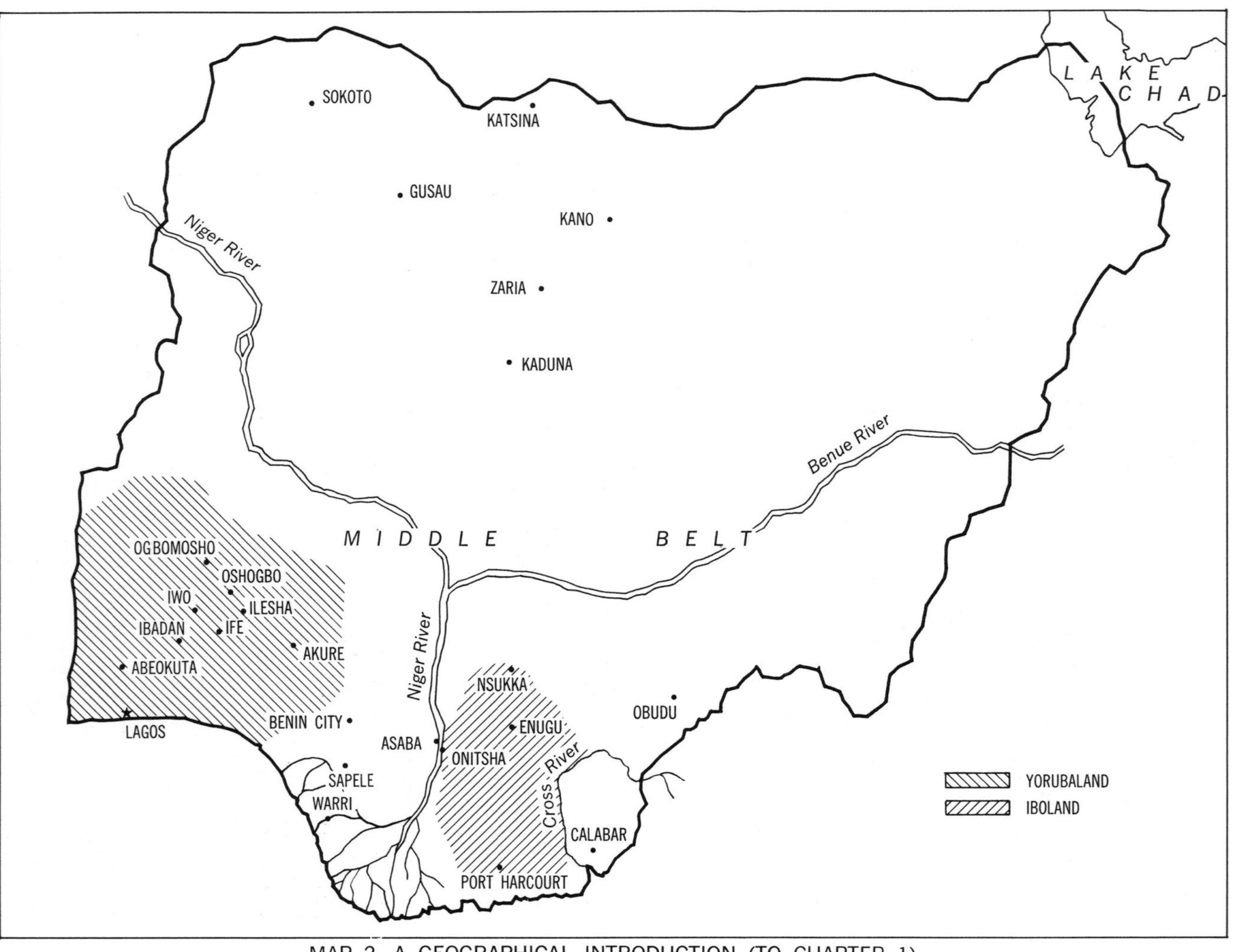

MAP 2. A GEOGRAPHICAL INTRODUCTION (TO CHAPTER 1)

returns in late September and October. The latter season is of less intensity and shorter duration. Over forty-seven years the yearly average for Lagos was 72.0 inches versus 51.2 inches for Kaduna and 33.3 inches for Kano.[11]

The (monthly means of) maximum temperatures increase, and (the mean annual) relative humidity decreases, from the coast northwards. Thus, Kano will have an average maximum temperature of 91.6°F. and a minimum annual relative humidity of 32 per cent vis-a-vis 87.3°F. and 73 per cent for Lagos, respectively.

Nigeria is divided into four regions or states, each of which is dominated by a different ethnic group, has its own premier and bicameral legislature, and has an economy that is highly dependent on the export of one distinct primary product.

The Western Region

Southern Nigeria is divided into the Eastern, Mid-Western, and Western Regions. The latter, with 30,454 square miles, is the wealthiest region on a per capita basis in the Federation. The West is bounded by the Northern Region, the Atlantic on the south, Dahomey on the west, and the Mid-West Region on the east.

Most of the 8 million inhabitants of the West live inland from the low-lying coastline of sandy beaches, calm lagoons, and mangrove swamps. Two-thirds of them are Yorubas, one of Nigeria's great tribal and ethnic groups. Their abode is the tropical rain forest that extends 60 to 100 miles northward, and the parkland savannah into which it gradually merges. The Ilesha Hills in the northeastern portion of the region are the highest points in the West, above 2,000 feet in elevation.[12] Central Yorubaland supplies almost all Nigeria's exports of cocoa. Additionally, tobacco is an important domestic cash crop north of the cocoa zone.

Lagos, Nigeria's capital, is situated on the coast and is the country's chief seaport. Predominantly Yoruba, and geographically part of the West, the 27-square-mile enclave has been administered since 1954 by the Federal Government as a Federal Territory, not unlike Washington, D.C. This city (estimated 1961 township population, 379,000)[13] is Nigeria's second most populous. Lagos is only one of several towns with a population in excess of 100,000. Besides Ibadan, the regional capital and largest city of tropical Africa, with 550,000 people,[14] there are the agglomerated farm villages of Ogbomosho, Ife, Oshogbo, Iwo, and Abeokuta. The existence of the seven, together with the estimate that 47 per cent of the Westerners live in towns over 5,000,[15] support the conclusion that the Yoruba are Africa's most urbanized people.

The Mid-West Region

The Mid-West is the country's newest and smallest, having come into being in the second half of 1963. Subsequent to a referendum held in the provinces of Benin and Delta on July 13, 1963, the fourth region of the Federal Republic was created.[16] Carved out of a formerly larger Western Region, its eastern border is the Niger River.[17]

Most of the 2 million residents of the region occupy the western part of the Niger delta. The majority are the Bini, or Edo-speaking people, and the minority are the Urhobos and Western Ibos. This area produces most of Nigeria's rubber, much of her timber, contributes to the exports of palm kernels and palm oil, and together with the Eastern Region has all of the country's discovered petroleum and natural gas reserves.

The capital and largest urban area of the Mid-West is Benin City, with some 54,000 people. Lying in a dense rain forest belt, this town was the seat of a dynasty that dates back more than 1,000 years. The region's other main centers are the seaports of Sapele (35,000) and Warri (20,000), and Asaba (18,000) on the Niger.

When most of the research for this book had been completed, Mid-Western Nigeria was only one of several proposed new regions. At the time of this writing, in early 1964, the new government is busy staffing its ministries. It will be some time before the regional marketing board and the development corporation are in full operation, and it will probably be longer before any meaningful regional statistics and data are gathered, collated, and published. Therefore, having called attention to the separate existence of this region, in most cases we will figuratively reincorporate Delta and Benin Provinces into Western Nigeria.

The Eastern Region

Nigeria's second smallest region has the greatest population density: 10 or more millions on 29,484 square miles. The pressure on the land is even greater than these figures, at first, indicate.[18] More than half of the areal total is fallow land or uncultivated bush and waste land. As in the West, in the 150-mile-transit from the ocean to the northern administrative boundary, a zone of 10 to 40 miles of mangrove swamps and tidal waterways is traversed. "Then, for the next 100 miles, the mangroves yield to the original tropical rain forest belt which is now mainly replaced by densely populated glades of oil palms."[19] The palm belt gradually gives way to tree-studded grassland. As one travels the 200 miles eastward from the Niger to the Federal Republic of Cameroon, a range of hills is met that runs southward from the northern boundary through Nsukka, the site of the new University of Nigeria, and Enugu, the regional capital. Further east is the hilly watershed of the Cross River, and finally the foothills of the Cameroons mountains. At Obudu, in the extreme northeast and at an elevation of 5,000 feet, the Eastern Nigeria Development Corporation has laid out a "dude ranch," one of several steps it is now undertaking to promote a tourist industry.

Second in population and in per capita income, the Eastern Region is dominated by the 5 or 6 million

Ibo who live in Owerri, Onitsha, Umuahia, Enugu, and Abakaliki Provinces and a portion of Port Harcourt Province. It is here in Iboland, that the region's four largest and most important cities are located: Port Harcourt (120,000),[20] Nigeria's second seaport, 41 miles up the Bonny River from the sea; Enugu (90,000), established in 1914 on the rail line near the coal fields; Onitsha (80,000), political hub of Iboland, and market and distribution center on the Niger; and Aba (65,000), commercial and growing industrial center.

At present, 90 per cent of the region's export earnings is provided by oil palm produce. Although other crops such as rice, cashew nuts, and coconuts show potential, it is rubber, among the newer crops, that will make its impact felt first. "The share of the Eastern Region in the Nigerian total [rubber output] in 1958 was 5.7 per cent. . . . Very large plantations near Calabar [in the southwest] have, however, still to mature, and this development is likely to make the Eastern Region the largest producer."[21]

The Northern Region

With more than three-quarters of the area of all Nigeria, or 281,782 square miles, and with a population of some 20 million, or about half of the country's population, the North is Nigeria's awakening giant. This land-locked region is surrounded on three sides by French-speaking Africa: Dahomey to the west, Niger to the north, and Cameroon to the east. Its southern boundary is below the line formed by the Niger and Benue Rivers.[22] This is an aftermath of the Fulani jihad, or Moslem holy war, in the first decade of the nineteenth century (see below).

Most of the region may be classified as tropical savannah grading into steppe. Above the twelfth parallel, particularly in the northwestern half of Sokoto Province and the northern half of Bornu, thorn scrub is the rule. The Sahara Desert begins just north of the town of Katsina. In addition to the two great rivers, two physical features break the regimen: the often bleak, mineral-bearing Jos Plateau of east-central Nigeria with its elevation rising to over 5,000 feet above sea level, 3,000 feet more than the general elevation in the North; and Lake Chad on the northeast border of Nigeria, a major source of fish.[23]

The northernmost provinces are those that are most densely populated. It is here that peanuts and cotton are grown, and cattle graze; and it is here that the Hausa (6 million)[24] and Fulani (3 million) hold sway. The southern, riverain portion of the region, generally spoken of as the "Middle Belt," is more sparsely populated, with fifty or less per square mile. War and slave-raiding in the past, and the continuing menace of the tsetse fly today, are the proximate causes. Not surprisingly, none of the North's large urban areas are located here.

The most important Northern cities are as follows: Kano City (140,000), for centuries a leading commercial center of the Western Sudan and now the major railhead for the groundnut [peanut] growing area; Kaduna (90,000), like Enugu a European creation fifty years old, the regional capital,[25] and a rising center of industry; Zaria (55,000), railroad junction and center of education; Jos (45,000), tin mining center; and Gusau (45,000), one of the several cotton "boom towns."

THE HISTORICAL BACKGROUND

What was the legacy in the economic field from Britain's tenure? It was colonial policy to limit the expenditures on internal development to a level that was set by the burden of public debt the administrators thought Nigeria could afford. Broad development did not commence until World War II, when Nigeria was cut off from her motherland. As far as foreign private investment was concerned, it was concentrated primarily in commercial activities of a trading nature,[26] and secondarily in mining, particularly tin. Yet, in the long run, the Nigerians were protected: Europeans were not permitted to buy land, placing Nigeria in a far more enviable position than, say, Kenya. Tragic confrontations of the races that have hindered national political and economic cooperation elsewhere in Africa have not occurred in Nigeria.

Nigeria obtained her independence 109 years after the British attacked the Kingdom of Lagos, on Christmas Day, 1851. In those years, Great Britain, slowly and fitfully, put together a nation where before the suzerainties of powerful tribal chiefs, kings, and emirs often clashed. An official decision to suppress the slave traffic along the Guinea Coast led to the introduction of British power in Nigeria during the first half of the nineteenth century. The exigencies of Britain's international trade, and her rivalry with France and Germany for African territory, kept her there.

The South: 1553-1807 - 1914

Seeking adventure, discovery, wealth, and converts, Portugal led Europe to Africa's West Coast in the early fifteenth century. By the second half of the sixteenth century, England was regularly dispatching ships to the Benin region, returning with palm oil, peppers, and ivory.[27] Not very much time had elapsed when Sir John Hawkins (1532-95) introduced England to the slave trade. Until 1807, when England abolished this human traffic, "Britain . . . controlled the lion's share of the trans-Atlantic slave trade."[28] Yet, through all those years, Nigerians, the African middlemen, remained sovereign in their coastal territories, or city-states.

Well into the first third of the nineteenth century, Europe was not aware of the connection between the delta area, the source of palm oil and slaves, and the Niger itself. Following in the tradition of Mungo Park, Denham, and Clapperton, the Lander Brothers in 1830, on a Colonial Office expedition, traced the course of the river from Bussa (Ilorin Province) to the sea. Their canoe trip coincided with the development of the steam engine, which meant that the

Niger was soon to be opened to river navigation on an important scale. But first the British had to dispose of the slavers who still plied the Guinea waters. For the latter, it was now a matter of economic warfare. "Success in inland trading would cut off their [human] supplies . . . a prospect they fought bitterly to prevent."[29] The African intermediaries, chief among them, King Kosoko of Lagos, joined in a last defense of these profitable dealings.

In doing his utmost to destroy the British influence in Western Nigeria, Kosoko invited retribution. So it was, after a three-day battle, on December 28, 1851, that Lagos was abandoned to the British. "A thousand warriors sent by the King of Dahomey to assist Kosoko did not arrive in time, and returned quietly when they found they were too late."[30] The beginning of the following year saw the installation of a puppet king and the signing of a treaty for the final abolition of the traffic in slaves in this last great Nigerian slave center. But this was not to be the end of the tale. The puppet died three weeks later, probably by poison, and threats against the British were renewed. So, on August 6, 1861, under the guns of the HMS Prometheus, anchored off Lagos, the town was annexed to the British Crown and was made a colony in the following year.

With the steamboat, the pacification of the coast, and the introduction of quinine in Nigeria in 1854, British merchants were ready to commercialize the Niger Valley. From 1857 to 1878 the number of trading posts increased from three to twenty-five, and "whereas the value of produce was about £9,000 in 1859, in 1878 it had risen to over £300,000."[31]

In six years Goldie Taubman (later Sir George Goldie), who had arrived in 1879, united the four largest British trading companies in the Niger Valley to form the United African Company (later the National African Company), drove his French competitors to cover, and presented Britain with a claim over the "Niger Districts" (ratified by the Berlin Conference of 1885). Britain was now in the scramble for territory with the Germans and the French.

Having acquired Lagos to protect her trading interests, she was now taking over more and more of Nigeria to protect her growing inland trade from European competitors. Moreover, inland, the Navy's gunboat diplomacy was not serviceable as it was along the coast.

With the closing of the nineteenth century, Goldie's progenitor of today's United Africa Company received in 1886, only to lose it thirteen years later, a Royal Charter as the Royal Niger Company. Yorubaland was attached to the Colony of Lagos as a British Protectorate in 1888; and in the delta and to the east as far as Calabar, the Oil[32] Rivers Protectorate was proclaimed, though not effectively, in 1885 and established as the Niger Coast Protectorate in 1893. Lastly, Benin was captured after severe fighting in 1897. Some minor administrative changes took place in 1906; otherwise, the situation was frozen until 1914. Thus, by bits and pieces, British control of present day Nigeria was extended northwards.

The North: 13th Century - 1804-1914

The cultural and linguistic group known as the Hausa, Hamitic and Negro in origin, has populated the land for at least a millenium. At first a group of seven pagan kingdoms, these people were, between the thirteenth and fifteenth centuries, overlain and, more or less, unified by Islam. As the years passed, a new people, the Fulani, peacefully migrated into Hausaland. They divided into two main groups: the Cow Fulani, remaining quiet and mostly pagan, and the sedentary, Town Fulani (the Fulanin Gida [of the compound]) intermarrying with the Hausa and adopting Islam. It was the latter who often became, at least in the European view, "fanatical in religion and racially arrogant."[33]

In 1804, a Fulani leader, Othman Dan Fodio, who had made the pilgrimage to Mecca, fomented a jihad so as to remove the lax Hausa rulers from their seats of power. By the time of Dan Fodio's death thirteen years later, all of Northern Nigeria had been swept by the Fulani cavalry. The rule of his son, Sultan Bello, was frequently punctuated by the rebellions of the descendants of former Hausa leaders, but it was in general a period of consolidation.

While the "pagans" of the south were being affected by European ideas, religion, technology, dress, etc., the north, with the exception of an occasional expedition, such as that of Clapperton, was not subjected to foreign influence. When the British did eventually penetrate north of the Rivers Niger and Benue, they found a feudal Fulani aristocracy in control of the society.

By 1857, as has been stated, the British had established three trading centers on the Niger. The northernmost was Lokoja, at the fork of the two great rivers. British influence did not really spread further northward until 1886, when the Royal Niger Company was formed. But even then, "no attempt was made . . . to deal with the powerful Fulani States, where misgovernment and tyranny flourished unchecked, accompanied by the worst form of slave-raiding."[34] This was the British rationalization for conquering the north; it was to be a military conquest, and the victors would treat the vanquished honorably.[35] In fact, with the imposition by Lugard of "Indirect Rule," by which Britain governed via the traditional rulers, the decentralized Moslem emirates remained ever powerful.[36]

Allegations of abuse of its commercial monopoly power, and the threats of French encroachment, led to the cancellation of the Royal Niger Company's Charter in 1899, for which the Company received £565,000 as compensation. The British Government also assumed full responsibility for the Company's outstanding £300,000 public debt. This was not all. The Company was also to receive one-half of the receipts of all mineral royalties in the territory between the Niger and a line drawn between Yola (on the Benue near the Federation of Cameroon) and Zinder (in Niger Republic)--for ninety-nine years.[37]

On the first of January, 1900, upon the raising of the Union Jack at Lokoja, the Protectorate of Northern Nigeria came into being. Sir Frederick Lugard, the first High Commissioner, proceeded to carry the "infidel" flag to the rest of the North; Kano was captured on February 3, and Sokoto on March 18, 1903. Local warfare was finished by 1906, although as late as 1909 towns that fired on political officers and the police were "punished."

Events followed one another now with rapidity. In 1912, returning to Nigeria from five years in Hong Kong as Governor, Lugard was appointed Governor of both the northern and southern sections. And then, fourteen years to the day after that Lokoja flag raising, Lugard was sworn in as Governor-General over the amalgamation of the Northern and Southern Protectorates. Just forty-six years prior to independence Nigeria had finally been unified.[38]

Nigeria: 1914-1960

In 1922, a Legislative Council for the Colony and the southern part of the Protectorate was established. It contained, albeit a minority, the first elected Africans in any legislature in British and tropical Africa. Subsequent to the end of World War II, the political tempo shifted from adagio to allegro. Relatively peacefully,[39] one constitutional conference followed another. The year 1946 saw the introduction of regional councils in the northern, eastern, and western groups of provinces; 1951 witnessed the granting of greater regional autonomy and the creation of a Council of Ministers (four from each region); and in 1954 Lagos became the capital of the new Federation, as the two southern regions continued on their way to self-government. In 1957, the House of Representatives unanimously demanded independence for Nigeria in 1959. In the same year the Western and Eastern Regions became self-governing, and the Northern Region followed suit two years later. The first Federal election was held on December 12, 1959, and three days after, Alhaji the Hon. Sir Abubakar Tafawa Balewa, who in August, 1957, as a Northern Peoples' Congress (N.P.C.) vice president had become the first Prime Minister of the Federation of Nigeria, was reappointed. The die was cast: he would lead his country to its freedom on October 1, 1960.[40]

Footnotes to Chapter 1

1. Eastern Nigeria Newsletter, Vol. 1, No. 11 (New York: Barnet and Reef Associates, Inc., December 1961), p. 2.

2. U.S., Congress, House, Committee on Foreign Affairs, Hearings, Activities of Private United States Organizations in Africa, 87th Congress, 1st Session, 1961, p. 238.

3. David E. Lilienthal, "Why Nigeria is 'Different,'" New York Times Magazine, June 11, 1961, p. 28.

4. Ayo Ogunsheye, "Nigeria's Economy," Nigeria Magazine, Special Independence Issue (October, 1960), p. 17.

5. Alhaji Zanna Bukar Dipcharima, the Federal Minister of Commerce and Industry, has been quoted as follows: "The Federal Government is not only determined that Nigeria shall be an industrial giant in the shortest time but also that Europeans should come to learn something of her industrial feats and tricks." (West African Pilot [Lagos], March 18, 1964, p. 3.)

6. On February 11, 1961, the plebiscite in the Southern Cameroons, formerly under British trusteeship, led, on October 1, 1961, to its joining the independent Federal Republic of Cameroon (vote for Nigeria, 97,741; for the Cameroon Republic, 233,571). On February 11 and 12, 1961, the Northern Cameroons voted by 146,296 to 97,659 to join the independent Federation of Nigeria. Renamed Sardauna Province, this territory became part of Northern Nigeria on June 15, 1961.

7. The 1952-53 census gave Nigeria, excluding the Southern Cameroons, a population of 30,417,000. The next complete census was undertaken in May, 1962. Because "the census figures did not receive the general approval of all four governmental leaders" it was nullified. (The Times [London], February 25, 1963, p. 9.)

The census was retaken during November, 1963. Preliminary results were released in late February, 1964: Northern Nigeria, 29,777,986; Eastern Nigeria, 12,388,646; Western Nigeria, 10,278,500; Mid-Western Nigeria, 2,533,337; and the Federal Capital of Lagos, 675,352. (West Africa, February 29, 1964, p. 243.) The total of 55,653,821 was once again the subject of controversy; two regional premiers having rejected the result. At the time of this writing further details are unavailable. The ultimate decision is a political once since parliamentary seats are apportioned on a population basis.

Compounding the 1952-53 figure at 2 per cent and rounding results in a sum of 38 million for 1963-64. (It will be noted that the Demographic Year Book of the United Nations is using a 1.9 per cent growth rate for Nigeria and the Population Reference Bureau 2.1 per cent for Africa.)

8. That is, excluding the countries bordering the Mediterranean Sea, and the Republic of South Africa.

9. Unpublished study of the National Income of Nigeria for the Period 1950-57, Prepared by E. F. Jackson and P. N. C. Okigbo, Federal Ministry of Economic Development, Lagos (in the files of the Ministry). W. F. Stolper, Ford Foundation economic adviser to the Ministry, with the assistance of L. Hansen and E. O. Iwuagwu, in March, 1961, extrapolated the Jackson-Okigbo estimates through 1960. The value added for (modern) manufacturing was estimated to be £15,650,000. The gross domestic product at market prices was given as £1,023,000,000, and the net income from abroad at £3.5 million. Therefore, the Nigerian GNP was estimated, in 1960, to be £1,026,500,000, or $2,874,200,000 (1957 market prices).

The 1950-57 figures, with accompanying text, has since been published. See Pius N. C. Okigbo,

Nigerian National Accounts: 1950-57 (Enugu: Eastern Nigeria Government Printer for Federal Ministry of Economic Development, 1962). Chapter two of the National Development Plan: 1962-68 (Lagos: Federal Ministry of Economic Development, 1962) includes some of the extrapolations by Stolper, et al.

10. During Independence celebrations in 1960, many of Port Harcourt's main streets were impassable, the result of rain-produced potholes.

11. At Ikeja (Lagos' airport), the mean monthly rainfall (inches) ranges from 1.0 in December, 5.6 in April, 10.8 in May, 18.1 in June, 11.1 in July, 2.7 in August, to 8.1 in October. Kaduna would show figures of 0.0, 2.7, 5.8, 7.0, 8.6, 12.3, and 3.0, while Kano would only have 0.0, 0.4, 2.5, 4.4, 8.0, 12.4, and 0.5. It should be emphasized that these are averages. As the amount of rainfall diminishes, so does its regularity. (K. M. Buchanan and J. C. Pugh, Land and People in Nigeria [London: University of London Press, 1955], p. 243.)

12. The tallest peak is 3,098 foot Mt. Orosun, an inselberg, 12 miles southwest of Akure.

13. Nigeria, Federal Office of Statistics, Digest of Statistics, Vol. 10, No. 3 (Lagos: July, 1961), p. 3. The Lagos growth rate is estimated at 4 per cent per annum. The 1963 census (preliminary) gives a figure of 675,352 for the Federal District. Metropolitan Lagos, therefore, would be approximately 1 million.

14. The 1952-53 census lists Ibadan with a population of 459,196. If it were to increase at 2 per cent per annum, there would be 570,000 inhabitants today. (Nigeria, Federal Office of Statistics, Annual Abstract of Statistics [Lagos, 1963], p. 25.) In all probability the growth has been even greater, possibly to more than 600,000.

15. Royal Institute of International Affairs, Nigeria: The Political and Economic Background (London: Oxford University Press, 1960), p. 19.

16. The Federal Prime Minister appointed Chief Dennis Osadebay, then N.C.N.C. [see footnote 36 below] President of the Federal Senate, as Administrator. Assisted by seventeen deputy administrators, the Chief ruled the interim government until February 3, 1964, when the electorate confirmed him as the region's first premier.

17. In 1914, the two protectorates of Northern and Southern Nigeria were amalgamated by Sir F. Lugard. "Sixteen years earlier, Flora Shaw, who later married Lugard, first suggested in an article for The Times (London) that the several British protectorates on the Niger be known collectively as Nigeria." (Michael Crowder, The Story of Nigeria [London: Faber and Faber, 1962], p. 19.)

18. "Some informal statistical work in 1959 in the Eastern Region produced a birth rate figure of 51 per thousand annually, which certainly places Iboland among those areas of the world which are multiplying most rapidly." (Ruben Frodin, A Note on Nigeria, West African Series, Vol. IV, No. 6 [New York: American Universities Field Staff, 1961], p. 6.)

19. Eastern Nigeria, Ministry of Information, Eastern Nigeria (Enugu, 1960), p. 1.

20. The 1952-53 census puts Port Harcourt's population at 71,634. More recently an Israeli firm of consultants, Eastern Nigeria Water Planning and Construction, Ltd. (in which the Eastern Region Government holds 51 per cent of the equity) made this estimate for 1960. (Eastern Nigeria, Ministry of Works, Report on Roads, Drainage and Sewerage in Port Harcourt [Enugu, September, 1961], p. 1.)

21. Economist Intelligence Unit, Investment Opportunities in Eastern Nigeria (London: The EIU Ltd., 1960), p. 10.

22. The Western Region has, time and again, claimed that those sections of Kabba and Ilorin Provinces which are extensions of Yorubaland should be ceded to it.

23. The World Bank study reported these estimates for 1952-53: 18,000 tons of fish from creeks and coastal waters, 16,000 from the rivers, and 8,000 (19 per cent) from Lake Chad. (International Bank for Reconstruction and Development, The Economic Development of Nigeria [Lagos: Federal Government Printer, 1954], p. 178.)

24. The author will not enter into an ethnographic discussion. The groups of tribes in the Northern Region who speak Hausa as their primary language are, in general practice, termed Hausas. This ancient, written language is a lingua franca throughout large areas of northwest Africa, especially the Western Sudan. The interested reader may wish to see Buchanan and Pugh, "The Human Pattern," op. cit., pp. 58-99.

25. Lord Lugard at one time had hoped to site the Federal capital at Kaduna.

26. For a thorough analysis of the activities of the great expatriate trading companies, see Peter T. Bauer's West African Trade (London: Cambridge University Press, 1954).

27. According to one source, "The first English ships reached the Bight of Benin in 1553." (E. I. Oliver, Nigeria: Economic and Commercial Conditions in Nigeria, Overseas Economic Survey [London: Her Majesty's Stationery Office, 1957], p. 1.)

28. K. O. Dike, 100 Years of British Rule in Nigeria: 1851-1951, 1956 Lugard Lectures, A Series of Six Radio Broadcasts (Lagos: Federal Ministry of Information, 1960), p. 9.

29. K. O. Dike, Trade and Politics in the Niger Delta: 1830-1885 (London: Oxford University Press, 1956), p. 61.

30. Alan Burns, History of Nigeria (5th ed.; London: George Allen and Unwin, Ltd., 1955), p. 122.

31. Dike, 100 Years of British Rule in Nigeria, p. 25.

32. Named in honor of the area's primary export, palm oil; and not after its subterranean wealth of mineral oil, which was discovered only in this century.

33. M. Perham, Lugard: The Years of Authority, 1898-1945 (Second Part of the Life of Frederick D. Lugard; London: Collins, 1960), p. 31.

34. Burns, op. cit., p. 154.

35. This is the Northern viewpoint especially. For example, it is set forth by one of the country's most powerful men (see footnote 36): "I do not think that there was any particular antipathy against them [the British]. It was the will of Allah that they should be there; they were not evil men and their administration was not harsh; in fact, we gained much from contact with them. . . ." (Sir Ahmadu Bello, My Life [Cambridge: Cambridge University Press, 1962], p. 2.)

36. To this day the North remains the domain of the Fulani aristocracy, with the Sardauna of Sokoto, Alhaji the Hon. Sir Ahmadu Bello, direct descendant of Dan Fodio, being the Premier of the Northern Region as well as President-General of the ruling party, the Northern Peoples' Congress. (Since 1959 the N.P.C. has been the senior partner in the coalition that is in power at the center in Lagos. With the addition of M.P.'s from the new Sardauna Province, the old Northern Cameroons, the N.P.C., from a numerical standpoint, is now in a position to form the Federal Government without the assistance of the N.C.N.C. [National Convention of Nigerian Citizens], the dominant party in the Eastern Region. To complete the picture, the Federal Opposition until 1962 was supplied by the A.G. [Action Group], who gather the bulk of their strength from Yorubaland in the Western Region. At this time there is no official opposition party at the center in Lagos. Finally, during March, 1964, Chief S. L. Akintola, Premier of the Western Region, formed the N.N.D.P. [Nigerian National Democratic Party] which may join a national government.)

Indeed, a student of one of these emirates, that of Zaria, recently reported, "By uniting under their Sultan [of Sokoto; not the Sardauna], the emirs are able to dominate the Northern elections and legislature without difficulty . . . and within the next few years we may witness an open restoration of the Fulani empire." (M. G. Smith, Government in Zazzau, 1800-1950 [London: Oxford University Press, 1960], pp. 249-250.)

37. The Company first reverted to an ordinary trading company, the Niger Company. Then in 1920, Lever Brothers, Ltd. took it over. Subsequently it was merged into the United Africa Company. UAC was founded in 1929 and is now the major African arm of two parent groups--the British Unilever Ltd. and the Dutch Unilever N.V.

As for the mineral royalties, this agreement was made three years prior to the discovery of the Jos tin fields. Throughout the years tin production increased. In 1917, "Lugard [the Governor] found himself . . . paying out £70,000 for that year and the sum was rising." (Perham, op. cit., p. 575.) "In 1949, the Company gave up its rights to mineral royalties in return for £1 million compensation from the Nigerian Government." (Bernard Blankenheimer, et al., Investment in Nigeria: Basic Information for U.S. Businessmen [Bureau of Foreign Commerce, U.S. Department of Commerce; Washington, D.C.: Government Printing Office, 1957], p. 58.)

38. The story of the effort to mold the north and the south into a cohesive, independent unit, viz., the variegated struggle against the British, and the tribal and political rivalries, is set forth in James S. Coleman's Nigeria: Background to Nationalism (Berkeley: University of California Press, 1958). A succeeding book, Richard L. Sklar's Nigerian Political Parties: Power in an Emergent African Nation (Princeton: Princeton University Press, 1963), carries the story up to Independence.

39. "The Nigerian independence movement was shaped in a climate of largely verbal jousting; incidents of violence over the years, once the fight for freedom gained momentum, were rare and of insignificant

proportions. The atmosphere in recent years has been marked by continuous negotiation and conferences." (Hugh H. Smythe and Mabel M. Smythe, The New Nigerian Elite [Stanford: Stanford University Press, 1960], p. 14.)

40. And Sir Abubakar remains the Prime Minister of the Federal Republic of Nigeria that was created on October 1, 1963. The Right Honorable Doctor Nnamdi Azikiwe, Nigeria's first Governor-General after Independence, was installed as President of the Republic on that date, thus replacing the Queen as Chief of State. Nigeria, however, chose to continue as a member of the Commonwealth of Nations.

PART II

THE FOUNDATIONS ON WHICH TO BUILD

CHAPTER 2 NATURAL RESOURCES FOR INDUSTRY

THE AGRICULTURAL BASE

If only one adjective is permitted to describe the Nigerian economy it would be "agrarian," as the figures in Table 1 so starkly substantiate. Although the ratio has been decreasing over the past decade, agricultural production still accounts for about 60 per cent of Nigeria's gross domestic product.

Table 1

The Composition of Nigerian Primary Production and Its Percentage of Gross Domestic Product at Factor Prices of 1957 (£ million)

	1950	1954	1957	1960
Tree and field crops	377.6	471.3	471.4	491.0
Livestock products	60.1	55.7	57.7	60.0
Fishing	9.7	10.2	13.3	16.0
Forest products	9.4	12.3	14.6	25.0
Total	456.8	549.5	557.0	592.0
GDP @ 1957 factor prices	686.7	872.2	909.7	993.0*
Primary Prod. as % of GDP	66.5%	63.0%	61.2%	59.6%

*GDP at market prices less an assumed figure of £30 million for indirect taxes _less_ subsidies.

Sources: E. F. Jackson and P. N. C. Okigbo, _National Income of Nigeria for the Period 1950-57_ (Lagos: Federal Ministry of Economic Development, 1960) (Mimeo.), and W. Stolper, _et al_., _Government Expenditures on Goods and Services_ (Lagos: Federal Ministry of Economic Development, 1961) (Mimeo.)

It is estimated that the majority of the male working population is engaged in agriculture: roughly 80 per cent in the North, 70 per cent in the West, and 75 per cent in the East. In addition, agriculture brings in 85 per cent of the country's export earnings.[1]

It is the export crops, earning more than four-fifths of the Republic's foreign exchange, and the domestic cash crops, having end-uses that necessitate industrial processing, which will receive our attention. The export crops may also require some processing prior to overseas shipment, as in the expression of palm oil. Yet, it is the place they occupy in Nigeria's balance-of-payments picture that makes them so important. For it is the foreign exchange receipts engendered by them which largely determine the quantity of capital goods that may be imported for industrial development purposes.

Approximately half of Nigeria's manufacturing industry is raw material-oriented (see Chapter 7 below). After accounting for the processing of tin ore and coal, and the refining of petroleum, the remaining portion of this category consists of abattoirs, oil seed mills, sawmills, soap plants, etc., all dependent on tree and field crops, and animal and forest products.

Despite leached soils in the south and an insufficient supply of water in many parts of the north, Nigeria must regard agriculture as the mainstay of her economy. Now, and for many years to come, farming will remain the country's major source of income and employment. Evidently, then, agricultural research, education, extension, and credit, as well as improved land use by such means as land registration, land consolidation, individual ownership, plantation enterprises, and farm resettlement, are of the utmost importance. These, together with the technical problems of the use of fertilizer and pesticides, the design and erection of suitable storage facilities, the eradication of the tsetse fly (which often prohibits the establishment of mixed-farming), the introduction of irrigation, and other such problems, are suitable subjects for intensive and rewarding study, but are beyond the scope of this work.

Table 2

Nigerian Output of Tree and Field Crops at Factor Prices of 1957 (£ million)

	1950	1954	1957	1960
Crops grown primarily for domestic use	301.3	375.0	360.7	370.0
root crops	184.7	201.0	197.1	(a)
cereals	81.6	134.1	129.7	(a)
kolanuts	3.9	4.1	4.9	(a)
beans and other	31.1	35.8	29.0	(a)
Crops grown primarily for export	76.3	96.3	110.7	121.0
groundnuts	16.3	26.4	40.5	25.2
cocoa	16.5	12.1	12.0	36.0
palm produce	29.6	35.4	32.5	33.7
cotton	4.0	9.4	9.9	7.0
rubber	2.0	3.1	5.6	8.4
soya beans	0.1	0.2	0.3	0.3
benniseed	0.3	0.6	0.6	0.8
bananas and plantains	6.8	8.2	8.5	8.8
other	0.7	0.9	0.8	0.8
of which:				
exports (b)	50.3	65.2	80.3	90.6
home consumption	26.0	31.1	30.4	30.4
Total of All Crops	377.6	471.3	471.4	491.0

(a) Figures not available.
(b) Including increases (and net of decreases) in stocks held by Marketing Boards.

Sources: E. F. Jackson and P. N. C. Okigbo, National Income of Nigeria for the Period 1950-57 (Lagos: Federal Ministry of Economic Development, 1960) (Mimeo.), and W. Stolper et al., Government Expenditures on Goods and Services (Lagos: Federal Ministry of Economic Development, 1961) (Mimeo.).

Unfortunately--and this is not an isolated instance--the exercise of regional prerogatives has inhibited coordinated action by government in this all-important field. Agriculture, an item on neither the exclusive nor the concurrent legislative lists of the Federal Constitution,[2] is residual, thereby remaining with the regions. One obvious corollary of this state of affairs is that there is no Federal Ministry of Agriculture.[3] Fortunately, non-governmental agencies, particularly the American Agency for International Development,[4] have numerous agricultural specialists in the field who provide much of the requisite, integrated, and directed effort in this sector of the economy.

Southern Tree Crops

Together with forestry and root crops (especially yams and cassava), tree crops form the basis of the economy of the south. The latter include the products of the oil palm, the cocoa tree, the rubber tree, plus those of the coconut palm, citrus trees, and the cashew nut tree.

Palm Oil and Palm Kernels

The products of a tree that is native to Nigeria and harvested the year round, palm oil and palm kernels are the basis of the Eastern Region's money economy, "providing 90% of the Region's export revenue."[5] As a whole, Nigeria supplies almost one-third of the world's palm oil exports, and about half of its palm kernel exports.

The oil is expressed from the outer part of the fruit either by a hand-press or by more sophisticated means at a small ("Pioneer") oil mill.[6] Composed primarily of glycerol and fatty acid, the oil is used domestically in the cooking of stews, and represents the southerners' main source of vitamin A. Industrially, the oil finds end uses in the manufacture of soap, candles and also margarine if the free fatty acid content is low enough, as well as in the tin-plating of steel food containers.

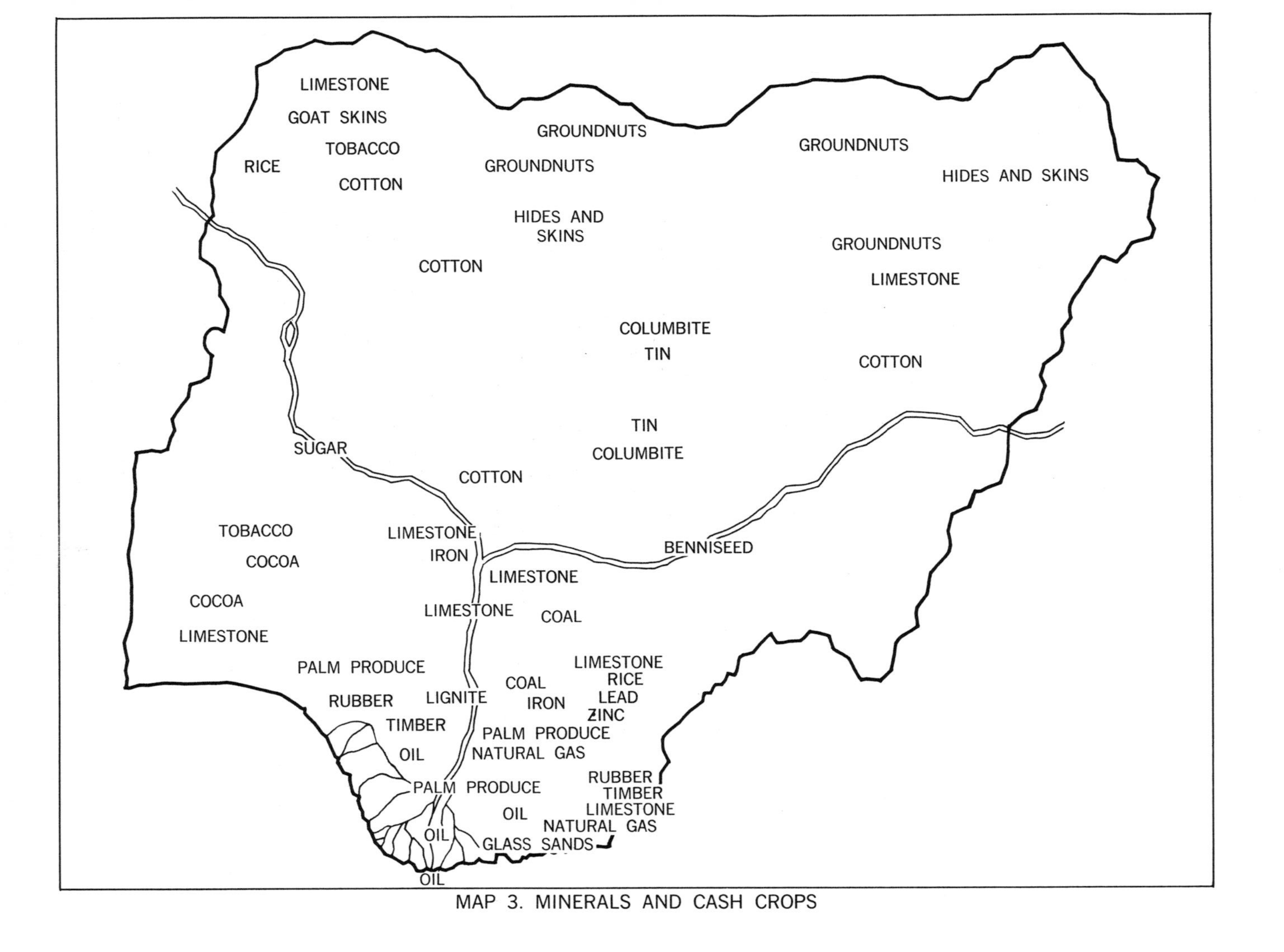

MAP 3. MINERALS AND CASH CROPS

The nut within the fruit is cracked either manually (usually by women), or at the Pioneer Mills, releasing the palm kernels. The high-grade oil that they provide is used in the manufacture of margarine. Because the extraction and refining processes are quite technical, and therefore highly specialized, the kernels have not, as yet, been commercially processed in Nigeria. Proposals for a local kernel industry are now under consideration.

Most of the trees are self-sown, hence called "wild," but they are individually owned. One government scheme aimed at the rehabilitation of the wild groves--thinning out and introducing cultivated varieties--is progressing slowly because of delayed payments of cash compensation.[7]

Cocoa

For 1961-62, the Food and Agriculture Organization estimated that Africa produced 73.7 per cent of the world's cocoa. Ghana and Nigeria produced 50.1 per cent and 23.3 per cent of the African share respectively.[8] For the past five years, Nigeria's crop, more than 90 per cent of which comes from Yorubaland in the Western Region, has been at a level about half that of Ghana's. Still, this places Nigeria second in the world with 17.2 per cent of world output.

The cocoa bean is the seed of the evergreen cacao tree. It was introduced into Nigeria in the latter half of the nineteenth century from its native Brazil via the island of São Tomé, a Portuguese possession about 300 miles south of Nigeria. The trees are planted in clearings in the formerly dense rainforest, thus affording protection from sun and rain; and produced almost entirely by individual farmers, its cultivation being developed with little or no scientific assistance.

After the harvest (the larger of the two each year takes place between October and February), the twenty to forty beans per pod are scooped out by hand, fermented for five to seven days, dried for another ten, and then are ready for export, and eventual processing into cocoa powder (which contains no cocoa butter) and chocolate (with cocoa butter, milk, and white sugar added).[9] In contradistinction to their use of palm oil, Nigerians consume very little of the cocoa.[10]

Rubber

At present, more than 90 per cent of Nigerian rubber grows in the eastern portion of the Western Region, now the Mid-West, an area less suitable than the Yoruba Provinces for the cultivation of cocoa. Climatic conditions in the Eastern Region are also very suitable for the planting of rubber trees, as was indicated earlier. With the encouragement of the Eastern Region Government, large rubber estates are now being developed in Calabar Province. The largest, the Dunlop Rubber Estate, covers approximately 21,000 acres, and has had an investment of £5 million since 1956. Five years later over half the area was cleared, and 3 million trees planted.[11]

Hevea rubber seedlings were first introduced into Nigeria around 1890. Production developed mainly on a peasant farming basis, in marked contrast to the development of plantations in Liberia and Congo (Léopoldville). Today there are approximately 100,000 small-holders on holdings of 2 to 4 acres. Estate acreage now in production accounts for only about 5 per cent of the total land under rubber. Production has increased more than twenty-fivefold since the mid-1930's; and since 1959 Nigeria has been the largest natural rubber producer in Africa and is now sixth in the world.[12]

Poor maintenance, overtapping (even slaughter tapping), and poor yields, because of unwillingness to replant, have plagued the industry. In 1957 the Western Government initiated its Rubber Improvement Campaign to increase the processed product. It takes five to six years before production can commence, and ten to eleven before full maturity is reached. So the farmers are reluctant to destroy the source of their current (though diminishing) income. It is likely that many of the subsidized high-yielding seedlings provided have gone to new farms.

Forestry

Benin Province is the main center of Nigeria's timber industry. It and some few other sections of the south supply most of the nation's internal needs plus the lumber, which places Nigeria among Africa's leading timber exporters.[13] The Cross River valley (Calabar in particular) of the East has a potential that should develop with the improvement of the area's communications.

At the confluence of three rivers, 70 miles from the sea, the United Africa Company (UAC) has erected a sawmill and plywood complex which makes Sapele (Delta Province) Nigeria's timber port as well as the site of West Africa's largest industrial undertaking. The nearby Benin tropical rainforests contain "a great diversity of forest trees and secondary growth of varying ages, and giant trees [the first branches often being over 100 feet from the ground] rarely occur as clumps or groups of a single type."[14] It is precisely this lack of continuous stands of one species, plus extensive farming in timber areas, that precludes the "jungle" areas of the tropics from being the unbroken vast expanses of mahogany and other valuable hardwoods which inhabitants of the temperate climes envision.

Northern Cash Crops

The Northern Region economy depends upon farming, the cultivation of cereals (guinea corn, a sorghum, and maize and millet), pulses, fibres, rice, tobacco, etc., and the practice of animal husbandry.

Groundnuts

This legume has been cultivated in the north for 400 years. Its value lies in its oil--43 per cent by weight of the decorticated nut. The groundnuts are produced by peasant cultivators in the northernmost provinces; normally, about 45 per cent of the crop comes from Kano Province alone. The nuts are shelled locally, more and more by hand machines, although a small portion is crushed in Kano City. Some peanuts are consumed locally, but for the most part they are shipped abroad. Nigeria is the world's largest exporter, usually accounting for 30 per cent of the total international trade.

Of all Nigeria's agricultural commodities, the groundnut has been the one most tied to the railroad, which reached Kano in 1912. Plantings are subject to the yearly rainfall fluctuations and the prospects for a good year for cereals. But shipments are dependent on the railroad's ability to transport the crop to port (see Chapter 4 below). With the opening of the railway extension to Maiduguri, in early 1965, Bornu's share of the crop--11 per cent in 1961-62--should increase.

Cotton

American (Middling 1" staple) Upland was introduced into the north from Uganda in 1912 by the British Cotton Growing Association (B.C.G.A.). This Nigerian Allen variety eventually brought Nigeria into the world cotton market as a minor exporter of lint and seed.

Cotton is grown primarily in Katsina, Sokoto, and Zaria Provinces by peasants, not on plantations. Its yield and quality are controlled by the seed distribution process. The B.C.G.A., as the agent for the Northern (and Western) Region Marketing Board(s), has established thirteen ginneries for the separation of the cotton and the seed. It is these ginneries that provide more than 90 per cent of the seed; selected strains produced in the cotton breeding section of the regional research station at Samaru (near Zaria City) can be rapidly disseminated. Samaru 26J (improved American Allen) developed in the mid-1950's, now has become the standard over all the north.

As with groundnuts, cotton production will expand in the northeast when the railroad extension is completed. Gombe, in particular, is expected to rank with the older centers of Zaria and Gusau as a major producer.

Tobacco

Since 1933, the year manufacture of cigarettes began in Ogbomosho, production of leaf tobacco has been continually increasing. Northern air-cured from Zaria and Sokoto Provinces and southern air-cured and flue-cured (10 per cent of the total crop) from Oyo Province of the West are the principal types grown. The Nigerian Tobacco Company, which was a private monopoly until 1964, provides free seedlings to peasant farmers who wish to begin growing this plant.

There are few commercial crops that are more sensitive to soil and climate environment than tobacco. Although conditions are favorable for its cultivation in Nigeria, it is doubtful that Nigeria will be able to compete in the export markets against the superior quality product from America and Southern Rhodesia.

Sugar Cane and Rice

These two crops are fairly minor today, but promise to gain more prominence in the next decade or so.

Zaria Province leads in the production of sugar cane. With no facilities at present for refining, most of the cane, grown on small plots, is chewed raw. However, the Northern Region Government and the Bookers Sugar Company of the U.K. are developing a large-scale sugar plantation on marshy ground south of the Niger, near Jebba; and a refinery will soon follow.

No similar great impetus is in store for rice, which of late has been increasing in importance. Today the majority of the crop, of both swamp and upland varieties, is grown in the north, but the Eastern Region is also making a concerted effort to increase production.

The World Bank mission thought that Sokoto Province offered good possibilities for expanded production in the fadamas--periodically flooded or inundated river-bottom land.[15] This is still true, although in 1960 the Sokoto Native Authority (local provincial government) almost became insolvent due to the failure of a rice mechanization scheme. A restricted growing season, fragmented land holdings, credit problems, and politics all had their part to play. In particular, the farmers were probably in debt prior to the start of the program; in general, it was a case of too much too quickly.

Abakaliki is the rice center of the East. After World War II, machine (diesel) hulling was introduced, and a directed effort by the government led to a tremendous increase in output and improvement in quality. A luxury a short time ago, rice is fast becoming a staple in an area that is experiencing population pressures.

What really excites southerners is the prospect of utilizing the mangrove swamps for rice production. Still, for both fresh water and salt water areas, a good deal of study and experimentation will be needed. Reclamation of the swamps will require large capital investments to prevent flooding and silting. Moreover, large-scale rice mechanization schemes will also entail many socio-economic problems: bringing people to the reclaimed areas, housing them, providing transport for the laborers, and so forth.[16]

Livestock and Fishing

It has been stated previously that animal husbandry is one of the northern economy's two main props. The south, too, would like to give its people animal protein and milk, and to make use of its citrus crop as an animal feed. But for the moment, the tsetse scourge relegates it to raising small, low-grade, disease-resistant types of cattle. More success is being achieved with poultry, notwithstanding numerous difficulties in this field also.[17]

Livestock

As Table 3 suggests, and newer figures do not exist, goats and sheep are quite prevalent all over the Federation, with pigs attracting ever more attention. The Northern Nigeria Development Corporation and UAC jointly run a profitable piggery at Minna, southwest of Kaduna in Niger Province, and a Lebanese expatriate in Kano, Mr. K. Maroun, operates Africa's largest piggery (22,500 head in 1963), shipping his excellent product to Lagos from this non-pork-eating center.

Table 3

Estimated Livestock in Nigeria--1960

Region	Cattle	Goats	Sheep	Pigs
Northern	6,500,000	11,000,000	3,000,000	150,000
Western	66,000	650,000	295,000	(a)
Eastern	160,000	1,370,000	800,000	20,000
Total	6,726,000	13,020,000	4,095,000	--

(a) Figure not available. It should be negligible.

Source: Nigeria, National Economic Council, *Economic Survey of Nigeria: 1959* (Lagos: Federal Government Printer, 1959), p. 45, adjusted by "guesstimates" of Northern and Western Ministries of Agriculture. (The Eastern Ministry would not attempt such an "educated" guess.)

Trypanosomiasis *brucei* is the form of African sleeping sickness that prevents the Fulani cattle from being raised in the Middle-Belt and the south. Even in most of the north there is some degree of risk. It is a risk that is a function of the fly concentration, which increases steadily southward.

The West African Institute of Trypanosomiasis Research (WAITR), with facilities at Kaduna and Vom (on Jos Plateau), is now treating one-half million head of cattle with prophylactic drugs on the northern migratory routes each year.[18] With education, control, and drugs, all costly, WAITR believes the opening of the Middle-Belt to cattle is within sight.

Whether mixed-farming should be started before cattle ranching is a question now being considered for the first time. In the meanwhile, Northern Region officials are more immediately concerned with the carrying capacity of the land, increasing the turnover of the herds to lower the percentage of old and useless animals, adding weight to the existing cattle, upgrading the quality of the hides, and improving the marketing channels, particularly those for milk.

There are few fields of endeavor that have as much application to the rest of tropical Africa. A successful quest for solutions to these many complex, but not hopeless, problems would have the broadest of consequences.

Fish

The south's coastal waters, creeks, and lagoons have been a traditional source of fish. In spite of additional catches from the rivers, Lake Chad, and, although gradually, the Atlantic, Nigeria still imports large quantities of dried ("stock") fish from Norway and Iceland. Lake Chad should offer substantially more fish in the future than at present. Its exact potential is not known, but the introduction of boats--present practice involves the use of papyrus rafts--education, research into breeding and migration patterns of the eleven or so edible species, and cooperation with the former-French territories that share this inland sea could bring a doubling of the catch in rather short order.[19]

THE MINERAL AND POWER BASE

The presence of substantial reserves of a variety of minerals and fuels is a desirable, though not a sufficient, condition for the development of modern industry. In this regard, Nigeria is in a fairly fortunate position. Present in varying amounts and grades are tin, columbium, coal and lignite, natural gas, petroleum, limestone, iron, lead, zinc, glass sands, ceramic clays, and zircon.

In all likelihood, petroleum, natural gas, limestone, and iron will have the greatest impact on Nigeria's future industrial development. Only a few years after the announcement that Nigeria had oil in commercial quantities, she is in fourth place among African producers,[20] her railroad is dieselizing, and a petroleum refinery is under construction. The Eastern Region, where all Nigeria's coal mining is carried on, contains both the first gas-powered generating station and Port Harcourt's Trans-Amadi Industrial Estate, whose factories are being supplied with nearby gas for power. The East and the West have cement mills in operation, and the North will soon join them. And a major component of Nigeria's Six Year Plan (1962-68) is a proposed steel mill. The development and utilization of these four domestic mineral resources is a step towards the modern industrial world Nigeria seeks to enter.

It follows that the contribution to the GDP of mining and oil exploration, which has recently been running at less than 11 per cent, will probably increase measurably in the next decade. (See Table 4.)

Table 4

Contribution of Mining and Oil Exploration to GNP (£ million) at Factor Prices of 1957

	Coal	Tinfields	Misc.	Oil Expl.	Total
1950	1.2	6.0	0.1	0.3	7.6
1951	1.0	6.2	-	0.4	7.6
1952	0.9	6.3	0.1	0.6	7.9
1953	1.4	5.8	0.1	0.6	7.9
1954	1.4	5.9	0.2	0.6	8.1
1955	1.7	6.2	0.4	0.7	9.0
1956	1.7	6.8	0.3	0.8	9.6
1957	1.7	6.5	0.2	1.0	9.4
1958					9.4
1959					9.6
1960					10.6

Sources: E. F. Jackson and P. N. C. Okigbo, National Income of Nigeria for the Period 1950-57 (Lagos: Federal Ministry of Economic Development, 1960) (Mimeo.); and W. Stolper, et al., Government Expenditures on Goods and Services (Lagos: Federal Ministry of Economic Development, 1961) (Mimeo.).

Petroleum

In 1957, three years after the IBRD devoted only one paragraph in its comprehensive study of Nigeria to mineral oils (including natural gas),[21] the Shell-BP Petroleum Development Company, a joint subsidiary of the Royal Dutch/Shell Group and the British Petroleum Company, Ltd., made encouraging finds at Oloibiri in the delta area (Yenagoa Province, 45 miles west of Port Harcourt) of the Eastern Region, and Afam (Umuahia Province), 25 miles to the east of Port Harcourt. Two years later, Oloibiri was proving a disappointment; output was falling, sand problems were developing, and water content was causing anxiety. But with the opening of the Bomu field, 14 miles south of Afam, and the development of the Ebubu field in Port Harcourt Province, Shell-BP announced in 1959 that oil in commercial quantities had been found in Nigeria. Thus ended a search begun in 1937, interrupted by the war, and requiring £61 million.[22]

The company has since opened Imo River (Umuahia Province) a few miles to the northwest of Afam, made major gas finds, struck oil in the Mid-Western Region (notably at Ughelli, in Delta Province a few miles to the east of Warri), and secured a prospecting lease for four 1,000-square-mile blocks of the continental shelf.[23] In addition, Shell-BP has constructed an oil terminal at the mouth of the Bonny River, 41 miles from Port Harcourt,[24] and is dredging a channel through the Bonny Bar to a depth of 35 feet.[25]

During December, 1963, crude oil was pumped to Bonny at an average rate of 82,820 barrels per day; and Shell-BP's total annual production for 1963 amounted to 28 million barrels or almost 4 million tons.[26] Shell-BP's originally announced target for 1970 of 70 million barrels per year is now forecast for 1967.[27]

The foregoing figures for Nigeria pertain only to Shell-BP. In 1960-61 Mobil Exploration (Nigeria) Ltd. was unsuccessful with four wells in the Badagri Creek area just west of Lagos. Nevertheless, it joined Tennessee Gas Transmission, Nigeria Gulf Oil Company Ltd., and a Caltex group (American Overseas Petroleum Ltd.) in 1961-62 to complete negotiations with the federal government for off-shore leases.[28] For, on January 18, 1962, Shell-BP had to give up 50 per cent of its oil mining leases to the federal government.[29] Possibly, Mobil _et al_. will make major discoveries in the strips they lease in the coming years. Indeed, Gulf struck oil with its first well in the western part of the Niger delta during January, 1964. Within fifteen years, Nigeria may be a major producer of crude.

Natural Gas

As so often is the case, considerable quantities of natural gas have been found in conjunction with the oil explorations. "The most important field is at Afam, producing 10 million cubic feet [at 1100 BTU per cubic foot] of gas per day; up to 50 million cubic feet of gas per day could be developed at short notice."[30] Shell-BP has also encountered good shows of gas at Ikpe in Uyo Province (Eastern Region), and Bomu, and it is not unlikely that discoveries will be made near Onitsha. At the present time, most of the gas associated with the production of petroleum, which is 75 to 98 per cent methane, is flared off at the well-heads at Bomu, etc.

Twenty million cubic feet of dehydrated "associated gas," however, is feeding the new electric power station at Afam each day via a six-and-one-half-mile-long pipeline that was completed in June, 1962. In addition, gas is now piped three and one-half miles to the Trans-Amadi Industrial Estate in Port Harcourt from Apara, and by July, 1964, a Shell-BP aluminum pipeline will carry gas from near Imo River to Aba eighteen and one-half miles away.[31]

Ultimately, a fertilizer manufacturing plant will be established in the East. Ammonia and nitrate can be made from the gas. But before such an operation is feasible, there will have to be a vastly expanded demand for nitrogenous fertilizers in Nigeria.[32]

Besides educating the farmers on the use of fertilizers, the government might consider making a guaranty to purchase a fixed percentage of the product of such a plant for distribution on a subsidized basis.

Coal and Lignite

Nigeria is the possessor of West Africa's only discovered (1909) coal reserves of any importance (see Table 5). The Enugu mines, opened in 1914, are the sole collieries in West Africa. But, unfortunately, the coal is low quality, sub-bituminous (40 per cent fixed carbon), and until recently not considered to be suitable for coking.[33]

Table 5

Reserves of Coal and Lignite in Nigeria

Place	Province and Region	Proved Reserves*
		267: COAL (in 1961)
Enugu	Enugu, East	42
Ezimo	Enugu, East	29
Orukpa	Benue, North	50
Okaba	Kabba, North	54
Ogboyoga	Kabba, North	82**
Inyi	Onitsha, East	10
		70: LIGNITE (in 1957)
Obomkpa	Benin, West	10
Asaba	Benin, West	60

* Millions of tons indicated by drillings.
**Too much stone for commercial exploitation. (Interview with Mr. C. C. E. Onoh, Chairman of Coal Corp., October 16, 1961, Enugu.)

Sources: Nigeria, Federal Ministry of Lands, Mines and Power, *Minerals and Industry in Nigeria* (Lagos: Federal Government Printer, 1957), pp. 18-19; and Nigeria, Ministry of Mines and Power, *The Coal Resources of Nigeria* (Bulletin No. 28; Kaduna: Geological Survey of Nigeria, 1961), p. 59.

The long-term outlook for the Nigerian Coal Corporation[34] is not sanguine: the railroad, which typically consumes about 50 per cent of the annual output, is scheduled to be completely dieselized by 1983. Moreover, the Electricity Corporation of Nigeria, its second large customer, will be almost completely converted to hydroelectric and gas power generation within a decade. Therefore, the last entries in Table 6 represent only a temporary half to a long downward trend. Indeed, the Obwetti mine was closed down in the 1962-63 financial year, and the Iva mine, which is the oldest and most uneconomical, will be closed by 1965.

Despite this foreboding, the corporation has continued the rationalization of its plant. At present, the new Ekulu mine is the most highly mechanized of the four mines in operation, and the overall producers' output per man-shift averaged 3.66 tons in 1962-63.[35] This is a follow-up of the IBRD Mission's finding that the drop in output per man-shift of face workers from 3.7 tons in 1929 to 1.24 tons in 1953 was ". . . more than can be accounted for by the deteriorating conditions."[36]

In the three-year period 1958-61, a 50 per cent cut in the labor force was accompanied by about a 200 per cent increase in efficiency. Still, in recent years, the corporation has suffered net losses. On March 31, 1963, the accumulated loss stood at £221,329.[37]

Government is faced with somewhat of a paradox. On the one hand, the corporation can maintain and increase efficiency only by further mechanizing. On the other hand, with the oil, hydroelectric, and gas picture being what it is, a decision to allocate further capital to coal may be of dubious validity.[38] Thus, in 1961, a holding action was decided on; the government announced a policy of no further retrenchment.

With regard to lignite, at Asaba "there are two thick lignites, a main seam averaging seventeen feet in thickness separated from an upper seam with a mean thickness of 8 feet by about 12 feet of clay shale."[39]

Although the lignite is workable, it is not yet economic to mine. Heavy rains which would affect the mines' roofs, a lack of communications with the industrial centers of the Eastern Region--the bridge across the Niger River will not be completed until the end of 1965--and an absence of demand combine as a reasonable explanation for non-exploitation.

Table 6

Coal Production*--1948-1962

Year	Amount (tons)
1948-49	610,283
1949-50	526,613
1950-51	583,433
1951-52	562,270
1952-53	613,374
1953-54	679,437
1954-55	675,918
1955-56	750,058
1956-57	790,146
1957-58	848,172
1958-59	905,397
1959-60	684,796
1960-61	565,681
1961-62	596,502
1962-63	608,330

*All production through 1957-58 was from three collieries, Hayes (or Okpara), Iva, and Obwetti (now closed down), with Ekulu and Sitting Pretty (or Ribadu) entering less than full-scale production in 1958-59. All five are near the city of Enugu.

Sources: E. I. Oliver, UK, Board of Trade, Nigeria: Economic and Commercial Conditions in Nigeria (Overseas Economic Survey; London: HMSO, 1957), p. 132; Nigeria, Ministry of Mines and Power, Annual Report of the Mines Division (Lagos: Federal Government Printer, 1961), p. 14; Nigerian Coal Corporation, Eleventh Annual Report for the Year 1960-61 (Enugu: Coal Corporation, 1961), p. 20; and Nigerian Coal Corporation, Draft Annual Report for the Year 1962-63 (Enugu: Coal Corporation, 1963), p. 9.

Hydroelectric Potential

Four stations on the Jos Plateau, with 21,000 kw. of installed capacity, represent Nigeria's present development of water power.

Plans, examined in Chapter 4 below, are in the offing for a multi-purpose project that will include dams on the Kaduna and Niger Rivers. For the first phase, the resulting power capacity is expected to be 960,000 kw. The scheme's practicability for power generation is affected by seasonal fluctuations in rainfall,[40] the fairly level topography, the sizeable distances from the main consuming centers, comparative costs of alternative energy sources, and the demand for electricity. In general, Nigeria is not considered to have a large hydroelectric potential vis-a-vis a number of other African lands.

Tin

The Jos Plateau and its surrounding area provide some 5 per cent of the world's supply of tin; this places Nigeria sixth among the Free-World tin suppliers. Until 1961, when the first domestic smelter commenced operation, all the high-grade cassiterite tin ore from the alluvial deposits was shipped to the United Kingdom.

With the fall of the Far East tin fields in Indonesia, Malaya, and Thailand to the Japanese in 1941, Nigeria took second place behind Bolivia in tin production. World War II proved a boon to the area around Jos, for "this devastating war . . . has given the tin mines an opportunity for more intensive and greater development than has ever been possible before."[41] But the supply is not inexhaustible. The consumption of this resource is shown in the fluctuating figure for proved reserves:

March 1955	136,279 tons
March 1959	101,509 tons
March 1960	95,223 tons
March 1962	111,074 tons.

New prospecting, production outside the declared reserves, and the location by drilling of alluvial deposits buried under a basalt capping up to 150-250 feet in depth have maintained the level of reserves over the 100,000-ton mark.

Columbium

Each year more than three-quarters of the world's production of this ingredient of high-temperature-resisting stainless steels is mined in conjunction with the Jos cassiterite. In fact, production rates of the two minerals often are inversely related, labor and equipment being directed in response to demand. The maximum production of columbite, the pentoxide ore of columbium (or, as it is also termed, niobium), occurred in 1954-55 when 3,152 tons were mined. This was due to the post-Korean stockpiling splurge in the United States.

At present consumption rates, the proved reserve as of March 1962 of 54,271 tons[42] should be adequate for at least another twenty-five years. Furthermore, "there are still large deposits of columbite which have not been properly explored and which will add considerably to these reserves. Columbite is widely disseminated . . . and the geological mapping of a great area of these reserves still needs to be finished."[43] Of course, if the price per ton was to go up markedly, additional reserves would be brought in rapidly. But high freight rates make it unlikely that Nigeria's columbium will be able to compete successfully with a new field in Canada.

Iron

Nigeria has extensive, though not high-grade, iron-ore deposits. These have recently taken on new significance with the decision to erect a small-scale steel plant within a year or so.

The World Bank report[44] referred to the two deposits that are under consideration: (1) proved reserves of 30 million tons on the Agbaja Plateau about 28 miles from Lokoja (Kabba Province, North) near the confluence of the Niger and the Benue, and (2) 40 million tons of the lateritic, sandy deposits near Enugu. The Lokoja ore contains 72½ per cent ferric oxide beneath a hard overburden of lateritic low-grade ore averaging 15 feet in thickness. The soft, friable ore has an average iron content of 50.78 per cent, and unfavorably high percentages of titanium dioxide (.54 per cent), phosphoric anhydride (2.15 per cent), and silica (6.68 per cent).[45] The iron content at Enugu is approximately 43 per cent, but contains larger quantities of silica, phosphorus, and titanium dioxide. Besides, the overburden per ton of ore recovered would be 3 times that at Lokoja,[46] taking 1.6 tons to release 1 ton of screened ore in excess of a quarter of an inch.

The Lokoja ore has been selected as the source of ore for the forthcoming domestic steel facility because it can consistently provide more than 47 per cent iron without screening, and because of its proximity to the Niger (closest point is one-half mile from the river).

As far as the world market is concerned, Nigeria's relatively inferior-grade iron ores are noncompetitive. Extraction difficulties and remoteness of the ore sites are compounding factors that bar their profitable mining.

Limestone

Of economic importance in the manufacture of steel, glass, and cement, limestone occurs throughout the Federation. But deposits suitable for use as a flux in iron manufacture, are not necessarily fit for the cement kiln or the glass furnace.

Portland cement (mainly calcium carbonate and clay; to a lesser extent gypsum) based on limestone quarried locally is now manufactured at Nkalagu, 32 miles northeast of Enugu, and at Ewekoro, on the Lagos-Abeokuta road. And a plant is under construction in the Northern Region near Sokoto City. Large deposits of pure crystalline limestone suitable for glass manufacture are situated at Jakura, 25 miles northwest of Lokoja, west of the Agbaja iron deposits, and at Ukpilla, 75 miles east of Akure in the Western Region. Commercial quantities of limestone are also found at Ashaka (Bauchi Province, Northern Region), on the Gongola River 48 miles north of Gombe, adjacent to the Maiduguri railroad extension, and at a location 3 miles west of Sokoto City.

Limestones containing considerable amounts of magnesium carbonate appear at Igbetti (Oyo Province, West), Elebu (Ilorin Province, North), Burum (Niger Province, North), and Itobe (Kabba Province, North). The Igbetti deposit is being tested with regard to its suitability for the manufacture of "terrazzo" tile and flooring,[47] while the Itobe limestone is of particular interest due to its location only 3 miles from the Niger River (20 miles south of Lokoja) and its proximity to the prospective steel-making site. Other thick beds of limestone are known near Awgu, south of Enugu, and on the Cross River near Calabar.

These facts indicate the large deposits available for future industrial purposes: (1) a minimum proved reserve of 20 million tons of consistent 98.5 per cent calcium carbonate is located at Jakura, and (2) the Nkalagu seam stretches as far as Igumale across the border into the Northern Region. In 1956, the Geological Survey reported that there are about 10 million tons of good limestone above the drainage level at Igumale, with additional reserves of 5 million tons for every 10 feet below this level.

Limestone is a bulky, low-value item. Since road building and construction are accelerating throughout the Federation, it is fortunate that cement-type limestones are available in widely scattered parts of the country.

Glass Sands

The Geological Survey is searching for glass sands near Bida (Niger Province) in the Northern Region, and in many parts of the Western Region.

Large deposits of silica sands have been found near Port Harcourt, Afam, and Enugu in the East, and probably are located elsewhere too in this region.

Due to the depth and hardness of the overburden at Enugu, the Port Harcourt sands, lying beneath 35 feet of soft, non-compacted soil, are the present source for the manufacture of glass containers. Borings, thus far, have indicated a ferric oxide content of .072-.110 per cent--above the limits specified for flint (clear) glass, though satisfactory for, say, beer bottles.

Borings at Imo River have been scheduled, and the extent and quality of this resource will have to await further investigation.

Other Minerals

In addition to clays, especially kaolin and feldspar, for ceramics, firebricks, brick and tile making, and as a mud in oil drilling, Nigeria has varying amounts of some other minerals of potential economic importance.

Over the years, lead and zinc have been mined locally on a small scale. A 350-mile long field stretches in a narrow belt from Ogoja Province (Eastern Region) through Benue and Adamawa Provinces to Bauchi Province (all in Northern Region). The lodes in the area of Abakaliki (Abakaliki Province, Eastern Region) have the most favorable prospects. High transportation costs and relatively low prices have heretofore deterred their development. With the current rise in prices of these metals, a U.K. firm is planning to commence mining in 1965.

The tinfields contain an abundance of zircon, the ore of zirconium. This minor metal is used in laboratories for high temperature applications and in the steel industry as an alloying element In its own right this element, a by-product of the tin and columbite mining, would not pay for its freight charges. At first, after the war, it was thought some of the deposits might have valuable concentrations of thorium. But shipments of this ore did not live up to expectations. Trial shipments to the United States in 1958-59, though, did prove satisfactory with respect to its high hafnium content, which averages twice the hafnium content of zircon from other sources. The resulting 1959-60 shipment of zircon zoomed to 1,575.1 tons. Unfortunately, two years afterward, exports of this mineral totaled only 415.2 tons.

Absent Minerals

Sedimentary rock formations in the south, especially, give Nigeria an important petroleum reserve. Very few nations have it both ways, so it is not surprising that there has been, to date, no discovery of workable gold, diamonds, manganese, or bauxite in Nigeria.

More unfortunately, there are no economic deposits of sulphur (or pyrites),[48] a basic element of the chemical industry, only a small quantity of salt and brines, and no borax, nitrate, sodium carbonate, sodium sulphate, potash, calcium and magnesium chlorides, iodine, etc. Furthermore, extensive prospecting by the Geological Survey has yielded only one phosphate deposit (at Oshosun, near Ifo Junction, about 27 miles from Lagos) of the slightest commercial significance,[49] and one low-grade asbestos deposit (at Shemi, Katsina Province, about 20 miles from Funtua).[50]

Petrochemicals

With respect to petrochemicals, Nigeria's economy has not reached the stage where her domestic needs for hydrocarbon derivatives will support a plant to produce ethylene and propylene glycols, and other organic compounds.[51] Eventually, the domestic plastics industry will probably supply the first major market for such a facility.

SUMMARY AND CONCLUSIONS

Agriculture is, and for many years will be, the mainstay of Nigeria's economy. With a diversified primary sector, Nigeria is not dependent on one export commodity as are many other underdeveloped lands.

Efforts in this sphere cannot be slackened. Indeed, an even greater exertion here should redound to the benefit of Nigeria's incipient manufacturing industry, since a large portion of Nigeria's secondary industry is now concentrated on the processing of agricultural raw materials.

Thus far, Nigeria is meeting with determined, if not always sufficient, endeavors on the agricultural front: the vicissitudes of the international commodity markets, the advancement of science, and the challenge of a growing domestic industry.

Auspiciously, Nigeria has a potential mineral base that promises to go a long way toward meeting her industrial aspirations. Some economists hypothesize that the new nations reap the advantages of the older nations' technological achievements. But a new petroleum producer, even if it should prove to be a second Venezuela, will not find itself in the advantageous position of the first,[52] for surplus crude is the order of the day.

There can be, moreover, little doubt that there are large reserves of natural gas in southern Nigeria. The supply of gas to industries being established in Port Harcourt and Aba is a reality; its provision to Enugu, and Onitsha, among others, is on the near horizon; and, the eventual distribution of this fuel to Lagos is not beyond the realm of probability.

Nigeria has the wherewithal for a modest domestic iron and steel industry, and can meet the growing demand for cement. Also, she has coal and lignite, and a moderate hydroelectric potential. But Nigeria cannot meet the need for the chemicals that are essential materials of almost every secondary industry as well as of modern agriculture. For these, she might always be dependent on imports.

Nigeria is faced with the problem of establishing priorities in a political context. Should natural gas be further developed? If so, even more coal miners will be thrown out of work. Should Asaba's lignite be used by the new steel mill? If so, political promises made in Enugu will not be met. Should the iron and steel mill be erected in the East? If so, political pledges of the Sardauna's government will not be discharged. And so on.

If priorities can be established in a reasonable and objective manner, and if they are followed, more or less faithfully, Nigeria will then have the means to utilize more efficiently her fairly wide range of agricultural and mineral resources in support of her inchoate manufacturing industry.

Footnotes to Chapter 2

1. "Agricultural Development since 1950," Nigeria Trade Journal, Special Independence Issue (September, 1960), p. 58.

2. Nigeria, Constitution of the Federation (Supplement to Official Gazette Extraordinary No. 71, Vol. 50, September 19, 1963 - Part A), Section 69.

3. All regions have Ministries of Agriculture. But even this does not necessarily lead to complete intra-regional coordination. The Northern Region, as a result of politics, the personalities involved, and custom, has divided the field between the Ministry of Agriculture and the Ministry of Animal Health and Forestry.

The Federal Ministry of Economic Development attempts, indirectly, to guide agricultural development policies and coordinate agricultural activities throughout the Federation by operating an Agricultural and Natural Resources Division.

4. In late 1961 the ICA was absorbed, together with the Development Loan Fund, by the new Agency for

International Development, a semi-autonomous agency of the U.S. Department of State. See Chapter 6 below.

5. Economist Intelligence Unit Ltd., op. cit., p. 10.

6. In April, 1963 the Eastern government ordered 1,000 hydraulic hand "stork" presses from the Netherlands that are capable of extracting 90 per cent of the palm oil. Supposedly, they are twice as efficient as traditional methods. If so, they will soon pose a threat for some of the marginal Pioneer Mills. (Barnet and Reef Associates, Inc., Eastern Nigeria Newsletter, Vol. 3, No. 1 [New York, April, 1963], p. 4.)

7. Eastern Nigeria, Ministry of Economic Planning, First Progress Report: Eastern Nigeria Development Plan, 1962-68 (Enugu: Government Printer, O.D. No. 15/1964), p. 6. The region's plan calls for a capital outlay of £1.92 million for this scheme. (Eastern Nigeria, Eastern Nigeria Development Plan, 1962-68 [Enugu: Government Printer, O.D. No. 8/1962], p. 21.) This contrasts with the 1958-59 subsidy of £634 in connection with the rehabilitation program to Eastern farmers. (F. Moore, et al., Prospects and Policies for Development of the Eastern Region of Nigeria [Report Prepared by a Ford Foundation Team; Enugu, 1960], p. 35.)

8. United Nations, Food and Agriculture Organization, Cocoa Statistics, Vol. 6, No. 4 (Rome: Food and Agriculture Organization, October, 1963), p. 5.

9. "Western Nigeria: Cocoa," Statistical and Economic Review (No. 18; London: United Africa Company, Ltd., September, 1956), pp. 1-41.

10. Whenever the writer offered a milk-chocolate candy bar to a Nigerian, he inevitably received a refusal: "No, it's too sweet."

11. "Eastern Region Survey," Daily Times (Lagos), October 23, 1961, p. 34.

12. "Natural Rubber Production in Nigeria," Rubber Trends (No. 7; London: Economist Intelligence Unit, Ltd., September, 1960), p. 23. African production was dominated in 1959 by Nigeria (37.5 per cent), Liberia (30.8 per cent), and Congo (Léopoldville) (28.6 per cent). (Economic Bulletin for Africa, op. cit., p. 49; and United Nations, Statistical Office, Monthly Bulletin of Statistics, Vol. XVIII, No. 2 [New York: United Nations, February, 1962], p. 15.)

13. The north's forest reserves, limited to savannah woodlands, are not sufficient to supply that region's timber needs, especially for fuel.

14. D. H. Buckle, "Timber Operations in West Africa," Unasylva, Vol. 13, No. 1 (Rome: Food and Agriculture Organization of the United Nations, 1959), p. 3.

15. IBRD, op. cit., p. 157.

16. A recent annual report of the Ministry of Agriculture reports that in 1959-60, "There was no marked improvement to response in tidal swamp rice cultivation in Calabar and the project was still largely patronised by the Federal Prisons Department." (Eastern Nigeria, Agriculture Division, Ministry of Agriculture, Annual Report: 1959-60 [Enugu: Government Printer, Official Document No. 2/1961], p. 11.)

17. All the governments are eager to introduce chicken farming on a large scale. An American AID livestock specialist, for instance, tells them that they are the easiest animals to start with; in less than a half a year egg production commences, and there is something to eat; not much land is required; and upkeep is fairly easy. Pig raising takes a bit longer and costs a bit more. Sheep and goats are more difficult to raise, and cattle the most exacting. (Interview with Mr. C. P. Wilder, adviser to the Western Region Ministry of Agriculture, Ibadan, September 26, 1961.) [It should be noted that other experts differ with Mr. Wilder.]

In the fall of 1961, an American in the Eastern Region, AID's Charles ("Chicken" to the local populace) Davis, distributed 20,000 one-day old chicks from the U.S. and the U.K. to five strategic "circle" farms (for eventual redistribution) and conducted training, devised feed formulae, conducted research, designed ventilated housing for the birds, etc. Technical assistance by AID in this field, as in others (see Chapter 6 below), has expanded since then.

18. Active immunization against this protozoon parasite by a vaccine is still only a dream. Only one vaccine has been developed against any protozoan--for East Coast (Africa) Fever [theileria parva], a tick-carried disease which attacks livestock--and that was after World War II. (Interviews with Mr. T. M. Leach, Deputy Director of WAITR, Kaduna, October 19 and 21, 1961.)

19. Interview with Mr. A. R. Maurer, Officer in Charge, the Northern Region Agricultural Research Station at Samaru, October 19, 1961.

20. After Algeria, Libya, and Egypt. By 1967, possibly Nigeria will surpass the latter.

21. IBRD, _op. cit._, p. 134.

22. Statement by P. McGlashan, Managing Director of Shell-BP (Nigeria), in _The Story of Oil in Nigeria_, Shell-BP Petroleum Development Co. of Nigeria Ltd., October 1, 1960, p. 3.

23. "There are reasonable expectations that in future years oil and gas will be found in commercial quantities in the continental shelf as far out to sea as present drilling technique permits." (Nigeria, Mines Division, Ministry of Mines and Power, _Annual Report for the Year ended 31 March, 1960_ [Lagos, 1961], p. 15.)

24. The four storage tanks--three of 110,000 bbl capacity, and the other, a floating-roof tank, of 84,000 bbl--are connected to the Eastern fields by an 18½-mile, 12-inch pipeline via the main collecting station at Bomu. (_The Shell Magazine_, Vol.

XLI, No. 655, London, July, 1961, p. 177.)

The capacity of the terminal is now being increased more than three-fold by the addition of two larger tanks to the original four. (Barclays Bank D.C.O., An Economic Survey: Nigeria [London, November, 1963], p. 24.) This is in anticipation of the terminal being connected to the Mid-Western fields by the £4 million trans-Nigeria trunk pipeline now under construction.

25. The stability of the experimental 12,000-yard-long scratch in the ocean floor made in 1960 was continuously observed through 1962. When the first phase appeared successful, it was decided to further dredge the channel to take larger tankers than those of 25.5 feet draught that can now reach the terminal. When the operation is finished, 33,000-ton, fully-loaded tankers will be able to sail from Bonny.

26. Barclays Bank D.C.O., Overseas Review (London, February, 1964), p. 54.

27. The earlier target was confirmed in an interview with Mr. P. E. L. Fellowes, Shell-BP (Nigeria) Director of Public Relations, Lagos, September 4, 1961. This daily rate of 200,000 bbl would be more than 38 per cent of Canada's 1960 rate (518,000 bbl/day) and slightly more than 7 per cent of Venezuela's 1960 production of 2,846,000 bbl per day. (F. G. Coqueron, et al., Annual Analysis of the Petroleum Industry: 1960 [New York: Chase Manhattan Bank, July, 1961], p. 29.) The Federal Minister of Mines and Power announced the altered date at a meeting with Shell-BP executives. (Nigerian Morning Post [Lagos], March 7, 1964, p. 1.)

28. Control of all minerals is vested in the State.

29. Therefore, the period 1959-61 saw the company expend a great effort in the direction of discovery: twenty-three exploration wells and eight appraisal wells were drilled in 1960, and seven of each in the first half of 1961. A major strike, at

a depth of over 14,558 feet--Africa's deepest--in the Nun River area of Yenagoa Province subsequent to the Ughelli find placed its emphasis in the Niger delta area.

30. Investment Opportunities in Eastern Nigeria, op. cit., p. 18.

31. West Africa (London), April 28, 1962, p. 471, and February 15, 1964, p. 191.

32. In 1962 Nigeria imported £253,178 of fertilizers. Less than one-third of this amount was nitrogenous. The total represented a decrease of £100,000 from two years before. (Nigeria, Federal Office of Statistics, Nigeria Trade Summary, Vol. 45, No. 12 [Lagos: Survey Department, December, 1960], pp. 9-11; and Vol. 47, No. 12, December, 1962, pp. 44, 60-61.)

33. Apparently some recent experiments may have altered the picture. See the discussion in Chapter 7 below.

34. A statutory corporation, established in 1950, which works and develops Nigeria's mines and distributes the coal. See Nigeria, The Laws of the Federation of Nigeria and Lagos, Rev. ed., Chapter 134, Nigerian Coal Corporation (Lagos: Federal Government Printer, 1959).

35. Nigerian Coal Corporation, Draft Annual Report for the Year 1962/63 (Enugu: Coal Corporation, 1963), p. 11.

36. IBRD, op. cit., p. 265.

37. Increased depreciation charges, write-offs of obsolete plant and equipment and stores, and payments connected to the retrenchment program, swelled the loss in 1960-61 to £185,000 which was above what might be expected in the following years. (Nigerian Coal Corporation, Eleventh Annual Report for the Year 1960-61 [Enugu: Coal Corporation, 1961], pp. 9-10.) Two years later the loss was £74,388. The

cumulative deficit was reduced, though, by cancelling the royalty liability from November, 1959 to March 31, 1962 of £254,834. (Nigerian Coal Corporation, 1962-63 Draft Annual Report, p. 8.)

38. For obvious reasons, the Coal Corporation is fighting the suggestion that lignite be used in the proposed Strategic-Udy steel plant (see Chapter 7 below).

39. Nigeria, Mines Department, Mining and Mineral Resources in Nigeria (Lagos: Federal Government Printer, 1957), p. 12.

40. The Jos stations have often been plagued by insufficient rainfall.

41. W. E. Sinclair, "Tin Mining in Nigeria," The South African Mining and Engineering Journal, August 14, 1943, p. 503.

42. Nigeria, Mines Division, Ministry of Mines and Power, Annual Report for the Year ended 31st March, 1962 (Lagos, 1963), p. 25.

43. Mining and Mineral Resources in Nigeria, op. cit., p. 4.

44. IBRD, op. cit., pp. 269-270.

45. Mining and Mineral Resources in Nigeria, op. cit., pp. 5-6.

46. Based on a report of Dr. F. G. Percival, a consulting engineer, in 1955 to the Department of Mines and Power, and quoted in a Compendium of Basic Information Relating to the Proposed Iron and Steel Industry and Market Survey of Iron and Steel Products, Prepared for the National Economic Council by the Production Engineering (PE) Management Group (Nigeria) Ltd., 1961.

47. Nigeria, Federal Ministry of Mines and Power, Annual Report of the Geological Survey for the Year 1958-59 (Lagos: Federal Government Printer, 1961), p. 10.

48. Nigeria's petroleum is sulphur-free.

49. See, particularly, G.S.N. Reports (unpubl.) No. 632, The Abeokuta Phosphates: A Conspectus by H. A. Jones (Ibadan, 25th October, 1957), and No. 634, The Bedded Phosphates of Abeokuta Province by H. A. Jones and A. N. Dempster (Ibadan, 11th July, 1959), in files of Geological Survey, Kaduna South. In answer to those who believe spectacular mineral finds will be discovered throughout the African continent as a matter of course, the Director of the Geological Survey says, "Africa is further along than most people think. . . . We are more advanced [with respect to mapping mineral deposits] than the Canadian Northwest was a few years back." (Interviews with Dr. R. R. E. Jacobson, October 20 and October 24, 1961, Kaduna South.)

50. Samples sent to the Imperial Institute (UK) have proven to be of poor quality with very weak fibres. Possibly it may be utilized as a filler for paint. (Interview with Mr. W. P. Gaskell, Chief Inspector of Mines, Federal Ministry of Mines and Power, September 16, 1961, Lagos.)

51. One main application of ethylene glycol is as an anti-freeze! Ethylene oxide is a starting material for the manufacture of, among other things, detergents. Until the spread of washing machines, Nigeria's domestically produced soap should satisfy her needs for a cleansing agent. Her one detergent plant--established in 1964--uses, in the main, imported raw materials.

52. "On the supply side, there are obviously strong and continuing incentives to produce and market extra low-cost crude from prolific producing areas. In addition, there is the increasing importance of new sources of supply, of newcomers to foreign production and of government demands for expanded output in virtually every producing country." (Walter Levy, "World Oil in Transition," The Economist [London], August 19, 1961, p. 725.)

CHAPTER 3 HUMAN RESOURCES FOR INDUSTRY

Great internal pressures are generating stresses within the Federation. A proliferation of tribes speaking two hundred languages, fifteen of which are major,[1] is the great divisive force plaguing the land. Each original region is dominated by a different political party: the three major tribal groups, Yoruba, Hausa-Fulani, and Ibo, still control the party machinery in the West, North, and East, respectively.

Religion also is a basis of division. The figures usually quoted for Nigeria are 44 per cent Moslem, 34 per cent Christian, and the remaining 22 per cent animist, "pagan," or "traditional."[2] Islam, the major religion of the North, is also making itself felt in the Western Region. It is more than likely the largest religious community in Ibadan, although less orthodox than those of the North, especially with regards to the status of women. Christianity is predominant in the south, Anglicans being in the majority in the West and Roman Catholics in the East; while the Middle-Belt[3] and the Niger delta are the last great centers of traditional beliefs.

Fortunately, the forces at work in Nigeria that emphasize her variety and her latent divisions, have so far been offset by a number of cohesive elements. These include the use of two lingua francas, English and Hausa, which play the role of unifying agents; a common colonial heritage; similar administrative structures; and a federal government that is gaining in national prestige with each passing year.

Differences in culture, language, and religion aside, Nigerians are starting up the path of industrialization with many burdens. They have a low standard of living--$80 was the approximate per capita share of the 1960 GNP (see Chapter 5 below). They are faced with a rigorous climate, and they are subject to all that the word "underdeveloped" connotes: disease, high infant mortality, malnutrition, primitive housing, illiteracy, little purchasing power, a fast growing population, urban unemployment and rural underemployment, and the almost complete absence of a middle class.

The whole imprecise science of economic development is about improving the lot of people. In part, this is accomplished by making better use of human resources, any nation's great asset. The problem of the upgrading of a people can and should be attacked on many fronts, as is being done today in Nigeria.

It would undoubtedly be an extremely difficult task to determine the return the Federation would or should receive on her investment in education. Yet, if Nigerians are to take advantage of new employment opportunities and also attract industry, a skilled labor force and a pool of managers must be created. As will be demonstrated, rapid steps are being taken in this direction, indeed perhaps too rapid!

Also important, from the national point of view, are community development schemes to construct roads and bridges that will give wider access to markets, turning swamp lands into rice paddies, and completing other projects.[4] Additionally, programs of agricultural extension, and alterations in the traditional ways of life, especially with respect to land tenure, are called for.

Again, for the purposes of this work, much of the foregoing cannot be dealt with directly. The quality and quantity of labor and management in Nigeria is the major concern here. Education, though, will be treated in some detail: (1) because it will affect, ultimately, Nigeria's ability to take advantage of her many economic opportunities--to increase her "absorptive capacity"; and (2) because it will illuminate a basic contradiction: the more that is spent by government on education, the less there is remaining for other capital investments that are supposed eventually to provide employment.

Health and welfare will also be discussed briefly. This is a subject that has an impact on the performance of the working force, from productivity to absenteeism. Further, as does education, it is one that compels government expenditure.

INDUSTRIAL LABOR IN NIGERIA

The 1952-53 census reported a male labor force of 8.25 million, of which 6 per cent were occupied in the trades and commerce, another 6 per cent were craftsmen and industrial workers, and 3 per cent government employees and professionals.[5]

In September, 1957, figures were calculated for undertakings employing at least ten persons of all races. The total number of males and females occupying managerial, administrative, and technical positions, as well as clerks, foremen, artisans, skilled and unskilled laborers, and apprentices, in processing and manufacturing, totaled 31,575.[6] Eighteen months later, the manufacturing enterprises registered with all the regional labor offices employed 45,206 people.[7] If it is assumed the male labor force reached 9 million in 1959, then it is seen that only 0.5 per cent was employed in manufacturing industry. Of these 45,000, approximately 3,000 may be considered to occupy management positions, from chargehand and foreman to engineer and administrator.

Labor Efficiency

It is a cliché to say that African labor is only apparently cheap labor, because the high cost of training and supervision required to achieve an adequate level of productivity more than offsets their low wages. A fairly recent publication of the Inter-African Labour Institute, in discussing the usual topics of health and nutrition, climate, incentives, etc.,[8] expounds the familiar. At the same time it omits almost wholly any discussion of Nigeria. Peter Kilby's essay, "African Labour Productivity Reconsidered,"[9] on the other hand, is based entirely on field work in Nigeria. Kilby concludes:

> First, the African does not possess any inherent incapacities or attitudes which are detrimental to efficient production. In fact, it can be argued that regarding continuous labour and repetitive operations he is particularly well-suited to modern production. Secondly, the African's willingness to work considerably exceeds [italics mine] that of labourers in developed countries. . . . Careful selection, monetary incentive and surveillance from higher management will reduce supervisory weaknesses to negligible proportions. Thus we may say that the quality of the African labour is adequate to meet the needs of the continent's developing economies, now and in the foreseeable future.

In discussing the efficiency of labor in an African milieu, the topics of absenteeism and turnover are usually broached. The writer's many conversations with expatriate managers throughout Nigeria bear this out while supporting Kilby's main conclusions:

> With the large machines, one man presses a button every forty-five to sixty seconds to clear it. . . . His output is the same as in the U.S.[10] [His pay is £150 per year.]

> With the standard stuff their work is very good considering their very low pay. . . . With the special stuff they're bloody awful [especially with respect to measurements].[11]

> We have very small labor turnover; our conditions of work are pretty good. . . . The standards we accepted ten years ago no longer hold.[12]

> Our supervisors report the men are doing a fairly good job; but it is not always very easy. . . . Labor turnover of the working force is less than 5 per cent per year. With the junior staff it is usually higher--they leave to improve their education.[13]

> It's difficult to make them feel responsible--they're playful; it takes much training. . . . Labor turnover is very, very low--they would like to keep their jobs; people are at the gates.[14]

> Considering the climate, absenteeism is quite low. Maybe [it exists] on the midnight shift and in the heavy rains--it's not a problem.[15]

> They can do the work quite easily--it's a simple process. They'll work if a European [the chief smelter] is with them.[16]

The foregoing corroborates the statement in the Westinghouse iron and steel feasibility study: "Productivity is satisfactory if adequate supervision is maintained."[17] Implicit in all this is the inference that Nigerians want to work. This is demonstrably true. Should an advertisement for a position be placed in the newspapers, hundreds and even thousands of applications will result. The cities are repositories of the unemployed. The worker knows he is replaceable, and with many mouths dependent upon him--the extended family system results in an elastic response of dependents as his wages increase--he is not one to wander.

It may be observed that managers, in general, do complain about a lack of employee loyalty. They are constantly shopping for a better offer, and will move on if they see an opportunity. The ebullient Ibos are singled out as typically thinking they can all be a "Zik"[18] some day. In the south, where most of the opportunity lies, motivation abounds

With regard to female production workers, the Bedford truck assembly plant in Apapa (Lagos) hired six in 1961. These blue-jeaned mechanics were given a commendatory rating by their supervisor.[19] The Kaduna Textile Mill hires no women: it is against the law for women to work at night, and the men raised a hullabaloo about their working day-shifts only. In all likelihood, women will not become an important factor in the industrial labor market, so long as a vast reserve of unemployed males exists.

Unionism in Nigeria

The period 1931-34 saw Nigeria's export earnings average only half of the 1928 figure. The ensuing financial difficulties resulted in cuts in government salaries, which, then as now, set the standard for all wages. The falling wages, and unemployment, led the railwaymen, miners, and others, to follow up the encouragement of trade unions in British West Africa by Sidney Webb, the Colonial Secretary in the Labour Government of 1929-31. But with economic recovery in 1934, the newborn labor dynamism faded

It was not until World War II that the first labor ordinances were passed. Rising prices in a wartime economy resulted in ninety-seven unions in 1945, when there had been nine in early 1941. The postwar labor unrest--prices were still rising, the unions were beginning to flex their muscles, and politics was becoming a prime issue--culminated in the "Enugu Shooting of 1949": twenty-one coal miners were shot dead when they clashed with armed police. Although the next decade witnessed a doubling of the total union membership, a split that occurred in 1949 "due largely to the pressure of militant political elements continued."[20] The breach was healed at times, only to be renewed once again. On October 13, 1961, it was announced that the long standing dispute between the Western-oriented Trades Union Congress of Nigeria and the left-leaning Nigeria Trades Union Congress (N.T.U.C.) had been settled.[21] But political ideology could not be forgotten for even a few years. In May, 1962, N.T.U.C. unions withdrew from the newly created United Labour Congress of Nigeria (U.L.C.). Thus, they rejected the U.L.C. decision to affiliate with the pro-Western International Confederation of Free Trade Unions.

Table 7

Growth of Nigerian Trade Unions

	Total Number of Unions	Total Membership
1940	7	---
1941	27	12,892
1942	80	26,275
1943	85	27,154
1944	91	30,000
1945	97	27,261
1946	100	52,747
1947	109	76,362
1948	127	90,864
1949-50	140	109,998
1950-51	144	144,358
1951-52	124	152,230
1952-53	131	143,282
1953-54	152	153,089
1954-55	177	165,130
1955-56	232	175,987
1956-57	270	198,265
1957-58	298	235,742
1958-59	318	254,097
1959-60	347	259,072
1960-61	360	274,126

Sources: J. I. Roper, Labour Problems in West Africa (London: Penguin Books, 1958), p. 107; Nigeria, Federal Department of Labour, Annual Report: 1958-59 (Lagos: Federal Government Printer, 1961), p. 39; and Nigeria, Federal Ministry of Labour, Annual Report for the Year 1960-61 (Lagos: Federal Ministry of Information Printing Division, 1964), p. 58.

Although the breach in the Nigerian labor movement had reappeared, the two rival congresses formed a Joint Action Committee (J.A.C.), which achieved a three-day quasi-General Strike in September, 1963. The strike was halted after the federal government agreed to appoint a commission of inquiry into wages and salaries. The governments' unwillingness to meet fully the commission's recommendations led, however, to a thirteen-day national strike in June, 1964. It is likely that further labor strife will occur as the J.A.C. gains victories, both economic and political. Only time will tell if the Nigerian labor movement is no longer to remain fractionalized and beset by apathy among much of its membership as it has been throughout most of its history.

Not inconsequentially, of the 274,126 union members in 1960-61, more than 141,000 were employees of government, including the statutory corporations. And the vast majority of the 10,000 or so unionized industrial workers are members of company unions, like the Shell-BP Workers' Union, Nigeria. In addition, Nigerian labor has been weakened by events beyond its control. Two examples of the latter are the regionalization of the government employees brought about by independence, and the financial problems of the coal miners' union due to the retrenchment in the mines. Perhaps, the legislation passed in 1960 allowing for the check-off enhanced the unions' outlook.[22] Management with a British tradition is not anti-union, and thus far seems willing to more than meet the minimum wages set by government.[23] In the long run, greater education, improvement in transportation and communications, experience, and a concentration on the needs of the workers,[24] rather than on international politics, should lead to a more responsible and effective labor movement in Nigeria.

EDUCATION AND TRAINING

Thus far all Nigerians are showing a marked enthusiasm for education. The youngsters want it, the oldsters want them to have it.[25] The subject of education is above politics by being championed by all. It is not surprising, then, to find that probably more has been accomplished since 1957 from the point of view of both plans and programs, on the one hand, and results, on the other hand, than in any other field. Since it is a non-controversial subject, the international agencies, foreign governments, and particularly the philanthropic foundations are expending their greatest efforts in this direction.

Primary and Secondary Education

In 1942, when the first ten-year plan for education was prepared, the total expenditure on education by government and the native authorities was £364,983;[26] there were 27,000 elementary students and 1,570 secondary students in the north, and 313,000 in elementary schools and 4,500 in secondary schools in the south. In 1958, two years before independence, the total enrollment in all Nigerian primary and secondary schools was 2,635,978.[27]

Since 1955, the West has provided six years of free primary education, beginning at the age of six, and maintains a policy of attempting to provide sufficient places for about 10 per cent of the successful primary school leavers.[28] The East also, for a time, instituted free primary education. In 1962 its primary enrollment of 1,266,566 (in 6,478 schools) exceeded that of the West by 157,000. But its secondary enrollment of 32,712 had not expanded proportionately, and was more than 100,000 less than in the West.[29]

Lagos, with its Western Region tradition, the financial support of the federal government (70 per cent of recurrent costs), and a starting age of five for free primary education, had 98,511 primary students in 1962, and its secondary enrollment reached 10 per cent. With a background of high land costs in the Federal Territory, and poor-quality sub-soils, which lead to expensive foundations, Lagos is now faced with providing schools for more than 138,000 primary students by 1970.[30]

The North, with a larger population than the south, has always lagged far behind in this field; it contributed some 12 per cent to the 1962 national total of 3,029,509 students.[31] A prime cause for the slow development was Moslem resistance to the Christian missionary educational efforts. But a new day is coming. The Sardauna's government wants not only to "Nigerianize" the civil service of the region, it wants to "Northernize" it. A 1961 White Paper[32] states that between 1970 and 1975, 25 per cent of the eligible age group will complete primary education (800,000 enrollment in 1970), and 10 per cent of these will go on to secondary education.[33]

In sum, the foregoing presents an impressive picture. The figures, though, do not show the preponderance of untrained teachers, and do not deal with the presence of under-age children in a grade, the quality of the syllabi, the size of the classes, and so forth. Nigerians, especially in the south, have an enthusiasm for education that all visitors are quick to notice. "This all too often is shown in an almost pathetic belief in the efficacy of a certificate or diploma in getting a job."[34] It will be shown in Chapter 6 that education expenses in the south, for the most part for primary education, are approaching 40 per cent of the regional recurrent (non-capital) budgets; the North's, with 22 per cent in 1963, will rise also.

University Education[35]

In addition to teacher training colleges, Nigeria has five growing universities. It was only in 1960 that Professor Federick Harbison of Princeton University estimated that Nigeria's university output per year was 300, and put her graduates returning from overseas at 700. This left a deficit of 1,000 to meet the minimum need for high-level manpower: including graduate teachers, engineers of all kinds, agricultural, forestry and fishery specialists, veterinarians, doctors, and scientists (for research institutes). Four years later, overseas and domestic institutions are supplying graduates in excess of this requirement. (Approximately 2,000 Nigerians are enrolled in American colleges and universities, and about 8,000 more are in the U.K.)

The University of Ibadan (UI), a federal institution, opened its doors in 1948 to 55 students. In 1963-64, this number had risen to 1,800 undergraduates who were working towards either a University of London degree or UI's own in 24 academic departments. UI also has a Department of Extra-Mural Studies, the Nigerian Institute of Social and Economic Research, a medical school,[36] and various institutes.

Following the lead of the North and East, the West established another university, more parochial in character, at Ife. It opened in 1962 with arts and social sciences in temporary buildings, and 244 students. The end of the decade should see 1,300 to 1,500 students studying agriculture, engineering, medicine, veterinary medicine, architecture, town planning, estate management, and dental surgery.

In the East, the University of Nigeria has been functioning at Nsukka, an hour's drive north of Enugu, since October, 1960. Based on the American land-grant system, and (on an AID contract) employing a large contingent from Michigan State University on its faculty, "Zik's Dream" is a burgeoning reality. In 1960-61 more than £2.75 million was expended on capital account. The 1,300 students in residence in 1962-63 should multiply four and a half times by 1972.

The Nigerian College of Arts, Science and Technology (NIGERCO), with branches in Zaria, Ibadan, and Enugu, was opened in 1952. This federal institution was established to provide work of non-degree nature. It was not long, however, before it deviated from this concept. The Zaria branch became the site of the engineering faculty of UI. The Ibadan branch amalgamated with the University at Ife, though eventually it may be transferred to UI, and the Enugu branch affiliated with the University of Nigeria. The Zaria branch, including the engineering school, together with the Agriculture Research Station at Samaru, the Veterinary Research Institute at Vom, the Institute of Administration at Zaria, and the Ahmadu Bello College, primarily a school of Koranic Studies, under construction in Kano, were assimilated in October, 1962, by the new Ahmadu Bello University of the North.

Lastly, in 1964, the University of Lagos commenced the construction of its physical plant. Two years earlier it opened at a temporary site. Following an Ashby proposal, the Faculty of Business and Social Sciences[37] offers evening courses as does the Faculty of Law. This represents a necessary innovation for this country. The new university also has Nigeria's second medical school, and will add an engineering faculty in late 1964.

Technical Training

In adapting her human resources to the requirements of an industrial milieu, Nigeria must supply vocational training on a large scale. This she is beginning to do. Aside from teacher training colleges and agriculture schools, the Federation is establishing a series of technical institutes and trade centers. An outstanding example of the former is the Yaba Technical Institute in Lagos. The success of it and others like it should go some way towards weakening Nigeria's strong bias toward literary and academic subjects.

The student at Yaba usually spends nine months at the college, fifteen months in industry, and then completes the "sandwich" course with another nine months at Yaba. At present, during any one time, there are 200 students in residence working towards the UK City and Guilds Institute Ordinary Certificates in mechanical engineering, electrical engineering, and building. The great majority of the students are sponsored by the public corporations, such as the Electricity Corporation of Nigeria, only a comparatively few by industrial firms.[38] Part-time day courses are being developed for about 240 students and an evening course will have 400 working for the Ordinary Certificate (six years), 170 enrolled in commerce and stenography, and 150 in miscellaneous course-work. By 1970 it is hoped that 300 per year will receive Ordinary Certificates and 100 more the Higher National Certificates of the UK.[39]

Similar institutes are in being at Enugu, Ibadan, and Kaduna; one is planned for Benin City, and two more are being considered for Kano and Port Harcourt. Moreover there are eight trade centers--one is attached to the Yaba Technical Institute--(known in the North as technical training schools), craft centers, secondary commercial schools, and an Emergency Science Training Center in Lagos. The major problem faced by all is the achievement of competent staffing. The industrial concerns will also have to lend their continued support, if the sandwich courses are to succeed.[40]

Industrial and commercial expatriate firms are, pari passu, setting up their own technical training schools to meet their particular needs. In this they are in company with the Electricity Corporation of Nigeria, the Nigerian Railway Corporation, and the Nigerian Ports Authority.[41] UAC's first training school was opened in 1954. Today it runs schools at Burutu, Kano, Aba, Sapele, and Lagos, and provides a five-year course for indentured apprentices, "booster" classes for craftsmen and supervisors, and courses in new techniques. In 1962, UAC set up a Territorial Training Centre for its administrative staff, both management and non-management. In the future, it will be expanded to include marketing, salesmanship, and senior accounts courses.

The Union Trading Company (UTC) of Switzerland conducts a motor training school in Enugu, taking boys from all over the Federation who have completed between six and eight years of schooling.[42]

Shell-BP runs its own large trade school in Port Harcourt. Selected graduates are then sent further on scholarships, especially to Yaba Technical Institute and the engineering school at Zaria. Additionally, it hires forty summer employees per year, many of them being their Zaria "scholars." This is of particular importance in a land where the engineering student has little opportunity to put to practice the theory he is learning. (Again, the students are not bound to Shell.) The Head of Personnel Planning for Shell-BP expressed a sentiment that is repeated ofttimes by the large industrial firms. "More and more we realize, the best people are those we train ourselves."[43]

The state of technical training today in Nigeria is considered "laughable" by some. But as smaller firms establish themselves they will require manpower that has the ability to step into technical and commercial positions. This bottleneck will only be ameliorated if vocational, technical, and commercial training is provided on a broad basis. The UAC's and the Shell's set up their schools because the trained manpower they required was not available. Today they claim, in general, that the future of Nigeria is, in good part, dependent on the quality of its human resources, and that the companies alone cannot bear the burden. Government, for its part, will have to create external economies in this field, especially for smaller firms. It will also have to adapt the U.K. course work to meet the needs of Nigeria. Greater emphasis on practical work will be necessary. At the more advanced level, one pernicious circle will be broken when enough industry has been established so that vacation time programs can absorb a meaningful number of students. For the time being, most of Nigeria's technical specialists will require "seasoning" abroad.

HEALTH AND WELFARE

Nigeria was once part of that section of West Africa known as the "White Man's Grave"--"Beware and take heed of the Bight of Benin/ There's few come out, though many go in." Today, the scourge of disease is primarily one that the Nigerian, and not the expatriate, faces. All the diseases of the temperate climes from measles to polio plus those that flourish in the tropics are present in Nigeria. For most Nigerians the rigors of the climate are compounded by an inadequately balanced diet. The European and the educated Nigerian boils and filters his water, takes malarial suppressants regularly,[44] receives an effective inoculation against yellow fever, and does not swim in and drink from rivers infested with the blood fluke that induces bilharzia.

In the last ten years, rural Nigeria has received especial attention with respect to health measures. In Northern Nigeria, a sulphone pill, dapsone, is being administered to more than 200,000 lepers; in the East, with the technical assistance of the WHO and materials from UNICEF, a yaws eradication campaign has been underway since 1954; in Western Nigeria, the number of smallpox vaccinations rose from 782,727 in 1954 to 3,045,525 in 1957.[45]

With a ratio of 1 qualified physician to 50,000 patients,[46] most of Nigeria's doctors are government employees. As with education, the regions' budgets are further taxed for necessary but non-developmental purposes. It might be noted that both the Western and Eastern Regions have committed themselves to the eventual introduction of a National Health Service.

The potential industrialist, then, is faced with problems of a different kind than he deals with in Europe and America. For example, it would be advisable to consider the establishment of a canteen for his employees, and the part-time employment, at least, of a medical practitioner. But even with a canteen, many of the employees will buy their _gari_ or cassava meal from the women hawking it at the factory gates.

Housing, too, is a factor bearing on the workers' productivity. New and improved housing is going up in the urban areas, with mud and wattle giving way to cement block construction. Yet, not unlike New York practices, landlords are crowding together the occupants of their dwellings in order to maximize profits.

The urban areas are growing rapidly (see Chapter 1 above). Nigeria's leading industrial area, Lagos, is notorious among Nigerians for its high cost of living, and rent is the main malefactor. If 1953 is taken as the base year, the group price index for accommodation averaged 186 in 1962.[47]

A word about social security is in order:

> At present, the only measures of social security in existence for workers are the workmen's compensation scheme under

> which workers are covered for accidents at work; limited provision under the Labour Code for sickness and maternity leave; pensions on retirement for public servants; and a small number of private employer Provident Funds and similar schemes.[48]

On April 1, 1962, all private employers of ten, or more workers, excluding the tin mines, had to commence the payment of matching contributions--the workers' and the employers' are at the rate of 3d. for every complete 5/- of wages--to the new National Provident Fund. The lump sum plus interest will be paid to the worker at age fifty-five or retirement from work whichever is later; provisions have also been made for payments when the worker emigrates permanently, has been out of work two years, etc.[49]

As the proportion of industrial workers in the population increases, and as the political power of the mass of the population makes itself felt with its newly acquired education, this and other schemes will assume greater importance. It will be part of the price of social stability. Sections of the press are already demanding the creation of a National Rent Control Board. So, as with education and public health, welfare and social services compete with purely developmental expenditures.

NIGERIAN MANAGEMENT AND ENTERPRISE

Availability

To paraphrase two American authorities, management can be considered an economic resource, a system of authority, or an elite. In the broadest sense it incorporates the functions of (1) risk undertaking and handling of uncertainty, (2) planning and innovation, (3) coordination, administration and control, and (4) routine supervision.[50] It has occasionally been the practice to differentiate the entrepreneur, who is the promoter and risk taker, from the manager, or professional administrator. In a country like Nigeria, where foreign investors have to provide both capital and know-how, once they have scouted out an industrial opportunity, the distinction is often academic.

It is management that will largely determine the productivity of the labor under its supervision. Foreign firms realize that the Nigerian governments frown upon expatriate management. Furthermore, they are well aware that it costs much more to maintain a European in Lagos than to employ a Nigerian in the same post. But not until local nationals are qualified to administer successfully the expatriate investments will local nationals assume these responsibilities. And, patently, Nigerians are not yet prepared to assume the role of "captains of industry." This is not to be interpreted as a criticism; industrial projects are new to Nigeria.

The Smythes list a roll-call of personalities who have made their mark in one or more of the following: real estate, rubber and cocoa, road transport, cotton, timber and lumber, trading, and building construction.[51] The industrial establishment is not listed because there was no tradition for it. Without industry, and economic development in general, there was a dearth of jobs for men with technical and vocational training. Not surprisingly, the colonial government, on the one hand, absorbed potential managerial manpower, and, on the other, reduced this potential by limiting the opportunity to acquire a technical education.

In 1954, an Oxford researcher saw the beginnings of an entrepreneurial class in the Nigerian owners of truck transport: "Industrialization requires the ability to deal with problems of fixed capital of this kind."[52] Hawkins was thinking specifically of the heavy wear and tear these lorries experienced on the rough Nigerian roads. In dealing with specific capital goods, the owner-operators had to consider depreciation, obsolescence, and maintenance of capital.

Some of the successful have entered light industry--tire retreading, printing--but the vast majority have done what successful businessmen have done from Iran to Chile: engage in speculative and very profitable residential building.

Expatriate business with its on-the-job training and internal promotion,[53] the technical training institutes, and universities both in Nigeria and abroad, the military and the governments, will supply qualified Nigerian managers in increasing numbers over the next decade. The creation of an entrepreneurial class willing to make the plunge into the industrial sector will be a more elusive goal. Hopefully, the Nwoke's[54] and the Eluchie's,[55] who begin as African businessmen engaged in small enterprises of a quasi-industrial nature and who transmute into full-fledged entrepreneurs, will proliferate. But the lack of credit and of knowledge are generally the major barriers. Therefore, in the near term, it is the Nigerians, successful in commerce and the law, who must be willing to take lower short-term profits than they have generally received,[56] if Nigerian enterprise is to develop on a significant scale. In the meantime, it is government, holding share capital "in trust" for the people, which will be the usual Nigerian partner of foreign capital in these ventures.

Organization of Production

As would be expected, individual proprietorships, while dominant in the crafts, and partnerships are not important production units in Nigerian manufacturing. It is the corporation that predominates. (The company may be either "private" or "public" [ownership] when a non-government organization; and is called a development corporation when it is a government organization.) The difficulty of raising capital on the large scale required by modern manufacturing usually militates against the other forms of organization. The Lagos Stock Exchange (see Chapter 6 below) is facilitating the transfer of ownership in, and the further raising of capital for, these corporations.

To complete the gamut, a word should be mentioned regarding producers' cooperatives. All the governments are promoting cooperation, from credit societies to consumers' cooperatives. But outside of craft and artisan societies (e.g., the Benin Ebony Carvers Co-operative Society, which has a workshop on the Yaba Industrial Estate) and cooperative fishing schemes, producers' cooperatives play a minor role. One activity in which they occasionally are able to overcome the usual difficulties faced by them[57] is primary production; a few Pioneer Oil Mills, for example, are now established on this basis in the East.

SUMMARY AND CONCLUSIONS

The largest recurrent expenditures by the regions are made on education. Statistically, the growth in both schools and students is impressive. It is, however, this very growth and concomitant expenditure that poses a great dilemma for Nigeria. To be sure, education is an investment as well as an expense. Universal schooling should improve the quality of the work produced by Nigerian labor; it should raise workers' motivations; and it should give them a background of knowledge to draw upon in making decisions. Thus, it should make them amenable to an industrial milieu of more complexity than now exists in their country. Still, it may be suggested that Nigeria is extending her primary education plant at the cost of secondary school facilities. Moreover, other worthwhile areas are necessarily neglected. Nigeria now graduates hundreds of thousands each year from her primary schools, most of whom cannot further their education. Unless more attention is paid to this situation, unless priorities are altered, Nigeria will soon be faced with a disillusioned, semi-educated mass of young people. The ultimate effect on Nigeria's vaunted stability is all too evident.

Expenditures by government on public health measures, as with education, is improving the quality of Nigeria's manpower, while adding to the already surplus labor force. Furthermore, tangible development projects are postponed. It is not suggested that it should be otherwise. But, again, sufficient thought by responsible Nigerians has not been given to the consequences of present day policies in the whole field of social welfare.

Turning to the Nigerian labor force, we should note that as more skill is required, more training and supervision will be needed. Maintenance "trouble-shooting" is exceedingly difficult for a people who have no tradition of playing with, and fixing, mechanical gadgets as children. Contrary to customary belief, European managers find their Nigerian workers' absenteeism and turnover rates low, due consideration having been made for the personnel procedures employed--often, none--and the rate of pay. Nigerians are willing, and even over-eager, to work in industrial establishments. Nevertheless, they are just as willing to "job-hop" as, say, Americans, in answer to greater monetary rewards.

At this juncture, it may be said that Nigeria's human resources will do more for industry than conversely. For one may justifiably conclude that Nigeria's labor, though not cheap, presents no barrier to the introduction of well-managed industry. With the labor surplus growing continuously, Nigerian laborers will continue to have an "incentive" to stay on the job. With unions in a relatively weak state, "make-work" rules and "featherbedding" are of no consequence. As with the belief in the menace to Europeans of disease, the currently accepted opinion abroad of Nigerian labor is ill informed and amounts to a myth.

But it is no legend that there is a scarcity of qualified African managers. Time, money, and education will deal with the problem. Meanwhile, expatriate corporations will have the added expenses of supplying non-Nigerian managers and operating expanded training programs. And budding Nigerian ventures will face a competitive situation with less than a reasonable chance of success.[58] Prosperous Nigerian entrepreneurs in other fields have, for the most part, steered clear of manufacturing. Until these vigorous men have a change of heart, fewer Nigerians will have an opportunity to acquire managerial skills. Beyond this, the development of industry will continue to be dependent on the Nigerian governments and expatriate firms.

Nigeria, then, is faced with the task of trying to industrialize, so that she may join the company of modern nations, and still escape some of the pitfalls that this catching-up entails: she must train her younger citizens while weighing the effects of ever-increasing government expenditures on education. At the same time, the education of most of the children only through primary school could result in a mass of dissatisfied, displaced would-be workers. She must provide for the welfare of her people, yet not bankrupt herself. And she must attract Nigerian entrepreneurs to manufacturing without erecting obstacles to foreign investment.

Footnotes to Chapter 3

1. English is the language of government, business, and the elite.

2. Dr. Frodin repeats Trimingham's estimate that 70 per cent of the Northern Region is Moslem. In all probability, the far northern provinces of Sokoto, Katsina, and Kano fall within the 90 per cent range. (R. Frodin, op. cit., p. 9; and J. S. Trimingham, Islam in West Africa [London: Oxford University Press, 1959], app. v.)

3. It is in the Middle-Belt that there are especially strong fears of economic discrimination, as well as of religious intolerance. While the new nation was celebrating its independence in early October, 1960, large-scale rioting was suppressed in Tivland, the Benue Province home of more than 3/4 million Tivs. These agriculturalists, who raise Nigeria's benniseed (sesame) crop, are very much in

favor of the creation of a new Middle-Belt Region, for they expect Moslem (Fulani-Hausa) domination now that the restraining influence of the British has been withdrawn.

In 1958 the Willink Commission recommended to the Secretary of State for the Colonies that no new regions be created until after Independence. (Great Britain, Report to Parliament by the Secretary of State for the Colonies, Nigeria: Report of the Commission appointed to enquire into the fears of Minorities and the means of allaying them [Cmnd. 505; London: Her Majesty's Stationery Office, 1958].) Chief O. Awolowo, Yoruba politician and leader, in his autobiography says that the Commission gave no thought at all to the danger to the entire Federation inherent in the size and population of the Northern Region. (O. Awolowo, AWO: the Autobiography of Chief Obafemi Awolowo [Cambridge: Cambridge University Press, 1960], p. 200.)

4. An interesting work in this field is I. C. Jackson's Advance in Africa: A Study of Community Development in Eastern Nigeria (London: Oxford University Press, 1956).

5. Statistics on the women, who, for example, outnumbered the men in trade, were not available.

6. Economic Survey of Nigeria, 1959, op. cit., p. 107. Including omissions, the total for all categories was 529,478; with 111,208 in construction and 62,630 in mining and quarrying. The armed forces, but not the police, are omitted. It was established that if firms of 5 to 9 employees were included only another 7,000 would be added to the figure for Nigeria and the Southern Cameroons. 1,327 females are included in the total.

7. Nigeria, Federal Department of Labour, Annual Report: 1958-59 (Lagos: Federal Government Printer, 1961), p. 29. 1,207 firms hiring less than 10 employees were included in the tabulation. More adequate and up-to-date statistics are not yet available.

8. Inter-African Labour Institute, The Human Factors of Productivity in Africa: A Preliminary Survey (2nd ed.; London: Commission for Technical Co-operation in Africa South of the Sahara, 1960).

9. The Economic Journal, LXXI (June, 1961), 273-291.

10. Interview with Mr. D. C. Mayer, Commercial Manager of the plastics firm, N.I.P.O.L., Ibadan, September 22, 1961.

11. Interview with Mr. R. T. L. Watson, Manager, Crittal-Hope [window-frames], Mushin (near Lagos), August 30, 1961.

12. Interview with Mr. R. E. Rowatt, Factory Manager, Nigerian Tobacco Company, Ibadan, September 19, 1961.

13. Interview with Mr. M. A. Nwankwo, Senior Industrial Relations Supervisor, Shell-BP, Port Harcourt, October 3, 1961.

14. Interview with Mr. H. Hansel, Technical Manager, Nigerian Breweries, Aba, October 6, 1961.

15. Interview with Mr. R. A. Mortimer, Commercial Manager, Kaduna Textile Mill, Kaduna South, October 20, 1961.

16. Interview with Mr. F. Dos Santos, Managing Director, Nigeria Enbel Tin Smelting Co., Ltd., Jos, October 27, 1961.

17. Westinghouse Electric International Co., et al., Report on the Feasibility of Establishing an Integrated Steel Mill in Nigeria, Prepared for the Federation of Nigeria (New York, 1961), Appendix XIII (Labor), p. 2. "It would seem difficult to sustain the charge of natural laziness and inefficiency of the Nigerian worker. In any case, it would be wrong to assume that labour is the only important factor in the maintenance of efficiency or the achievement of high industrial productivity. In Nigeria, as

elsewhere, organizational and technical factors such as proper supervision and equipment, factory layout, and the system of distribution and co-ordination of work, may be equally, or at times even more, important." (T. M. Yesufu, An Introduction to Industrial Relations in Nigeria [London: Oxford University Press, 1962], p. 115.)

18. A reference to Nnamdi Azikiwe, Nigeria's first native-born Governor-General and first President.

19. Interview with Mr. C. A. Ince, Commercial Manager, UAC Bedford truck assembly plant, Apapa, September 15, 1961.

20. J. I. Roper, op. cit., p. 76. "It would be helpful to remember that the trade unionists in African countries are not just workers, but ardent anti-colonial nationalists as well." (T. M. Yesufu, op. cit., p. 152.)

21. Daily Times (Lagos), October 13, 1961, p. 1.

22. The check-off is non-compulsory. The union under the law must meet a number of requirements, such as submitting a statement of accounts to the Federal Minister of Labour.

23. As of June, 1964, there is no law re minimum wages or overtime. Moral suasion only can be exerted. The Federal Minister of Labour recommends forty-four hours in general, and frowns on overtime work. In the East and West, employees in government, during 1962--and there have been no general increases since then--received a minimum of 5/- a day for a 44-hour week; in the North there were provincial rates. The federal government paid a minimum daily rate of 5/10d. in Lagos and between 3/10d. and 4/3d. elsewhere. The Morgan Wages Commission of Inquiry released its report during the course of the national strike in the first week of June, 1964. Its recommendations would effectively raise wages throughout the country. On June 29, 1964, the unions and the government completed their negotiating over this issue. "Labor won a $28-a-month minimum wage for

Government employees. . . . The Government agreed to introduce legislation making the minimum wage binding on private companies and setting up permanent boards for compulsory arbitration." (The New York Times, June 30, 1964, p. 9.)

24. Much of the manhandling on the Apapa docks is performed by unorganized laborers who work seven days a week. (This, however, is changing.)

25. More to improve their economic lot than to acquire learning per se.

26. Nigeria, Advisory Committee on Education in the Colonies, Ten-Year Education Plan (S.P. No. 6/1944; Lagos: Federal Government Printer, 1949), p. 1.

27. Nigeria, Annual Abstract of Statistics, op. cit., pp. 159, 163, 164.

28. Western Nigeria, Western Region Development Plan: 1960-65 (S.P. No. 17 of 1959; Ibadan: Government Printer, 1959), p. 10, and Wéstern Nigeria, Western Nigeria Development Plan: 1962-68 (S.P. No. 8 of 1962; Ibadan: Government Printer, 1962), p. 40.

29. Data obtained from Federal Ministry of Education, March 1964. Primary education is provided from the age of six. In 1960, due to financial difficulties, the entry age of five was discontinued after a trial of three years. But as births are not generally registered there is no reliable way of determining the age of the pupils; so minimum age is not really an effective barrier. The Eastern Region has met, unlike the Western Region, acute financial strains in attempting to introduce free education. In 1958 it reintroduced fees in the later primary years after a forgiveness of just one year, and on January 1, 1962, these were increased. Two years later, the East reduced the primary school period from seven to six years. (Eastern Nigeria, Ministry of Education, Policy for Education [Enugu: Government Printer, O.D. No. 7/1963], p. 4.)

In 1960, before this belt-tightening the

Eastern primary enrollment was 1,422,068, (Daily Times [Lagos], October 23, 1961, p. 36.) and exceeded that of the West by almost 300,000.

30. If the entry level is raised by one year, this figure would drop to 120,000. These figures are projected in J. N. Archer's Education Development in Nigeria: 1961-70, a document prepared in 1961 to phase and cost the Ashby proposals. (See Nigeria, Federal Ministry of Education, Investment in Education [Lagos: Federal Government Printer, 1960].) The Ashby Report includes a manpower (high-level) survey by Prof. Frederick Harbison of Princeton.

31. "In a southerly province . . . the percentage of children getting secondary education is approximately 0.6%. . . . Another province, in the north of the Region . . . [the figure is] approximately 0.07%." (Northern Nigeria, Ministry of Education, A Short Survey of Education in Northern Nigeria, by D. H. Williams [Kaduna: Government Printer, 1960], pp. 58-59.)

32. West Africa (London), July 29, 1961, p. 835.

33. O. Osanyintolu in a review, pointed out that the "Government's intention is to accelerate progress in the backward areas only [the Provinces that accepted missionary and private education will receive only limited assistance for new secondary schools]." (Daily Times [Lagos], August 24, 1961, p. 5.)

34. A. C. Callaway, School Leavers and the Developing Economy of Nigeria (Ibadan: 1961, Mimeographed), p. 6.

35. For simplicity, the writer is omitting a discussion of the English-style Sixth Forms which supply a two-year post-School Certificate education necessary for entrance into many UK universities, as well as the University of Ibadan.

36. The year 1960 saw the first graduating class of thirteen doctors. Its near-term objective is fifty per year.

37. A Ford Foundation study called for a full-time, resident management center in Lagos. (Dr. S. Hoslett, Working Paper on the Proposed Nigerian Center of Management and Administration [Mimeo.] [Lagos: Ford Foundation, 1961].) Apparently, the University of Lagos will incorporate this suggestion. Since its inception, the Faculty of Business and Social Sciences has been under the direction of a team from New York University.

38. Shell-BP recently donated £500,000 to Yaba's expansion program.

39. Archer, op. cit., p. 86.

40. Major firms, e.g., United Africa Company, Union Trading Company, Mobil, Glaxo-Allenbury, etc., have been supporting the Supervision and Management Training Department which was established in July, 1959, and is a tenant on the grounds of the Yaba Technical Institute. Courses include Supervision and Management, Organization and Administration, Foremanship, Office Supervision, Sales Supervision, and the British Institute of Management (B.I.M.) exams in the evening. The Production Engineering Management Group (Nigeria) Ltd. has run the Department for the Federal Ministry of Education since its inception.

By April, 1964, 1,600 men and women, almost all Nigerians, had attended full-time, non-resident courses. Candidates for full-time courses are only accepted if nominated and sponsored by their employers. The Supervision and Management courses, in three weeks, cover Planning and Control, Human Relations, Finance, Nigerian Economics, Industrial Economics, Method Improvement, etc. At the request of Mr. P. C. Dawson, the Head of the Department, the writer, on August 7, 1961, partook in two seminars dealing with the Economic Development of Nigeria. The students ranged in age from twenty-five to forty-nine and held such positions as Senior

Assistant Works Manager of the Nigerian Railway Corp. and Chief Costing Clerk of G. B. Ollivant (Nigeria) Ltd.

41. NPA, for instance, conducts a five-year course in its training center at Apapa (Lagos) similar to that given at Yaba.

42. This course consists of a three-months apprenticeship, eight months of class, one year in the workshop, eight months in the class, one year in the shop, and two months of class followed by a final exam. The boys, who receive free room and expenses, are not bound to UTC at the end of the period. (Interview with Mr. H. Jaggi, Manager, UTC Motors Department, Enugu, October 12, 1961.)

43. Interview with Mr. D. N. Leich, a fourteen-year veteran in Nigeria with Shell, Government and University, October 3, 1961, Port Harcourt.

44. If he is an American he will screen in his house. The Nigerians, like their former British mentors, do not favor screens.

45. It will be some time before vital statistics, such as the infant mortality rate, are compiled on a universal basis. In rural areas, a compulsory system would be impossible without an appropriate staff. Even the available figures are outdated. In October, 1961, the most recent annual reports were for 1953-54 in the Northern Region (Kaduna, 1956), 1957 in the Western Region (Ibadan, S.P. No. 1/1961), and 1958 in the Eastern Region (Enugu, Official Document No. 11/1961).

46. Statement of Federal Minister of Health, Daily Express (Lagos), September 1, 1961, p. 5. In 1957, the largest city--Ibadan--had eight private medical practitioners.

47. Nigeria, Federal Office of Statistics, Digest of Statistics, Vol. 12, No. 4 (Lagos: October, 1963), p. 75. In Enugu, during the second quinquennium of the 1950's, rents rose by 26 per cent. (Nigeria, Federal Office of Statistics, Report on

the Enugu Rent Enquiry: June 1959 [Lagos: Mimeographed, 1960], p. 3.)

48. From a radio broadcast by the Federal Minister of Labour on September 10, 1961. The full text appears in the West African Pilot (Yaba), September 12, 1961, p. 4.

49. See National Provident Fund Act, 1961: Supplement to Official Gazette Extraordinary No. 47, Vol. 48, 30th June 1961 - Part A.

50. Frederick Harbison and Charles A. Myers, Management in the Industrial World: An International Analysis (New York: McGraw-Hill, 1959), Chapters 1-5.

51. Smythe and Smythe, op. cit., p. 85.

52. E. K. Hawkins, Road Transport in Nigeria: A Study in African Enterprise (London: Oxford University Press, 1958).

53. In 1961, UAC had eight Nigerians in Senior Executive positions, i.e., controlling large bodies of the management. Interview with Mr. J. B. Davis, Chairman, Lagos, September 7, 1961.

54. It is claimed that S. I. Nwoke, a tailor, started with one bag of flour in 1941; in June, 1961, his Ezinwa Bakery Industry produced 45,326 loaves of bread. Interview with A. U. Nwoke, commercial manager, Aba, October 7, 1961.

55. Managing Director of Elusos Electrical Works, a tenant on the Yaba ("nesting") Industrial Estate, a nursery of sorts for Nigerian industrial enterprises. In six years--more than two on the estate--he grew to the point where he employed twenty-eight young apprentices as armature and coil winders. Interview with Mr. Eluchi, Yaba, August 8, 1961.

56. In a noteworthy case, immediately after independence, private homes in Lagos' European suburb of Ikoyi fetched rents five years in advance, all in cash, at the time the lease was signed.

57. "Capital has been difficult to obtain . . . [and] improvements in efficiency may mean the destruction of the jobs of the workers." (A general statement by Arthur R. Burns, in Comparative Economic Organization [New York: Prentice-Hall, 1955], p. 186.

58. Faulty keeping of accounts has led to the death of many a small Nigerian business. Likewise, lack of an inventory control system has too many times spelled disaster.

CHAPTER 4 INFRASTRUCTURE--THE OVERHEAD CAPITAL OF AN EMERGING NATION

Industries establishing themselves in east-central North America give only minimum consideration to the existence of adequate electricity and water supply, or to the adequacy of road and rail routes and connections. They take these external economies almost for granted. In the underdeveloped world, these services--or lack thereof--play an important part in the decision on plant location. Before building its sawmill at Sapele, the United Africa Company had already constructed hundreds of miles of roads, as well as bridges across the non-fordable streams, in the surrounding forest area. But concerns with less financial backing cannot make these enormous outlays. They can only await the provision of an adequate infrastructure before establishing themselves in an underdeveloped country.

How far and how well Nigeria has progressed in providing the transportation and communication networks and the power, water, and sewage disposal facilities for industry is the subject matter of this chapter.

TRANSPORT

Roads

Nigeria's 45,498 miles of road[1] give it a road density of almost 1 mile per 8 square miles, relatively high for Africa. Of the total, 7,706 miles, or approximately 17 per cent, were surfaced with bituminous asphalt by 1962. Only nine years earlier the corresponding figure had been 1,113 miles, or less than 5 per cent of a total of 27,758 miles.[2] During this period the number of motor vehicles registered in Nigeria experienced an even greater growth rate.

From 1908, when two motor vehicles were imported for the first time, to 1940, road construction in Nigeria proceeded by fits and starts. The traditional barriers of the Benue and Niger Rivers, and the tsetse-infested Middle-Belt, as well as the fear of competition with the railroad, World War I, and the depression all contributed to this state of affairs. As late as 1937, the only tarred road outside townships was from Lagos to Abeokuta (65 miles).[3] In 1940, with the fall of France, military considerations came to the fore, and brought about the construction of an all-season road between Jebba, on the Niger River, and Bida, and on other sections of the Lagos-Kano Road. Also, major improvements were made in the route from Port Harcourt to Fort Lamy (capital of Chad Republic) via Jos and Maiduguri.

Table 8

Road Vehicles in Nigeria

	Comm'l	Private Cars*	Motor Cycles	Total
Jan. 1953	11,014	9,511	1,216	21,741**
Jan. 1955	12,642	13,973	1,810	28,425
Jan. 1957	16,367	19,823	3,395	39,585
Jan. 1959	17,430	23,451	4,935	45,816
Jan. 1961	23,908	36,761	11,151	71,820
Jan. 1962	24,036	38,852	12,242	75,130

* Includes taxis
**Includes Southern Cameroons

Sources: Stanford Research Institute, The Economic Co-ordination of Transport Development in Nigeria (Menlo Park: S.R.I., 1961), p. 145; and Nigeria, Digest of Statistics, Vol. 12, No. 4 (Lagos: Federal Office of Statistics, October, 1963), p. 65.

The postwar period saw no letup in activity. Today, the trunk roads forming a grid network are in the final stages of completion. The "A" roads, two north-south (Lagos and Port Harcourt to northern boundary) and four east-west, are constructed and maintained by the Federal Ministry of Works. They link the federal and regional capitals with the largest cities and neighboring countries. The "B" roads are constructed by the regional governments, and maintained by their ministries of works or other local authorities. They link the provincial (or divisional) headquarters with each other, the "A" roads, the railroad, and the ports. Additional roads, constructed and maintained by local authorities, complete Nigeria's road map.

Table 9

Roads by Category and Region (miles)--1960

	"A"	Of Which Tarred	"B"	Tarred	Local	Tarred	Total	Of Which Tarred
NR*	4,057	1,350	2,184	452	13,856	200	20,097	2,002
WR	819	672	1,007	985	10,070	361	11,896	2,018
ER	688	495	1,473	500	11,865	63	14,026	1,058
Lagos	-	-	-	-	-	-	196	166
Total	5,564	2,517	4,664	1,937	35,791	624	46,215	5,244

*Sub-totals are provisional.

Sources: Stanford Research Institute, The Economic Co-ordination of Transport Development in Nigeria (Menlo Park: S.R.I. 1961), p 137; and Nigeria, Digest of Statistics, Vol. 10, No. 2 (Lagos: Federal Office of Statistics, 1961), p. 63.

The Stanford team, in its 1961 report, stated that road transport in the preceding year carried 62 per cent of the freight-traffic (ton-miles) and more than 90 per cent of the passengers.[4] (Appendix B of their report lists seventeen of the bigger Nigerian trucking firms, which had fleets of from 23 to 160 lorries.) Short-distance traffic, notably trucking of Western Region cocoa, which is hauled to Apapa (Lagos' port); movement of valuable items that necessitate quicker than rail delivery; and east-west freight in the south (where there is no railroad) are not the only goods traveling by road rather than by rail. For north-south items of a more heavy and/or bulky nature, in relation to value, are road-users too.

Nigeria has an inventory of thousands of bridges over 20 feet in length, the majority of which are of reinforced concrete and/or steel. But, in 1964 only two crossed the major rivers:[5] the 1,945-foot Jebba Bridge across the Niger on the Ibadan-Kaduna road, built in 1915, and the 2,854-foot Makurdi Bridge across the Benue on the Enugu-Jos route, opened in 1932. Both carry rail traffic as well. At present, the Dumez Construction Company of Paris is working on the £5 million, 4,800-foot-long,[6] Niger River Bridge (Lagos to Enugu route) between Onitsha in the East and a point 4 miles south of Asaba in the Mid-Western Region. Opening for traffic is scheduled for September, 1965.

The past decade has been a period of rapid road construction. In addition, the complete changeover, since 1955, to the sale of gasoline from fixed pumps at filling stations has increased "the effective payload of lorries by relieving them of the unwelcome burden of a drum of petrol."[7] But Nigeria is still faced with a series of highway problems, chiefly the many single-lane bridges and unsurfaced stretches on the trunk road network, and the intrusion of political considerations into the construction/maintenance decision-making process.

In 1964, the road system of Nigeria, though not yet completed according to plan, is adequate for the needs of industry. It links cities and villages not connected by other means of transport, and it serves all areas of the nation. There will continue to be much progress. To take a single example, the Niger Bridge at Onitsha will expedite the flow of traffic and allow twenty-four hour service across the river, whereas the ferry now operates only during daylight. This improvement should significantly expedite commerce between the Eastern Region and the rest of the south. If there is any barrier to road use by industry, it is the high vehicle insurance rates, which average three times those in the U.K. The high cost of insurance is primarily due to poor driving standards, and unsafe, overloaded trucks on the highways. Improved traffic law enforcement should ameliorate this situation.

The Railroad

In Chapter 2 reference was made to the importance of the railroad in the development of cotton and groundnut cultivation in the north. This is a prime example of the economic expansion brought about by the introduction of modern transport. Indeed, from the time of Lugard, the railroad was considered as the key to the opening of the north and a means of ensuring law enforcement. Today, 90 per cent of its revenues is received from traffic to and from the north.

The Nigerian railway started from Lagos (Iddo) in 1898, and reached Ibadan in 1901 and Jebba in 1909. Two years after, the Baro-Kano line (serving the Niger by river from Burutu in the delta) was completed, and in 1912 joined the Lagos line at Minna. The Jebba Bridge replaced the ferry in 1915, completing the continuous line from Lagos to Kano via Kaduna. In the East, the Port Harcourt line was extended to Enugu in 1916 because English coal was unavailable, and was completed to Kaduna in 1932 with the opening of the Makurdi Bridge across the Benue River. At the end of 1959 the system comprised 1,770 miles of single, 3'6"-gauge track extending as far as Kaura Namoda in Sokoto Province, by a branch from Zaria, and to Nguru in Bornu by a continuation of the Kano line.[8]

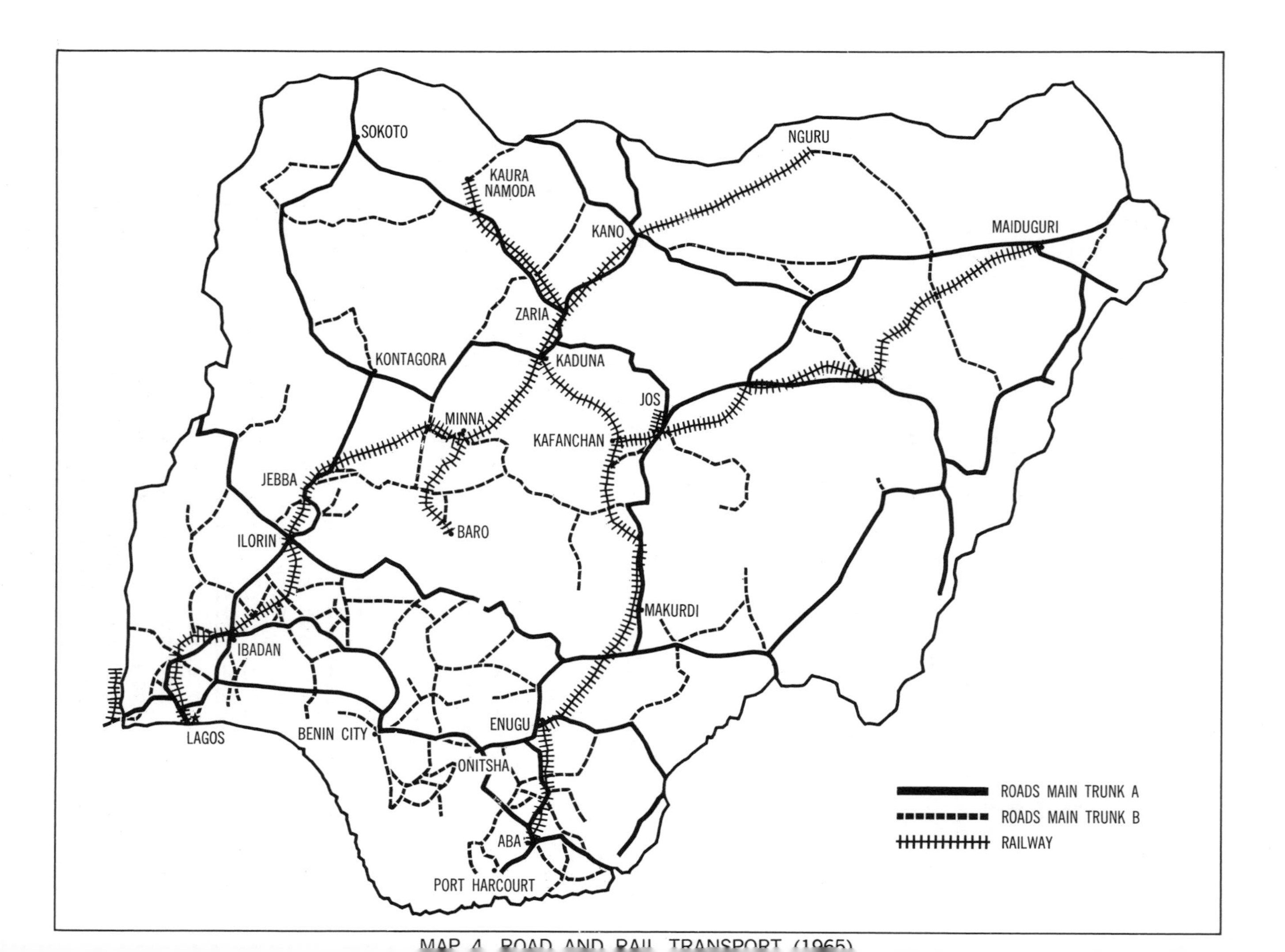

MAP 4. ROAD AND RAIL TRANSPORT (1965)

Table 10

Railroad Traffic Within Nigeria--1946-62

	Freight		Passengers	
Year	Tons (000)	Net Ton-miles (mn)	No. (000)	Passenger-miles (mn)
1946-47	1,394	473	6,256	297
1948-49	1,385	534	6,197	326
1950-51	1,225	536	5,585	357
1952-53	1,543	687	5,516	351
1954-55	1,983	937	5,451	349
1956-57	2,052	1,099	7,271	445
1958-59	2,353	1,214	7,015	372
1959-60	2,052	1,103	7,991	358
1960-61	2,054	1,040	9,822	434
1961-62	2,381	1,280	11,061	482
1962-63	2,209	1,298	12,006	516

Sources: Stanford Research Institute, The Economic Co-ordination of Transport Development in Nigeria (Menlo Park: S.R.I., 1961), p. 77; and Nigerian Railway Corporation, Report and Accounts for the Year Ended 31st March, 1963 (Ebute Metta: Railway Printer, 1963), pp. 93-94.

On August 27, 1958, with the "cutting the first sod" ceremony of the Bornu Extension, the first major addition since pre-war days was begun. The 397 miles from Kuru, on the Kafanchan-Jos branch of the eastern line, via Gombe to Maiduguri, is costing at least double the £10 million loan obtained from the World Bank.[9] On August 14, 1961, the first 107 miles to Bauchi opened for goods traffic; Gombe, 102.5 miles further on, was served by freight traffic on December 27, 1962, and passenger traffic on April 11, 1963. Maiduguri is now scheduled to be reached by late 1964 or early 1965. And sometime in the 1970's, the line might well be extended to Fort Lamy in Chad.

From its inception the railroad has been a

government operation;[10] and since 1955 it has been administered by the Nigerian Railway Corporation (NRC), an autonomous statutory public corporation.[11] In 1954, the IBRD noted that the railway was unable to move all the traffic offered, "evidenced strongly by groundnut 'pyramids' in Kano," and that insufficient stock, poor maintenance, and labor problems were the chief difficulties. "One bright spot," the report went on to say, "is the favourable financial situation."[12] Today, some improvements have been made,[13] pyramids are a rarity out of season, labor is still a problem, and the corporation is running a deficit![14]

In response to the change in the railway's financial fortune the government appointed the Elias Commission in 1960 to investigate the corporation. The commission's report[15] made twenty-four recommendations including an acceleration of the corporation's Nigerianization policy. Although no immediate cut of significant proportions was suggested in the membership of the Nigerian Union of Railwaymen,[16] the staff was reduced by some 2,600 in the ensuing 2 years. This was in line with section 208 of the report, which stated that the railroad "should be run as a commercial concern which should, as far as possible, be made to pay its way."

In 1962, the long awaited Stanford Research Institute transportation study was made public. It cites the railroad's undercapacity, slow speeds,[17] and other deficiencies. But primarily it argues that road-users should pay for a greater share of the road maintenance and capital costs. Government implicitly has supported this conclusion by since raising taxes on fuels and lubricants, license fees, and import duties on vehicles. If we assume that the railroad can correspondingly increase its operating efficiency, the prospects for the corporation are measurably improved. In any case, industry now has to pay higher costs for its transportation, because the railroad is able to obtain certain higher rates than it could in 1961. To be sure, it is still charging out-of-pocket costs,[18] or even lower, on some bulk items.

In a preceding chapter, mention was made of the corporation's dieselization program. With a lack of watering and coaling facilities on the Bornu extension, it was dieselized from the start.[19] The overall program was put into operation in 1955; by March 31, 1963, 43 of the 245 main-line locomotives were diesels.[20] The figures are less disproportionate when it is realized that the steam locomotives, 18 years old on the average, are out of operation more than 50 per cent of the time.

A word may be added about railroad sidings. With a traffic guarantee, often not fulfilled, and with payment by a manufacturer, the corporation will construct the siding to the plant site.[21]

Air Transport

Once-a-week mail flights from Khartoum to Kano and Lagos, in 1936, inaugurated commercial aviation in Nigeria. But it was a world war that once again provided the impetus for great activity. In 1940-41, twenty-four airports plus numerous landing strips were constructed. In 1946 the West African Airways Corporation was established to serve the four British colonies. This it did until Ghana elected to discontinue her participation after independence. So, in 1958, the Nigerian Airways (W.A.A.C.) Ltd., a private limited liability company, was formed.[22]

Today, Nigerian Airways serves Lagos, Ibadan, Benin City, Port Harcourt, Enugu, Calabar, Kaduna, Jos, Kano, Sokoto, Gusau, Maiduguri, and Yola on its internal F.27 passenger and DC-3 freight services. Externally, it flies from Dakar to Léopoldville, and, operating a charter-pooled, partnership agreement with B.O.A.C., it flies VC-10's from London and other major European cities to the international airports at Kano and Ikeja (Lagos). In addition, many of the leading international carriers connect Nigeria to the outside world. The continual multiplication of jet services since October, 1961, may eventually relegate Kano to a Shannon or a Gander, which are now usually overflown. Also, consideration will have to be given to bringing Port Harcourt up to international standards.

The Nigerian aviation picture obscures some recent conflicting moves by government. Service was improved when the grass fields, particularly at Enugu, were "hardened," thus allowing flights after heavy rains, and when the passenger fleet of seven obsolescent DC-3's was replaced by five Fokker F.27 Friendship airliners from Holland in 1963. Yet, at the same time, cuts were made in many of the services[23] leading to a fall in traffic. The demand may be there, for often reservations are quite hard to come by.

Table 11

Total Air Traffic Within Nigeria
(ton-miles)--1949-62

Year	Load	Revenue Load Factor (%)
1949-50	257,822	51
1950-51	487,729	61
1951-52	627,484	62
1952-53	657,642	68
1953-54	1,058,871	62
1954-55	1,073,546	59
1955-56	1,103,196	65
1956-57	1,349,524	62
1957-58	1,478,688	59
1958-59	1,790,776	58
1959-60	1,655,023	64
1960-61	1,498,930	72
1961-62	1,486,560	n.a.
1962-63	1,700,256	n.a.

Sources: Stanford Research Institute, The Economic Co-ordination of Transport Development in Nigeria (Menlo Park: S.R.I., 1961), p. 244, and Nigeria, Digest of Statistics, Vol. 12, No. 4 (Lagos: Federal Office of Statistics), p. 61.

Funds that could be spent on a restoration of the cancelled internal flights are, in part, being spent for national prestige. In 1961, the government bought out the private interests in the Nigerian Airways, and undertook negotiations for the purchase of international equipment. Further, some Nigerians are advocating flights across the Atlantic.[24] It is unlikely that this route can be maintained on a profitable basis, unless some pooling arrangement with a profit-making international carrier is effectuated.

Nigeria is also served by four private contractors. The two largest are Aero Contractors of Nigeria, Ltd., formed in 1960 and flying Pipers and Dorniers, and Pan African Airlines (Nigeria) Ltd., which appeared on the scene in 1961 with two twin Beechcrafts and a C-46.[25]

River Transport

The two main rivers, situated as they are, do not serve the major population centers. The three fleets[26] based at Warri and Burutu in 1960 carried less than 4 per cent of the river, road, and rail freight total.

Niger River Transport's downstream traffic includes groundnuts (45.7 per cent), palm kernels (25.2 per cent), and cotton lint (12.2 per cent), while its upstream traffic--a bit more than half the downstream total--is based mainly on cement (51.2 per cent), and salt (18.6 per cent).[27]

At present, the Niger and the Benue are open for navigation on a seasonal basis. The Niger rises in the mountains of Sierra Leone, 2,550 miles from the sea. Yet, it has only 35 per cent of its annual discharge left by the time it leaves the inland delta in Mali. From mid-April through part of June, only the stretch to Onitsha (232 miles from the Escravos Bar and the sea) is navigable by boats with limited draughts. It is not until November, at the end of the "Black Flood" period, that the Niger is open to

Baro (434 miles). At the height of the "Baro Season," which ends by early April, Jebba (556 miles) can be reached.

Table 12

Nigerian Surface Freight Traffic
(mns. ton-miles)--1953-60

Year	Rail	Road	River*	Total
1953	687	840	88	1,615
1954	775	1,020	95	1,880
1955	937	1,200	99	2,236
1956	1,002	1,380	101	2,483
1957	1,099	1,500	110	2,709
1958	1,065	1,710	100	2,875
1959	1,214	1,830	120	3,164
1960	1,103	2,010	120	3,233

*Excluding canoe transport.

Source: Stanford Research Institute, The Economic Co-ordination of Transport Development in Nigeria (Menlo Park: S.R.I., 1961), p. 55.

The second distinct season, "The Benue Season," occurs in a non-overlapping period: June through part of October or November.[28] The Benue River, the Niger's largest tributary by far, rises 4,400 feet above sea level on the Adamawa Plateau of neighboring Cameroon. In the first 20 miles the Benue falls 2,500 feet, but in the last 700 miles, to the confluence with the Niger at Lokoja (362 miles), it has a fall of only 570 feet.

With the construction of a multi-purpose dam on the Niger, the NEDECO staff foresees, "in many years," the opening of the Niger to navigation for nine months of the year through Sokoto Province and into Niger Republic as far as Niamey and Tillabéri. Dams on the Benue, at Lagdo, 40 miles above Garua, and at Yola, would double the length of the present shipping season of Yola and Numan. It is unlikely that any consideration will be given to the latter two dams during the 1960's.[29]

Table 13

Nigeria's Ports on the Niger and Benue

	Approx. Annual Tonnage	Covered Storage (tons)	Facilities
Warri	100,000	12,000	Q,B,L,M
Burutu	350,000	40,000	Q, M,T
Onitsha (a)	80,000	25,000	Q, L,M,T
Idah (b)	20,000	6,000	L
Lokoja	10,000	8,000	L, T
Baro	75,000	10,000	L, R
Makurdi	12,000	10,000	L, R
Ibi	3,000	4,000	L
Numan	7,000	8,000	L
Yola (c)	8,000	9,000	L
(Garua (d)	35,000	17,000(e)	Q, L,M,T)

Q = quay, B = berth, T = petrol tanks, L = man-handling, M = mechanical handling, R = railroad connection

(a) Includes Asaba; (b) Includes Agenebode;
(c) Includes Dalmare; (d) In Cameroon;
(e) Away from waterside.

Source: NEDECO, River Studies and Recommendations on Improvement of Niger and Benue (Amsterdam: North-Holland Publishing Co., 1959), p. 687.

Meanwhile, the fleets are being modernized, new technology, for example the push-tow, being introduced, and plans being drawn up for quays and berths at Baro. The problems remain of expediting the handling, usually by man, of goods at most of the ports; and the eroding of banks at the ports, which some day will have to be replaced by permanent jetties and quays. If the rate structure can be shifted downward, the major difficulty, lack of upstream traffic, may ease.[30]

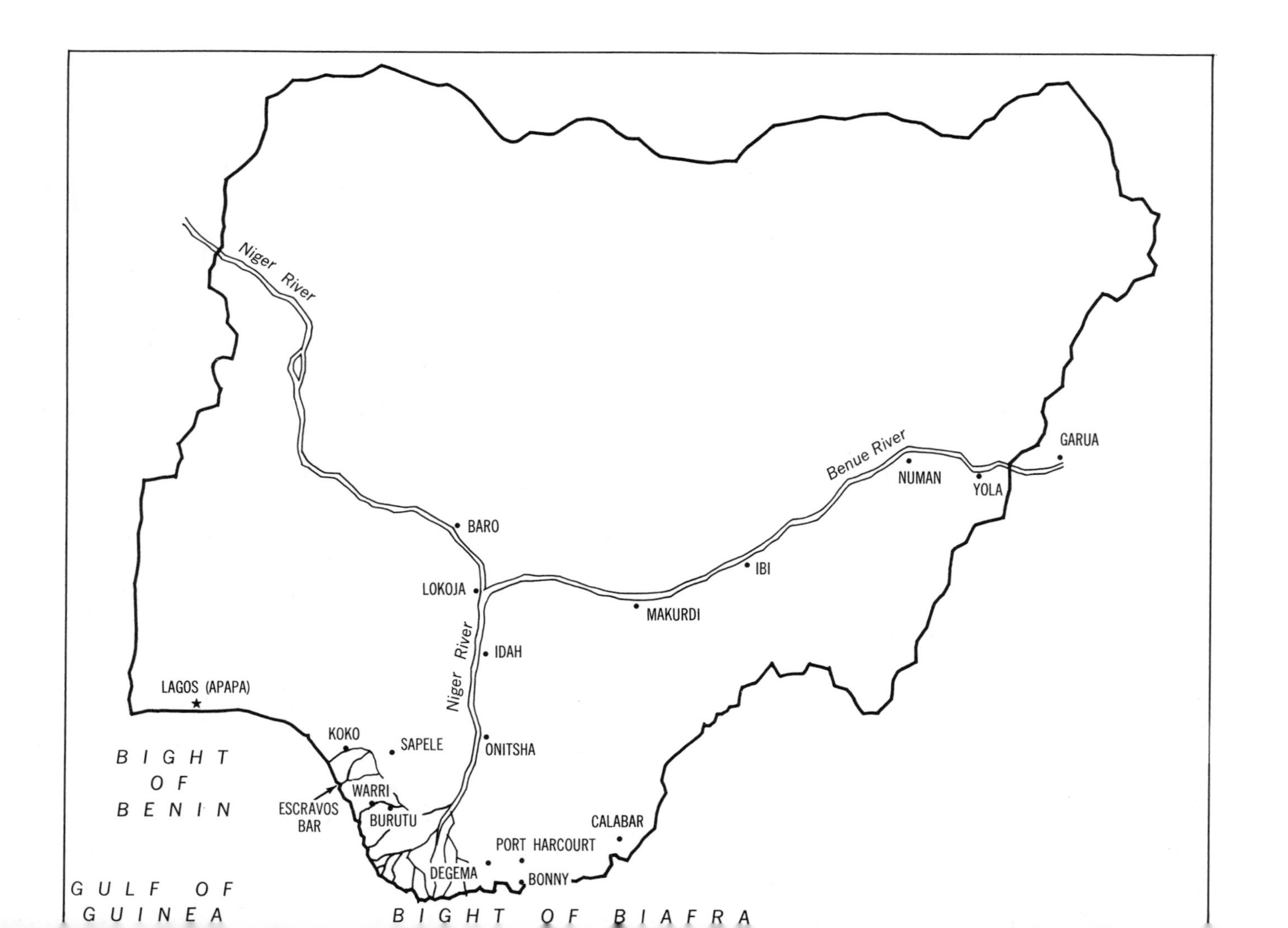
Niger River
GARUA
Benue River
NUMAN
YOLA
BARO
IBI
LOKOJA
MAKURDI
Niger River
IDAH
LAGOS (APAPA)
KOKO
SAPELE
ONITSHA
BIGHT OF BENIN
WARRI
ESCRAVOS BAR
BURUTU
CALABAR
PORT HARCOURT
DEGEMA
BONNY
GULF OF GUINEA
BIGHT OF BIAFRA

Ocean Ports

The operation of the ports, lighthouses, buoyage, etc., has, since April, 1955, been the responsibility of the Nigerian Ports Authority (NPA), a statutory corporation formed under the Ports Ordinance of 1954.[31]

Nigeria's leading ports are all obstructed by bars, and, with the exception of Lagos, are located on rivers or creeks, connected to the sea by tricky channels. Dredging the 11-foot bar which blocked the channel to Lagos Harbour was begun in 1899. Until 1913, when the entrance to the harbor was opened--coincident with completion of the rail line to Kano--all cargo destined for Lagos had to be unloaded at Forcados, 142 miles to the southeast, and transshipped into light-draught steamers for the trips through the lagoons and creeks to Lagos. By 1917, the entrance was dredged to 20 feet and ocean vessels first visited Lagos. To maintain the entrance and the channel to Lagos itself, several miles from the bar, two moles[32] and a training bank had to be constructed from stone quarried 60 miles away. In 1964, the depth of the bar is maintained at 30 feet, with Apapa Channel at 27 feet and Customs Channel at 26 feet.

Customs Wharf, adjacent to the heart of Lagos Island's commercial district, has three berths for imports to Lagos only. Apapa quay across the harbor was connected to the railroad in 1926. Between 1952 and 1956, the quay was extended by reclamation a half mile into the harbor. Today Apapa has nine berths plus bulk oil, petroleum, and lighter berths. With six ships often in the harbor awaiting a berth, in addition to the ships anchored outside the bar in the Bight of Benin, the NPA has commenced construction of four more berths on the Apapa side, by means of a further extension. A connecting quay across the roadstead to Customs Wharf would provide for a total of at least thirty berths.[33]

Table 14

Number of Ships Entering Nigerian Ports--1955-62*

Port	1955	1956	1957	1958	1959	1960	1961	1962
Lagos	1,351	1,437	1,522	2,027	2,213	2,126	2,233	2,174
Port Harcourt	467	487	556	695	722	886	847	939
Sapele	n.a.	n.a.	354	231	288	296	276	335
Warri	n.a.	n.a.	171	131	190	189	172	187
Burutu	n.a.	n.a.	238	228	241	276	246	159
Calabar	n.a.	n.a.	208	215	248	223	205	178
Degema	n.a.	n.a.	91	65	94	80	62	75
Bonny	-	-	-	-	-	-	176	198
Total	-	-	3,140	3,592	3,996	4,076	4,217	4,245

*In the eight years shown, the net registered tonnage of all ships entering Lagos and Port Harcourt increased from 3,397,868 and 1,075,357 to 5,547,776 and 2,639,451, respectively.

Source: Nigerian Ports Authority, Annual Reports for Years Ended March 31, 1961 and March 31, 1963 (Lagos: NPA, 1961 and 1963), p. 130 and p. 89.

Table 15

Tonnage of Cargo Handled at Nigerian Ports ('000's long tons)

Year	Lagos	Port Harcourt	Sapele	Warri	Burutu	Calabar	Degema	Bonny	Total
1937*	941	236	68	88	187	143	-	-	1,663
1938*	677	192	59	76	153	122	-	-	1,279
1946*	1,035	409	57	31	63	93	25	-	1,713
1948	1,379	477	169	71	180	149	94	-	2,519
1950	1,831	518	250	93	158	137	82	-	3,069
1952	2,052	662	204	91	181	171	79	-	3,440
1954	2,230	793	309	126	200	198	79	-	3,935
1956	2,962	1,070	383	130	215	184	88	-	5,032
1958	3,155	1,410	299	114	190	174	83	-	5,425
1960	3,603	2,088	477	141	164	149	75	-	6,699
1961	3,595	1,390	415	123	134	127	35	2,707	8,525
1962	3,521	1,451	396	137	100	108	41	3,377	9,131

*Excludes cargo shipped coastwise.

Sources: Nigeria, Annual Abstract of Statistics: 1960 (Lagos: Federal Office of Statistics, 1960), pp. 46-47; and Nigerian Ports Authority, Annual Reports for Years Ended March 31, 1961-63 (Lagos: NPA, 1961-63), p. 142, p. 148, and p. 102.

Port Harcourt, Nigeria's second port, was largely unoccupied before 1912. In a span of some fifty years it has, as the terminus of the eastern railroad to the north, achieved prominence by serving the coal mines of Enugu and the tin fields of Jos. Now that the railroad is being extended to Maiduguri, and oil is being exported in ever larger quantities, the port should expand its operations rapidly. Oil exports are pumped to the terminal (see Chapter 2 above) constructed at Bonny Island inside the bar, some 41 miles downstream from the port. Therefore, the oil exports play an indirect, albeit very important part in Port Harcourt's future. As Tables 14 and 15 indicate, Bonny has become a major contributor to the port totals since it began loading crude oil for export in April, 1961.

It is the dredging, carried out by Shell-BP under a long-term agreement with the NPA, that is so vital. The present draught of 21 feet has been extended to 25½ feet at the bar. By 1965, depths of 35 feet at the bar, 30 feet at Okrika, the oil refining site, and 28 feet at Port Harcourt are envisioned. Eventually, Shell-BP hopes to have tankers requiring 50 feet of water using its terminal.

Most of the facilities the IBRD team visited were constructed in 1928. Since 1954, three extra deepwater berths, making a total of seven, and a lighter berth have been constructed, the covered storage space has been doubled, and cranes and mechanical handling equipment have been introduced. And, in 1963, work started on the modernization of the old berths.[34]

Sapele is 63 miles from the Escravos Bar via the River Escravos, Nana Creek, and the Benin River, a tortuous route that has a depth of only 16 feet in some places. Koko, on the Benin River, was re-opened as a custom's port in June of 1959. Five years later, one deep-water berth is almost completed. So far, Koko's traffic has consisted of bulk palm oil shipped coastwise to Lagos.

Burutu and Warri are the other "Delta Ports"; they are situated 5 miles and 27 miles, respectively, from the Forcados Bar. Burutu is owned and operated by UAC, but is open to all ships requiring its use. It acts as the base for the company's river fleet. Warri is the base for the John Holt and Company (Nigeria) river fleet.

In 1899, the Forcados Bar was used by ships of 20 feet draught. But by 1934, silting had reduced the limit to 12 to 14 feet. Four years later the Escravos Bar, in a better position with respect to wind and swell, was opened, after being dredged to 14 feet. Further dredging was not successful. Starting in 1953, NEDECO carried out investigations of the Niger River delta. As a result, work began in 1959 on a 5-mile breakwater, and was soon followed by dredging in the lee of the mole. Completed in late 1963, at a cost of £10 million, the Escravos Estuary is serving all four ports.[35] These, in turn, will form a link with inland navigation to provide a waterway reaching 1,000 miles into Africa. The delta rivers are being made less hazardous, and more suitable for larger units. With decreasing costs, freight carried should increase significantly.

The remaining ports are Degema, reached by the Bonny River, and Calabar, on the river of that name 5 miles from the main entrance channel to the Cross River.[36] In the last few years some oil palm produce normally shipped from Degema has been transported by road instead to Port Harcourt. Calabar was once the headquarters of the Oil Rivers Protectorate. Today, especially after the loss of much of its hinterland in the Southern Cameroons, it has been on the decline. Perhaps the 1963 A.I.D. loan of $8.6 million for a highway 71 miles to the north, including a bridge over the Cross River, will alter this town's fortunes. Timber and rubber areas will have access to the sea.

Shipping

The Nigerian National Shipping Line was formed in 1959 by the federal government in partnership with Elder Dempster Lines Limited, and Palm Line Limited, a subsidiary of UAC. On September 1, 1961, as she did with the airline, Nigeria took over complete ownership by purchasing the equity interests of her two partners.[37] Serving Europe, the line's fleet of three ships has grown to sixteen by 1964, including eight on charter.

COMMUNICATION

It may seem to be an anachronism that Nigeria has had direct dialing telephone service between Lagos and Ibadan since October of 1960. Yet when a nation enters the twentieth century it does so with a vengeance, adopting all the latest manifestations of apparent modernity.

As in most European countries, the Posts and Telegraphs Department of the Ministry of Communications operates the internal media of telephone, telegraph, and the mail. From 1950 through 1961, the number of postal agencies and post offices increased from 594 to 1,384, and postal articles handled grew from 63.8 million to 116.7 million; the number of operating telephone instruments more than quadrupled to 48,919 in the same period.[38]

In December, 1963, the Western Electric Company, under A.I.D. auspices, completed a comprehensive telecommunications study for the Federal Ministry of Communications. Should this report be accepted by the government, and it appears that it will, within ten years Nigeria shall be very well off in this field indeed: an applicant for telephone service will be able to have the instrument installed in one week's time. A subscriber will be able to reach any other telephone in Nigeria within thirty seconds via dialing. There will be twenty-four hour service throughout the country The government will provide this service while earning a profit. And four international switching stations will be installed to meet the needs of Nigeria in this field.[39]

The IBRD report[40] approved the expansion of the VHF (very high frequency) radio telephone system beyond the Lagos-Ibadan link. The costly job of maintaining land lines in the forest areas, which are subject to frequent lightning storms, were thus to be made unnecessary. By 1964, the VHF main line communications system connected the major centers, a micro-wave system had been installed between Lagos and Ibadan, thirty cities with 75 per cent of Nigeria's telephones had automatic telephone exchanges, the Morse key was rapidly being replaced by teleprinters, and soon telephone calls to much of Africa would not need to be relayed via London and Paris.[41]

Since 1936, Nigeria has had wired broadcasting, or re-diffusion. In 1949, the first wireless broadcasting station was set up, and on April 1, 1957, the Nigeria Broadcasting Corporation (N.B.C.) was established with a charter patterned after the B.B.C. Today the N.B.C. operates a national service based in Lagos, plus three regional services located in the three capitals--all on the air fifteen to sixteen hours each day. But that is not all. During 1962, the National Broadcasting Corporation, Ltd., an RCA subsidiary, began transmission on Nigeria's external broadcasting service ("The Voice of Nigeria") to her neighbors. And to complete the picture, N.B.C., with the technical assistance of the Radio Corporation of America, commenced television transmission from Lagos in early 1962. Each of the regional governments, by the end of 1963, not only had its own broadcasting service, it also had its own television service.[42] No doubt these are only initial steps: a national television service will follow.

This is a striking manifestation of modernity. Moreover, it is a demonstration of regional emulation; a rivalry that will be seen again in the discussion of industry.

GENERATION AND DISTRIBUTION OF ELECTRICITY

At this time, Nigeria has little in the way of low-cost power facilities in operation. The Niger Dam and the gas fields are potential sources of relatively inexpensive power, which will act as an attracting force to industry.

The Electricity Corporation of Nigeria

The Electricity Corporation of Nigeria (ECN), another of the statutory public corporations, was established in 1951 as the successor to the governments' undertakings, and, in 1952, to those of four native authorities.[43] The IBRD report noted, "Although the 165.2 million kWh of electric power generated in 1952-53 was double the output in 1944 and four times that in 1941, it amounted to only 5 kWh *per capita*."[44] With the exception of private companies on the Jos Plateau and at Sapele (see below), and power generated by some industrial concerns for their own use, electricity was, and is, provided by the ECN. In 1952-53, the ECN had one plant with an installed capacity in excess of 5,000 kw. (or 5 mw.), its other installations were widely scattered, and it was faced with a large recurring annual deficit.

By 1964, the situation was considerably altered. The corporation had added a new 6 mw. plant at Kano; had installed the Ijora oil-fired "B" station (86.25 mw. serving Lagos; had opened the Oji River coal-fired station (25.5 mw.), which is located on the Onitsha-Enugu road and is fed by an overhead cable conveyor from the Enugu mines; and had completed the Afam natural gas station (20 mw.) to serve the Port Harcourt-Aba area. Moreover, plans had been completed to add thermal capacity throughout much of the Federation: 14 mw. at Ibadan, 35 mw. at Afam, 14 mw. at Lagos, 6 mw. at Sokoto, 5 mw. at Port Harcourt, 15 mw. at Kaduna, and 60 mw. at Ughelli, the site of a major gas field. This was all done in advance of commissioning Phase 1 of the Niger Dam project.

Where no inter-urban lines existed in 1953, 500 miles of transmission lines had been erected by 1962, including the Lagos-Ibadan, Afam-Port Harcourt-Aba, and Onitsha-Enugu-Nsukka systems. It is in the south, with its concentration of population, that another 340 miles is being constructed. The Western grid has connected across the Northern border with Ilorin; in the East, Umuahia and Calabar are hooking up with a grid connecting Oji to Afam. In the vast North, site of the dam project, no lines have been constructed, although work has begun on one between

Kaduna and Kano via Zaria. This section will eventually be extended to the Niger Dam via Jebba. By that time the various transmission networks will be tied together into one national electricity grid. The other major towns in the Northern Region, e g., Maiduguri, Sokoto, Gusau, Jos, Gombe, Lokoja, etc., will not, however, be connected to this national grid.

Subsequent to the 15 per cent rate increases of 1956, the ECN's operating deficits have disappeared. In the period from 1959 through 1962, surpluses varying from £705,971 to £1,305,755 were produced.[45]

The accompanying tables indicate: that ECN's sales will have increased tenfold in eleven years, with figures of a comparable magnitude for installed capacity; that residential users are holding their own vis-à-vis the commercial and industrial group; and that six urban areas recently consumed 81.8 per cent of the total, with one, Lagos, using 41.2 per cent.

Of interest, particularly to the Coal Corporation, is that the generating capacity installed or under construction in 1962 and 1963 amounted to twenty-four undertakings, and of these, twenty-three were either diesel or gas units. It would seem that oil, gas, and hydro-power will run Nigeria's generators of tomorrow, except for the immediate vicinity of Enugu. And even Enugu will soon find itself on the same grid as Afam.

Rates vary in different parts of the country. Blankenheimer calculated, in 1957, that charges--and the rates have not changed since then--incurred by a monthly demand of 200 hours for 1,000 kw. would be $0.016 per kw-h. for an individual user in an American city of more than 50,000 and $0.0375 in Lagos. "For a smaller industrial plant of 30 kilowatts, these charges would be $0.0550 and $0.0267 in Nigeria and the United States, respectively."[46]

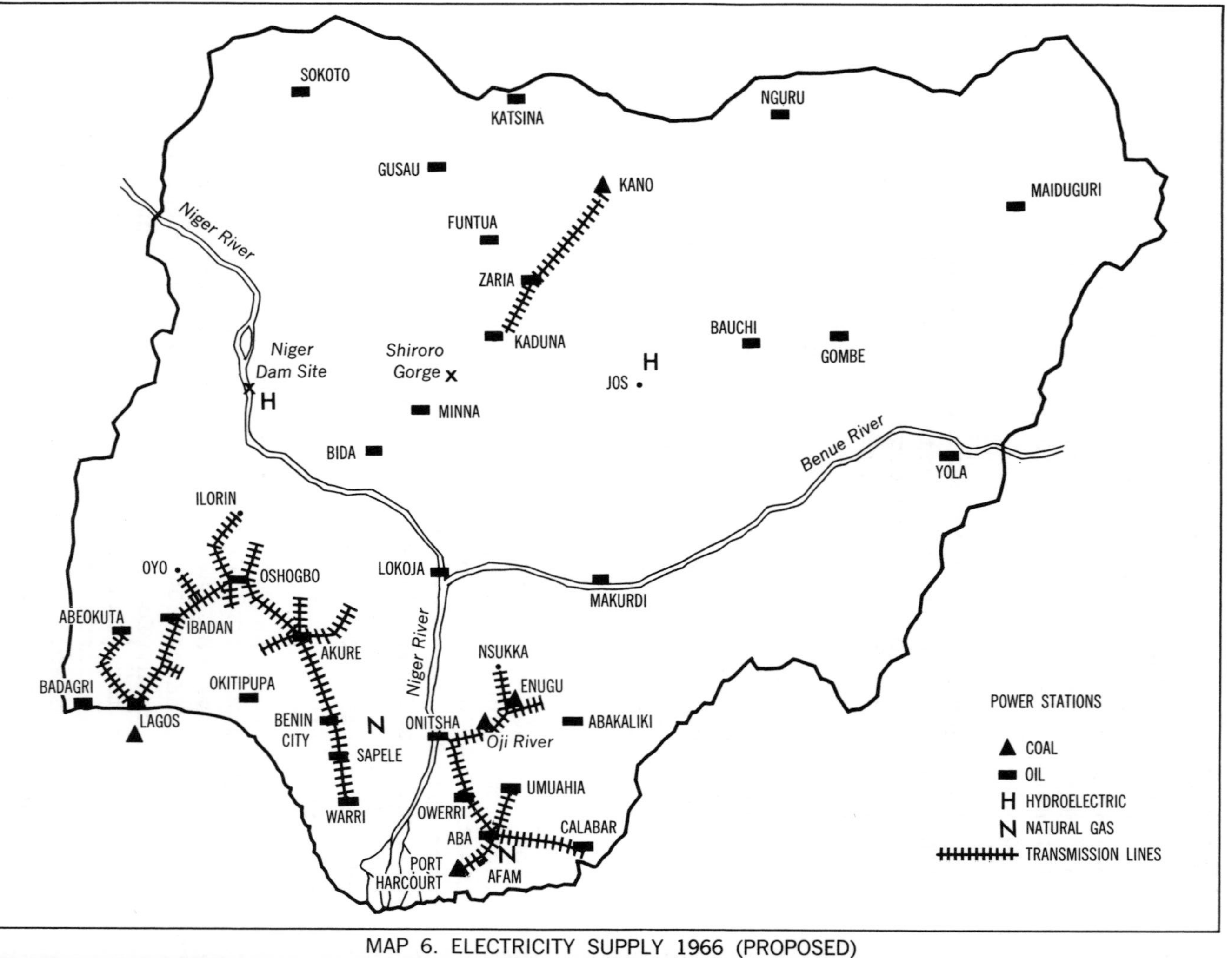

MAP 6. ELECTRICITY SUPPLY 1966 (PROPOSED)

TABLE 16

Uses of Electricity (Sales in mns of Kw-h.)

	Res.	Com./Ind'l.	Street	Misc.	Total
51-52	19.93	28.30	.83	4.80	53.87
53-54	42.92	45.07	1.76	.21	89.96
55-56	61.04	53.84	2.69	16.90	134.47
57-58	88.02	102.56	3.59	1.26	195.43
59-60	122.33	158.36	5.16	1.16	287.00
60-61	151.09	203.25	5.27	.70	360.31
61-62	179.28	252.32	5.90	.71	438.21
62-63	204.86	311.44	6.53	.89	523.72

Sources: G. E. Wyatt, The Price of Electricity in Nigeria (Lagos: ECN, February 1961), p. 7; and Electricity Corporation of Nigeria, Annual Reports for the Years ended 31st March, 1961-63 (Lagos: ECN, 1962-63), p. 66, p. 62, and p. 54.

Table 17

Geographical Distribution of Electricity Sales (1962-63)

Place	Kw-h. Sold
Lagos	215,777,828
Kaduna	34,312,633
Kano	32,380,969
Enugu/Nsukka/Onitsha	68,086,602
Port Harcourt	36,785,947
Ibadan	41,215,251
Total North	95,577,671
Total East	121,136,147
Total West	91,224,880
Total Nigeria	523,716,526

Source: Nigeria, Electricity Corporation of Nigeria, Annual Report: 1962-63 (Lagos: ECN, 1963), pp. 53-54.

Table 18

ECN Power Capacity and Electricity
Sales (a)--1951-63

	Inst. Capac. (mw.)	Max. D. (mw.)	Sales (b) (mns kw-h.)
1951-2	25.18	14.46	53.87
1952-3	34.29	19.00	76.96
1953-4	38.67	24.03	89.96
1954-5	42.93	29.10	110.71
1955-6	62.00	39.92	134.47
1956-7	85.39	44.02	158.31
1957-8	93.89	55.50	195.43
1958-9	102.42	65.70	242.24
1959-60	134.57	74.75	287.00
1960-1	181.00	95.00	360.30
1961-2	187.00	110.12	438.21
1962-3	215.00	127.93	523.72
1963-4(c)	240.00	155.00	585.79

(a) Units sold $<$ units sent out $<$ units generated. In 1962-63 the figures were 523.72, 626.88, 659.41. All figures through 1960-61 include Southern Cameroons.

(b) Includes power purchased in bulk and sold by ECN.

(c) General Manager's projection.

Sources: G. E. Wyatt, The Price of Electricity in Nigeria (Lagos: ECN, February 1961), p. 8; and Electricity Corporation of Nigeria, Annual Report for the Year ended 31st March, 1963 (Lagos: ECN, 1963), p. 57.

Private Generation of Electricity

The Nigerian Electricity Supply Corporation (NESCO) supplies electricity from its four hydroelectric stations on the Jos Plateau to the nearby mines, and to the ECN for distribution to the latter's customers in Jos, Vom, and Bukuru. In addition, a number of industrial enterprises generate their own power when the ECN agrees it cannot make supplies available. Of these, the UAC's African Timber and Plywood Company stands out. It too, until late 1962, sold in bulk to the ECN for distribution to the Sapele area.

In 1962-63, NESCO sold 98.16 million kw-h., vs. 51.57 million three years before, a 90 per cent increase.[47] Were it not for shortages of water (see the next section), the results would have been even more favorable. As a result, the ECN approved an application by NESCO to establish in 1963 a thermal plant at Bukuru of 4,220 kw.

Potential Power Sources

It has already been noted that the gas fields of the south offer immense possibilities for development. The Afam and Ughelli turbine generators were only the first steps. It was somewhat fortuitous that the Niger Dam scheme was under investigation at a time when full realization of the gas situation had not been reached. With Volta and Aswan in the minds of many, a plan for damming Nigeria's main river was soon forthcoming.

The scheme for the dam project has changed in the last few years with respect to size, number of dams or phases, sites, and so forth. Present plans call for three complementary dams: at Kainji and Jebba on the Niger River, and at Shiroro Gorge on the Kaduna River. Kainji is approximately 65 miles upriver from Jebba and 20 miles downstream for Sokoto Province where the border intersects the river. It is about 244 miles north-northeast of Lagos and 298 miles southwest of Kano. Shiroro Gorge is 55 miles southwest of Kaduna and approximately 130 miles from the confluence of the Kaduna and Niger Rivers.

Only Phase 1, the Kainji Dam, is included in the 1962-68 six-year plan. This dam, with an initial power capacity of 320 mw., will cost approximately £68 million, more than half of which will involve the expenditure of foreign exchange. This figure includes the cost of the generators, transmission lines to the grid connecting Lagos and Kano, and navigation locks and channels. A commission, the Niger Dams Authority (NDA), patterned after the TVA, was set up on September 13, 1962. The NDA will sell power to the ECN which, in turn, expects to bear more than half of the local capital costs of the project. The main civil works contract was let during February, 1964, to the Italian firm, Impregilo, that has been involved in the construction of Kariba (Rhodesia), Rosieres (Sudan), and Volta (Ghana). At this time a five-year construction schedule is foreseen. Financing support has been offered by the IBRD, United States, Italy, United Kingdom, and the Netherlands.

In 1969, when the first four 80 mw. units come into operation, most of the existing thermal capacity will be placed on reserve. By 1980, the other eight units, making a total for the Niger Dam at Kainji of 960 mw., should be installed. Phase 2, a second dam on the Niger at Jebba, is scheduled for 1983 (after a thorough review at that time). At 1961 prices, the cost of this proposed 500 mw.-maximum-capacity structure is estimated in the range of £36 million.[48] This dam will "complete navigation control of the Niger from the Dahomey border downstream to the confluence with the Benue, and also provide a valuable additional road bridge across the Niger near the existing north-south road."[49]

Phase 3, the Shiroro Dam, is, like the Benue dam at Yola, no more than a vision at this juncture. Originally this was to have comprised the second phase. Whether or not it will have a power capacity of 480 mw. as set forth by a U.K. consulting firm[50] is open to conjecture. In any case, the main purpose of the first two phases is to supply cheaper electricity for Nigeria's development, with navigation a secondary consideration. (Flood control, irrigation, and improved fishing are also put forth as resulting benefits of the project.) Phase 3 would regulate the discharge of the Kaduna River, whose peak occurs six to eight weeks earlier than the Niger's, into the Niger, thereby improving navigation on the main stream.

Faced with the newly discovered sulphur-free natural gas reserves, some planners are suggesting that the East, supplemented by Enugu coal, and the Niger delta be fed by gas-produced power.

In the fiscal year of 1962 Nigeria produced 785.8 million kw-h. of electricity.[51] This amount--more than was actually consumed--amounts to only 20 kw-h. per capita, less than two-fifths of the corresponding Ghanaian figure for the period 1955-57.[52] Still, it is an amazing increase from the situation in 1948 when the ratio of kw-h. to each Nigerian was a meager 4.4.[53] And, with the exception of occasional power fluctuations and failures, industry in the major urban centers appears to receive electricity sufficient for its needs.

As for the future expansion of electric generating capacity, Nigeria has passed a fork in the road. The decision to go ahead with Phase 1 of the Niger/Kaduna dams project is of importance to the long-run stability of the economy, particularly in a period of growing balance-of-payments difficulties. The procurement of capital equipment for this project will involve a great expenditure of foreign exchange. Furthermore, assuming that additional installed capacity of the magnitude of the Kainji Dam will soon be required,[54] the question arises whether or not the dam scheme, after making adjustment for the benefits to navigation, etc., will provide electricity to Nigeria on a more economic basis than will a combination of gas and oil. Presumably this has been answered in the affirmative.

WATER FOR INDUSTRY

All industry uses some water. Some industry uses a lot of water. Included in the second category are breweries, textile bleaching facilities, oil seed crushing plants, tanneries, and steel mills. Lack of water may be a limiting factor. Even where it is available it may entail large capital expenditures to bring it to the user.

Lagos

In 1959-60, consumption averaged 10 million gallons per day (m.g.d.), or 83 per cent of the maximum capacity of the distribution system.[55] Extensions to the trunk mains and distribution system are now in progress. At the completion of this program, Lagos will receive a firm 20 m.g.d. of potable water from two nearby rivers. An A.I.D.-financed study is to make projections for the future. All in all, as far as supply is concerned, Lagos is faced with no immediate problems. In the long run, the current sources may need to be augmented.

Western Region

In October, 1961, Ibadan had no water for new industry.[56] Consumption already equaled the maximum output of 4 m.g.d., even though this riverine supply had been doubled in 1957. A December, 1963, A.I.D. loan will contribute towards 9 m.g.d. more by 1968.[57]

Including Ibadan, the major portion of the region's manufacturing industry is located in the outskirts of Lagos, viz., Mushin and Ikeja. At present, in 1964, Ikeja obtains its water from the Lagos system. Since 1962, Ikeja and Mushin have been able to draw a maximum of 6 m.g.d. from Lagos. For this privilege, the West contributed £310,000 for capital construction.

Other areas, e.g., Warri, maintain boreholes as their source of supply. In sum, water for industry appears to be, or soon will be, available in ample amounts throughout the West (and Mid-West).

Eastern Region

With rates as low as 2/6d. per 1,000 gallons for industrial users (one-third less than the West, and the cheapest in Nigeria), the East, with the exception of Abakaliki Province and the extreme western side of Ogoja Province, is in a position to meet all near-term requirements.[58]

Port Harcourt's capacity of 3.5 m.g.d. should reach 7.5 m.g.d. by 1968. Its main source of supply is from six new boreholes near the airport.

The region's three other large centers, Aba, Enugu, and Onitsha, are now consuming water at a rate equal to the capacity of their respective systems. Construction of extensions are underway at all three. Boreholes may be drilled in most sections of the region with the exception of the Abakaliki area where there are shales for an unknown depth. In order to secure water of normal salinity and with no sulphates, industry has not always found it necessary to wait for the public works department. A case in point is Aba. The Lever Brothers soap plant draws extremely soft water from a nearby river. The adjacent brewery, requiring purer water, utilizes boreholes, since the low pH [acidic] may easily be raised by treatment.

In September, 1961, an engineering firm commenced work on a fourteen-month study that resulted in an Eastern Region master plan for the supply of water for drinking, industry, and irrigation.[59] (Simultaneously, a Russian hydrologist under United Nations auspices investigated the Abakaliki area.) Assuming that the long-term outlook is as bright as the present, the only significant problem remaining is providing the funds as required by the plan.

Northern Region

It is in parts of the North, which have up to five months with no rainfall, that the lack of sufficient water may thwart industrial planning and aspirations.

The preceding section cited NESCO's inability to sell additional electricity on the plateau in recent years for lack of enough water. In late 1961, the tin smelter in Jos had three electric furnaces on the floor and five more on order. Yet there was only enough electricity for one furnace, with a promise for no more than a second.[60]

A tannery proposed for Zaria will require 350,000 gallons per day versus the present capacity of 800,000 gallons per day. Even with the added 600,000 gallons-per-day-capacity under construction, it would consume one-quarter of the city's supply. A similar project is scheduled for Maiduguri, where only 500,000 gallons per day are in supply and no further construction is in progress (although .5 m.g.d. additional capacity is projected).

In 1962, when the Kaduna Textile Mill started bleaching operations, its water consumption quadrupled to 200,000 gallons per day. In 1962, also, the Nigeria Breweries' Kaduna branch, which had been bottling mineral waters for six years, added a brewery operation.[61] Moreover, new textile mills are being established. No problems should arise because the city's water supply capacity is being enlarged from 1.2 m.g.d. to 4.67 m.g.d., and should attain 7.5 m.g.d. by 1970.

Kano, the North's largest city, has a capacity of 1.7 m.g.d. with no major additional capacity in work. Other cities, such as Gusau, Sokoto, Jos, and Ilorin, do not have extensions in progress although they are projected.[62]

In Bornu and Sokoto Provinces, artesian supplies are probably available in the vast sedimentary rock formations.[63]

The IBRD reported[64] that in 1954-55 urban water supplies received no funds because allocations listed in the Ten Year Plan of Development and Welfare (1946-55) had been exhausted. It cannot yet be determined whether the section of the Northern Region Development Plan for 1962-68 devoted to urban water supplies will be adequate vis-a-vis the government's policy of establishing industry all over the region.[65]

SEWAGE DISPOSAL

In 1964, there is no legislation in effect in Nigeria with respect to effluents and trade wastes. The Lagos area empties into the lagoon. The Ikeja area is very porous and can handle the small quantities of industrial wastes it receives, but Ibadan's industrial estate will require treatment since the ground is less porous.

The expenses involved have inhibited action in this field.[66] Should legislation be passed in the East, plants located on the new Trans-Amadi Industrial Estate in Port Harcourt will have to provide separate treatment for their wastes and then discharge the treated effluent into an adjoining creek.

SUMMARY AND CONCLUSIONS

Nigeria, although a new nation, has a comparatively well-developed infrastructure. She is particularly on the move in the field of transport. Roads and bridges are being built, the railroad is being extended, the airline has received a new fleet of planes, and the ports of Lagos and Port Harcourt are being continuously expanded and modernized. Also the Niger Dam scheme will improve river navigation, and the Escravos Bar project is increasing the importance of the four delta ports.

The traditional rail and river transportation networks served the trade between colony and mother country, carrying minerals and agricultural produce to the sea. However, the railroad mileage from Lagos to Enugu, a distance of 477 miles by road, is 979 miles via Kaduna Junction. Of necessity, perishable, small, light, compact, and high-valued items travel between the Eastern and Western Regions by air and road. This east-west traffic in the south will be facilitated by the opening of the Onitsha Bridge across the Niger in 1965.

The railroads in the United States and Britain are meeting greater and greater competition from the road. With the exception of the wide expanses in the north, where the roads, more than competitors, serve as feeders to the railroad, this situation also obtains in Nigeria. Still, the railroad has always enjoyed the shelter provided by restrictions placed on road traffic. The railroad, for example, is exempt from the tax on diesel oil. Thus, although the road-users have not been paying full maintenance and capital costs of the road network, neither has the railroad been free of accepting subventions.

In any case, all present industrial areas are relatively well served by a variety of transport. Even so, with respect to costs, the north is penalized by its long distance from the sea. This is somewhat compensated by the cheaper modes of transport, which connect it to the ports and internal markets of the south.

All areas where industry is located, or soon will be, are at least adequately served by communications facilities and media, as well as by electricity. With respect to the latter, the rate structure is not likely to inhibit the introduction of new ventures.

Throughout the south, water, too, can be supplied to any industry that is established during the next decade. This assumes that the capital funds necessary for extensions of present-day capacity will be forthcoming.

But with the exception of those urban areas, such as Lokoja, Idah, and Makurdi, that border the Niger and Benue Rivers, the majority of the Northern Region will have to await investigation before it can be ascertained whether and how water may be produced at places planning large-scale, water-consuming industry. In 1964, supplies in hand do not exist in many northern towns sufficient to satisfy current and prospective demands. What the future holds for them in regard to water for industry is, for the time being at least, a matter of guesswork. Finally, also for the moment, industry's conscience and pocketbook will determine what is done with its trade wastes.

In sum, though an underdeveloped country, Nigeria has progressed to the stage where her infrastructure is adequate for the establishment of industry in almost any major urban area. Moreover, the external economies will become more attractive as Nigeria adds to every category of her overhead capital.

Footnotes to Chapter 4

1. 1962 figure from Nigeria, Digest of Statistics, Vol. 12, No. 4, op. cit., p. 63.

2. UAC, Statistical and Economic Review, No. 14 (London, September, 1954), p. 18.

3. Nigeria, Federal Ministry of Information, Our Communications: Highways and Bridges (Lagos: Ministry of Information, 1958), p. 11.

4. H. Robinson, et al., The Economic Co-ordination of Transport Development in Nigeria, a report prepared by the Stanford Research Institute for the Joint Planning Committee, National Economic Council, Federation of Nigeria (Menlo Park: 1961), pp. 38 and 112. There is a minimum of inter-urban bus service; "Mammy Wagons," locally made wooden bodies on imported five-ton chasses, can adequately carry most of the road passenger traffic plus short-haul freight.

5. And only one connected Lagos Island with the mainland. A second Lagos bridge is now in the design stage.

6. There will be 75 ft. clearance between the underside of the carriageway and the highest water level; therefore it will not be a drawbridge. The writer visited the site on October 13, 1961.

7. UAC, Statistical and Economic Review, Vol. 25, March, 1961, op. cit., p. 39.

8. Service on the narrow gauge Jos-Zaria line serving the tin fields was discontinued on September 13, 1957.

9. A description of the route and the country through which it passes is contained in the comprehensive study prepared by K. L. Crawford, Deputy Chief Superintendent of the Nigerian Railway Corporation. (Nigerian Railway Corporation, Bauchi-Bornu Railway Extension: Review of Revenue Potential [Ebute Metta: Railway Printer, 1960], 148 pp.)

10. "The railways of Nigeria were started in the period of reaction from laissez-faire, they were state railways from the first." (L. C. A. Knowles, The Economic Development of the British Overseas Empire [New York: Albert and Charles Boni, 1925], p. 491.) More likely the prospects for profitable traffic were not apparent to private investors. "The lines were in measure economic speculations, being built partly for administrative and philanthropic purposes." (A. McPhee, The Economic Revolution in British West Africa [London: George Routledge and Sons, Ltd., 1926], p. 111).

11. See Nigeria, The Laws of the Federation of Nigeria and Lagos, Chapter 139, Nigerian Railway Corporation (Rev. ed.; Lagos: Government Printer, 1959).

12. IBRD, op. cit., p. 296.

13. Relaying, re-sleepering, and reballasting programs are in progress.

14. £1,349,639 for 1959-60, £2,335,369 for 1960-61, £1,063,985 for 1961-62, and £940,285 for 1962-63, before taxation. (Nigerian Railway Corporation, Reports and Accounts for the Years Ended 31st March, 1960, 1961, 1962, and 1963 [Ebute Metta: Railway Printer, 1961-63], p. 51, p. 5, p. 5, and p. 5.) In 1961 and 1962, the corporation achieved net working surpluses. However, interest payable on short-term borrowings plus capital liabilities resulted in over-all net operating deficits.

15. Nigeria, Report of the Elias Commission of Inquiry into the Administration, Economics, and Industrial Relations of the NRC (Lagos: Federal Government Printer, 1960), pp. 62-65. See also Nigeria, Statement by the Government of the Fed. of Nigeria on the Report of the Elias Commission. . . (S.P. 7/60; Lagos: Government Printer, 1960) which proposed to await the release of the Stanford Research Institute Report before making economic decisions.

16. At the time, this union composed half of Nigeria's federal civil servants.

17. Express passenger service from Lagos to Ibadan (120 miles) is 5 3/4 hours ($2\frac{1}{2}$ hours by car), 24 1/4 hours to Kaduna Junction, and 31 hours to Kano. (Nigerian Railway Corporation, Railway Public Time Table [Ebute Metta: Railway Printer, March 11, 1961], p. 20.) These figures still hold true in 1964.

18. Out-of-pocket costs, for example, would exclude depreciation charges, since the purchase of new equipment does not enter the short-run cash budget.

19. On August 24, 1961, the first four of seven locomotives arrived. They are capable of hauling 500 tons over the 2 per cent grades on the Kafanchan-Jos line. (West African Pilot [Yaba], August 25, 1961, p. 2.)

20. Nigerian Railway Corporation, Annual Report for 1962-63, op. cit., p. 32. In mid-1964 the NRC placed an order for twenty-nine additional diesels.

21. The guarantee is requested because more crossings add to the maintenance cost of the line. Interview with Mr. J. C. Mertens, Deputy Chief Superintendent (Operating and Commercial), Nigerian Railway Corporation, Ebute Metta, August 28, 1961.

22. The federal government had 51 per cent of the equity shares, the Elder Dempster Lines 33 per cent and B.O.A.C. 16 per cent. (E. H. Coleman, How Aviation Came to Nigeria [Lagos: Federal Ministry of Information, 1960], p. 16.) It might be noted that the initials W.A.A.C. were retained for the purpose of goodwill.

23. In 1959 and 1960 these direct flights were discontinued: Benin City-Port Harcourt, Calabar-Enugu, Calabar-Kano, Enugu-Makurdi, Jos-Lagos, Jos-Makurdi, Kaduna-Zaria, Kano-Zaria. (During the same period Lagos-Port Harcourt flights were increased from four to seven per week, and by April, 1964, to eleven per week.)

24. In all this Nigeria is deeply affected by Ghana whose Russian-piloted Ilyushin turbo-props land at Ikeja and fly to Moscow. It is ironic that Ghana, the apostle of Pan-Africanism, dissolved the old W.A.A.C., thereby leading to a duplication of equipment, especially on the international runs.

25. The cargo plane was introduced in late 1961, primarily for the shipment of meat from the north to Lagos. On January 1, 1963, Aero Contractors Ltd. had five aircraft and Pan African Airways Ltd. six.

26. UAC's Niger River Transport carries more than double the combined ton-mileage of [John] Holt's Transport Ltd. and the Niger Benue Transport Company.

27. "General" commodities comprise 19.1 per cent of the upstream total. The percentages are based on 1959-60 traffic. S.R.I., _op. cit_., p. 216.

28. "Ships must have cleared the river by [the steep fall in October] . . . , but it is very difficult to predict the exact time of this fall. As a result, most of the ships must leave the Benue well before the beginning of the sudden drop in water-level, thus shortening the navigable season considerably." This statement is from the most thorough and authoritative examination of these two rivers, within Nigeria, ever undertaken. (Netherlands Engineering Consultants [NEDECO], _River Studies and Recommendations on Improvement of Niger and Benue_ [Amsterdam: North-Holland Publishing Co., 1959], p. 70.) The two seasons differ because the Benue is further south. Thus it is affected by more intense rains that start earlier.

29. Interview with Mr. Blackburn-Kane, Deputy Permanent Secretary, Federal Ministry of Transportation and Aviation, September 30, 1961, Lagos.

30. The cost per ton-mile should be one-half to one-third of the railroad's; today it is on the order of 1:1.

31. Nigeria, _The Laws of the Federation of Nigeria and Lagos_, Chapter 155, _Ports_ (Rev. ed.;

Lagos: Federal Government Printer, 1959). It might be noted that the NPA has realized a sizeable net revenue in each of the last six years, the greatest being £977,004 in 1961-62. (Nigerian Ports Authority, Annual Reports for 1958-59, 1960-61, and 1962-63 [Lagos: NPA, 1959, 1961, and 1963], p. 106, p. 125, and p. 83.)

32. A stone breakwater.

33. "With the creeks, there is no real limit." (Interview with Mr. J. F. Lane, NPA Chief Traffic and Commercial Manager for all ports, Apapa, September 9, 1961.) The government provided grants for much of the capital costs of the past wharf extensions, etc. The present work is being financed, in part, by a loan of $13.5 million from the World Bank.

34. Three years ago it was stated that work was scheduled to start on four additional berths, bringing Port Harcourt within two of Lagos. (Interview with Mr. C. F. D. Wallace, NPA General Manager, September 5, 1961, Lagos.) Apparently, the decrease in tonnage handled in 1961 and 1962 (see Table 15) has delayed these plans.

35. Planned allowable draught is now 22 feet vis-à-vis the previous depth of 12 feet. The cost of the Escravos Bar project is being allocated as follows: 25 per cent to river transport (Department of Inland Waterways) and 75 per cent to ocean transport (NPA).

36. NEDECO studies of the eastern and western portions of the delta were finished during 1962.

37. The Federal Minister of Transport plans to expand the fleet to twenty ships by 1967. (West Africa [London], February 24, 1962, p. 217.) This could be accomplished sooner should the National Line purchase the Guinea Gulf Line of John Holt--it has four vessels.

38. Annual Abstract of Statistics, op. cit., pp. 111-112, and Nigeria, Annual Report of the Posts

and Telegraphs Department for the Year 1957-58 (Lagos: Federal Government Printer, 1960), p. 7.

39. Statement by the Federal Minister of Communications, the Hon. O. Akinfosile, at the presentation of the Western Electric study by the American Ambassador, the Hon. Joseph Palmer II. (Repeated on Channel 10, Lagos, December 6, 1963.)

40. IBRD, op. cit., p. 359.

41. Nigerian External Telecommunications Ltd. is constructing a new transmitting station at Ikorodu, about 20 miles from Lagos, at a cost of £800,000. (Barclays Bank D.C.O., Overseas Review [London, August, 1963], p. 64.)

42. Benin City, too, will have its own N.B.C. broadcasting station by the end of 1964. In May, 1964, television transmitters were operating in Lagos, Ibadan (also serving Lagos), Enugu, Aba (Eastern Region), and Kaduna. The Northern Region plans to construct one at Kano also.

43. See Nigeria, The Laws of the Federation of Nigeria and Lagos, Chapter 58, Electricity Corporation of Nigeria (Rev. ed.; Lagos: Government Printer, 1959).

44. IBRD, op. cit., p. 32.

45. Nigeria, Electricity Corporation of Nigeria, Manpower Review, No. 12 (August, 1961), p. 1, and Annual Reports for the Years ended 31st March 1962 and 1963 (Lagos: ECN, 1962 and 1963), p. 9.

46. Blankenheimer, op. cit., p. 69. Since inflation in Nigeria has exceeded that in the U.S., the real difference in the rates, as a proportion of all costs, has decreased in the intervening years.

47. The Economist (London), September 30, 1961, p. 1295, and Nigerian Electricity Supply Corporation, Ltd., Chairman's Review for the year ended 28 February, 1963 (London, October 25, 1963).

48. Nigeria, Electricity Corporation of Nigeria, Niger Dams Project (a seven-volume report prepared for the federal government), Vol. 4, Part 6 ("Jebba and Shiroro Projects") (The Hague and London: Netherlands Engineering Consultants and Balfour, Beatty & Company, Ltd., April, 1961), p. 6-4.

49. Ibid., Vol. 1, Part 1 ("General"), p. 1-46.

50. Sir Alexander Gibb and Partners (in association with Preece, Cardew and Rider), Report on Hydro-Electric Development of the Kaduna River at the Shiroro Gorge (London, February, 1961).

51. Digest of Statistics, Vol. 12, No. 4, op. cit., p. 68.

52. UN, Economic Survey of Africa Since 1950, op. cit., p. 133.

53. Ibid.

54. Nigeria's maximum demand has been estimated at 155 mw. for 1963-64. Using an annual increment of 20 per cent, which is greater than that used by Mr. Wyatt in Table 18, a maximum demand of 667 mw. would be attained in 1971-72, exclusive of the standby capacity of 33 per cent. An installed capacity of 1,000 mw. would be required by that date. The 20 per cent annual increment would seem to be a reasonable figure, especially in light of the experience of the IBRD estimate of 16.5 per cent. The World Bank estimated a peak load of 53.3 mw. for 1960 versus the actual maximum demand of 95 mw. (IBRD, op. cit., p. 290.)

55. Nigeria, Federal Ministry of Works and Surveys, Annual Report on the Works Division: 1959-60 (Lagos: Federal Printing Division, 1962), p. 19. Water was drawn from polluted wells until 1916, "when a pure supply of pipe-borne water was laid on." (McPhee, op. cit., p. 288.)

56. Interview with Mr. S. O. Fadahunsi, Chief Water Engineer, Western Region Ministry of Works and Transport, September 27, 1961, Ibadan.

57. Originally, the 1960-65 Western Region Development Program called for 16 m.g.d. more, the first half of which was to be completed by 1964. (Letter from Mr. Fadahunsi to the writer, dated January 10, 1962.)

58. Interview with Mr. D. S. Benton, Chief Water Engineer, Eastern Region Ministry of Works, October 16, 1961, Enugu. The Port Harcourt Town Council collected for its water at the rate of 3/- per 1,000 gallons. Firms who were pumping their own water, e.g., for cooling welding machines, were being charged a "nominal" £40/year by the town. This regional decision was made because it was felt the new modern works would be underutilized otherwise.

59. Interview with Mr. A. Turecki, Chief Engineer, Eastern Nigeria Water Planning and Construction Ltd., October 10, 1961, Enugu.

60. Interview with Mr. F. Dos Santos, loc. cit.

61. Water will be consumed indirectly too, as in the washing of bottles.

62. With the exception of Kano and Katsina Provinces which have their own advisors, the provinces established Water Resources Committees of men from government and business. They are looking into the water requirements of the next twenty years, assessing growth of town and industry, and are to provide a detailed survey of sources of water. (Interview with Mr. E. Jones, Permanent Secretary, Northern Region Ministry of Works, October 24, 1961, Kaduna.)

63. Measurements to determine rates of extraction will take many years, and the question, "Where is the water from?" will have to be answered.

64. IBRD, op. cit , p. 220.

65. The plan merely calls for expansion of urban water supplies and provides £3,510,170 for thirteen items. (Nigeria, National Development

Plan: 1962-68 [Lagos: Federal Ministry of Economic Development, 1962], pp. 158-159.) Apropos is this quotation: "The construction of the new trunk distribution main in Kano was completed, but lack of funds with the Native Authority prevented the carrying out of the other necessary extensions to the scheme." (Northern Region, Ministry of Works, Annual Report: 1959-60 [Kaduna: Government Printer, 1961], p. 5.)

66. Only at the University of Nigeria in Nsukka has the first modern sewerage treatment plant been constructed. Otherwise, there is no pipe-borne sewage system in use in any town or city in Nigeria.

CHAPTER 5 MARKETS AT HOME AND ABROAD

Since the days of Adam Smith the "extent of the market" has been of basic interest to economists. Manufacturing enterprises and, of course, nations are vitally concerned with this subject.

Nigeria is a country of at least 40 million in population. But a great number of citizens is not a sufficient condition for large-scale buying of consumer goods, particularly durables. Purchasing power, too, is essential; for without it, the desire for goods will not be translated into effective demand.

Nigeria finds herself in a somewhat different position with regard to foreign markets. Competition from other lands, tariffs, quotas, treaties, and so on, as well as tradition, play important roles in determining what Nigeria will receive for her exports. Improvement in quality has often offset the lower prices received by Nigeria which resulted from increased world production of primary produce. Yet this advantage may be of only short duration, since competitors can follow this same path.

With respect to the home market, the amount and distribution of the national income will affect, among others, the type and number of manufacturing enterprises that may be established in Nigeria. The amount of consumer expenditures will relate to the funds available for fixed investment. Additionally, the method used to distribute industry's output will determine to what extent industry is able to meet the existing effective demand.

The extent of the market for the output of

manufactured goods is a particular concern of industry, and this topic will be fully explored. It also will be worthwhile to examine briefly two topics pertaining to Nigeria's foreign markets. These are (1) the value, composition and destination of Nigerian merchandise exports, and (2) Nigeria's possible relations to the European Common Market. Although they may be considered of a more peripheral nature than the preceding material, they will afford a fuller understanding of the relation of exports to Nigeria's balance of payments.

THE NIGERIAN HOME MARKET

National Income and Distribution

Using figures developed earlier, the 1960 GNP of £1,026.5 million divided by a population of 35.6 million equals £28/16/7d. or $80.72 per capita (in terms of 1957 market prices). In 1956 and 1957, depreciation ran at an average annual rate of 50.1 per cent of gross investment.[1] At this rate, depreciation in 1960 was £79.16 million.[2] If it is assumed that indirect taxes net of subsidies was £30 million, then the national income of Nigeria in 1960 was in the vicinity of £917.34 million. Thus the income per head was only £25/15/2d., or $72.13.

It is generally presumed that about 75 per cent of the male labor force of 9 million is engaged in agriculture, forestry, and animal husbandry.[3] Undoubtedly, a majority of women also are engaged in agriculture. Nigeria is not saddled with the problem of absentee landlords, nor has she many large landowners. Therefore, since the national income figures omit certain services performed by members of the rural household, like the drawing of water, it may be justifiably assumed that the typical income of the farmer and the per capita figure above are of the same magnitude.[4]

The foregoing suggests that the vast majority of the population receives, real or imputed, not much more than the low income of approximately $6 per month. Also, the comparatively small number of officials, etc., indicates that there are very few Nigerians who are wealthy in American, or even European, terms. Even the professionals receive salaries that cannot be termed munificent. For example, the expatriate chief engineer of the NRC earns £3,300 per year, including overseas pay.

Generally speaking, in the absence of contradictory evidence, the distribution of national income seems to be fairly even throughout the population.[5]

In 1952-53 the census reported 30.4 millions in the present boundaries of the Federation, and Jackson and Okigbo calculated the GDP at £829.5 million in 1957 market prices. Thus, while the population has increased by a minimum of 2 per cent per year, the GDP has experienced a growth rate at constant prices of 3 per cent. At these rates, the per capita share of GDP will not reach $100 (in 1957 prices) until 1984.[6] Of course, each successive year will find the income distributed even less homogeneously as a differentiated class structure makes its appearance.[7] Possibly, as more attention is given to a land tenure that encourages individual initiative, farm settlement that attracts the educated back to the land, and agricultural extension and credit that enable farmers to take advantage of scientific advances, the rural/peasant class will advance with the rest of the nation. Beside accelerating the development process, the inequality in the distribution of the national income between classes will thereby be minimized.

Demand and Consumption

The literature is replete with references to the "demonstration effect" and the "revolution of rising expectations." In general, the picture that is conveyed fits the Nigerian scene, especially in the urban areas. There are at least 30,000 non-Africans,[8] one-third of whom are British, mostly in positions of authority, scattered throughout the Federation. Their constant exhibition of the requisites and comforts of Western Civilization prompts emulation. So, it follows that workers and office boys buy bicycles and radios, and the elite purchase automobiles and television sets.

It may be anticipated that as their income grows urbanites will demand more and more of the goods consumed by more affluent societies the world over: goods ranging from umbrellas to wrist watches, from bread to beer, and from books to phonograph records. As should be expected, consumers' expenditures now absorb the major portion of the national product, 85 per cent of the GDP in 1960. After accounting for the government's share of total consumption, little remains for capital formation from domestic sources. Moreover, as income rises, wants are translated into effective demand. The implications that arise with respect to the internal financing of industrial development, and the composition and level of imports will be dealt with in the next chapter.

Table 19

Percentage Distribution of Consumers' Expenditures--1960

Food	69.0%	Clothing	8.5%
Drink	1.9	Other Non-Durables*	3.8
Tobacco	1.9	Durables	3.6
Fuel and Light	0.9	Misc. Services*	3.9
Education	4.6	(of which,	
Travel	2.1	housing	1.6)

*Figures based on the share these categories claimed in 1957. Education may be overstated.

Source: W. Stolper, et al., Government Expenditures on Goods and Services (Lagos: Federal Ministry of Economic Development, 1961) (Mimeo).

Table 19 highlights in capsule form the large proportion, almost four-fifths, of total expenditures that consumers must allocate to food, clothing,

Table 20

Consumers' Expenditures in 1960 at 1957 Retail Prices

	£ mn		£ mn		£ mn
Food; home produced:		Tobacco:		Clothing; imported:	
agricult. produce	492.0	home produced	10.4	apparel*	51.1
meat	25.0	imported	6.2	footwear	7.1
fish	14.0	Total Tobacco	16.6	Total Clothing	73.7
other animal pro-					
duce	31.0	Education	?	Other Non-Durables	?
				e.g. soap, books	
Food; imported:		Travel:			
fish	12.6	buses and lor-		Durable Goods:	
bread	5.0	ries	20.4	motor cars & cycles	10.3
salt	3.3	running private		bicycles	3.3
sugar	7.0	cars	4.0	hollowware	8.2
misc. mfrd. food	10.8	rail	0.9	radios, clocks, etc.	5.1
Total Food	600.9	other	0.2	furn. & 'frigerators	4.2
		Total Travel	25.5	others	.5
Drink:				Total Durables	31.6
home produced	10.6	Fuel and Light	7.5		
imported	6.7			Misc. Services	?
Total Drink	17.3	Clothing; home		e.g. housing	
		produced:			
		apparel*	13.0	Total Consumer	
		footwear	2.5	Expenditures	870.

*Figures adjusted to equal totals given by Stolper et. al.

Source: W. Stolper et al., Government Expenditures on Goods and Services (Lagos:

and shelter.[9] If most Nigerians were to purchase a more fully-balanced diet, one that included milk and meat, the amount of personal income that remained for fuel and light, education, and transport to a job would necessarily diminish.

Channels of Distribution

This topic has been the subject of many studies, the most comprehensive being P. T. Bauer's West African Trade.[10] Here, it is sufficient to state that goods move to consumers in all conceivable ways: from the woman traders who dispense cigarettes one at a time, to the many Kingsway Department Stores, complete with escalators in Lagos and Ibadan, which are operated by UAC in the major cities of the country. The market women conduct their business with a minimum of working capital, often replenishing their stocks daily from middlemen, wholesalers (including stores and factories), and importers. The big stores, being well appointed and stocked, require large investments of capital. The former are usually prepared to bargain; the latter sell at a fixed price.[11]

The great non-African trading firms and agencies not only distribute the bulk of the manufactured finished goods, but also import most of the diversified items coming into Nigeria, and they are the only companies that maintain technical servicing facilities. The most important companies are UAC, Paterson,-Zochonis, John Holt, A. G. Leventis, UTC, S.C.O.A., C.F.A.O., Chellerams, and Mandilas and Karaberis. "Heavy technical equipment, therefore, probably can be successfully marketed only through existing expatriate companies."[12] African businessmen, too, are beginning to import directly from abroad for their wholesale/retail operations. This is evident after questioning a random number of proprietors of stalls in the great Onitsha Market, and after observing the goods sold by African ventures in Lagos and Ibadan. But, nevertheless, the manufacturer of asbestos-cement roofing in Nigeria needs a sales organization that covers the widely scattered and limited market. He finds that only the trading companies that used to import this item can fill the need.[13]

The market for many items produced by the modern manufacturing industry exists only in a relatively few Nigerian urban centers, which are large centers of commerce and/or government and which contain most of the expatriate and African consumers of these goods. In these centers, with their press, radio, television, and motion picture houses, advertising is carried out in a manner not so different from Europe before the days of Nielsen, i.e., dependent on "hunch and flare."[14] Throughout the country, billboards abound, and, as in the city, much emphasis is placed on brand consciousness. Until recently, with few goods of high quality (particularly with respect to durability in a tropical environment) and limited competition, brand loyalty was supposedly a characteristic of the African consumer. Today, with increasing competition, acceptable quality is likely to become the norm. Also, slogans like "Made in Nigeria" may well carry more importance as a national identity develops among the people, although nationalism and a preference for national goods do not always go together.

A final word may be written regarding "hire purchase," the British term for installment buying. A few independent finance companies, in addition to UAC and John Holt which handle their own, operate in the field of extending credit for the purchase of durables such as automobiles, television sets, radios, air-conditioners, refrigerators, cameras, stationary engines, and so forth. It is automobile purchases, however, which supply their <u>raison d'être</u>. UTC sold approximately 240 passenger vehicles in Enugu alone during 1960, mostly to government employees. In 1964, civil servants are still receiving monthly car allowances.[15]

EXPORTS

Composition and Direction of Trade

Much of Chapter 2 dealt with the agricultural produce and minerals that comprise the bulk of Nigeria's export list. Table 21 summarizes the

Table 21

Composition of Exports: Quantity, Value and Percentage of Total Value of Domestic Exports--Selected Years

	1954	1956	1958	1960	1961	1963*
raw cocoa beans						
tons	98,373	117,133	87,244	153,925	183,911	175,000
£ mn	39.260	23.984	26.668	35.057	33.746	32.360
%	26.8	18.1	20.1	21.8	19.5	17.5
hides and skins						
cwt	180,056	170,843	163,996	189,245	196,180	160,000
£mn	3.020	3.260	3.349	4.299	4.127	4.200
%	2.1	2.5	2.5	2.9	2.4	2.3
groundnuts						
tons	427,868	448,084	513,179	331,913	493,860	614,000
£ mn	29.900	27.764	26.948	21.956	32.233	36.590
%	20.4	21.0	20.3	13.6	18.6	19.2
groundnut oil						
tons	30,634	35,107	39,591	46,624	45,213	69,000
£ mn	3.757	4.095	3.747	5.296	4.992	6.550
%	2.6	3.1	2.8	3.3	2.9	3.5
groundnut cake						
tons	40,776	42,471	58,347	53,270	74,680	85,000
£ mn	1.460	1.239	1.179	1.557	1.931	2.740
%	1.0	.9	.9	.9	1.1	1.5
palm kernels						
tons	464,111	451,070	441,223	418,040	410,628	398,000
£ mn	22.791	20.440	20.450	25.097	19.889	20.280
%	15.6	15.5	15.4	15.6	11.5	11.0

Table 21--Continued

	1954	1956	1958	1960	1961	1963*
palm oil						
tons	208,482	195,237	170,508	183,366	164,592	126,000
£ mn	13.431	14.866	12.663	13.182	13.227	9.370
%	9.2	11.2	9.5	8.2	7.6	5.1
cotton seeds						
tons	36,578	37,338	60,314	39,937	72,919	66,000
£ mn	.645	.951	1.091	1.039	1.906	1.430
%	.4	.7	.8	.6	1.1	.8
raw cotton						
tons	25,959	27,852	33,705	26,865	47,935	40,000
£ mn	7.350	7.113	7.845	5.905	11.120	9.520
%	5.0	5.4	5.9	3.7	6.4	5.2
rubber, crude and crepe						
tons	20,397	38,032	41,130	57,167	55,093	63,000
£ mn	2.849	6.382	7.617	14.241	11.019	11.770
%	1.9	4.8	5.7	8.9	6.3	6.4
timber - logs						
'000 cu ft	10,254	10,616	15,335	22,021	20,304	18,472
£ mn	2.781	2.551	4.141	5.918	5.479	5.379
%	1.9	1.9	3.1	3.7	3.2	2.9
timber - sawn						
'000 cu ft	1,282	1,744	2,223	2,119	2,200	2,732
£ mn	.728	.987	1.211	1.118	1.243	1.363
%	.5	.7	.9	.7	.7	.7
tin ore and concentrates, and metal**						
tons	10,308	13,364	7,627	10,658	10,410	9,673

Table 21--Continued

	1954	1956	1958	1960	1961	1963*
columbite ore and concentrates						
tons	2,525	2,405	737	3,334	1,839	1,599
£ mn	5.142	1.762	.457	2.121	1.165	.748
%	3.5	1.3	.3	1.3	.7	.4
coal						
tons	25,596	98,393	98,248	26,780	51,041	8,031
£ mn	.052	.277	.446	.127	.243	.038
%	.04	.2	.4	.08	.1	.02
petroleum						
mn tons	-	-	.245	.828	2.228	3.695
£ mn	-	-	.978	4.408	11.545	20.140
%	-	-	.7	2.7	6.7	10.9
manufactured goods***						
£ mn	1.057	1.114	1.208	1.506	1.600	1.798
%	.7	.8	.9	.9	.9	.97

* Provisional figures.

** 1963 figures are for metal.

***Plywood and leather are largest contributors. Exports from Southern Cameroons are excluded as of 4th Quarter, 1960.

Sources: Nigeria, Department of Statistics, Trade Report: 1958 (Lagos: Federal Government Printer, 1960), pp. 198-246; Nigeria, Federal Office of Statistics, Abstract of Statistics: 1960 (Lagos: Federal Government Printer, 1960), p. 34; Nigeria, Federal Office of Statistics, Nigeria Trade Summary, Vol. 45, No. 12 (Lagos: Federal Government Printer, December 1960), pp. 30-36; Nigeria, Nigeria Trade Journal (Lagos: Federal Ministry of Information, June 1962), p. 79; Barclays Bank D.C.O., Overseas Review (London, May 1962), p. 62; and provisional data from Federal Office of Statistics, May 25, 1964.

contribution--revenue and per cent of the total--of the more important items. One factor stands out, namely, that manufactured goods have never amounted to 1 per cent of the total value of exports. This is in contrast with 36.0 - 54.9 per cent of the exports of primary products that require some processing prior to overseas shipment, processing such as cotton ginning, tin smelting, expressing palm and groundnut oil, dressing and concentrating mineral ores, sawing timber, extracting palm kernels, and creping rubber latex. It was shown above that much of the manufacturing extant in Nigeria is oriented to serve the demand of Nigerian consumers. Now, the second major category can be added, that is, the segment of industry that processes natural resources. In essence, it serves the demand of foreign consumers.

Table 22 indicates the continual growth in value, at current prices, of Nigerian exports. In 1960, total exports were 16 per cent of the GNP, approximately what it was a decade before. So, in spite of the well known price fluctuations of raw materials in the international markets, Nigeria has been able to maintain a quite consistent ratio of exports to GNP. Nigeria's prime advantage as opposed to many of the other tropical African and of Latin American nations is the diversity of her exports; in the past decade, no item exceeded 26.8 per cent of the total, and, in 1963, the largest contribution, that of groundnut products, was 24.2 per cent, with the three main categories totaling 47.7 per cent. By improving quality, and introducing rubber and petroleum as important exports, Nigeria has thus far been able to resist the worsening commodity terms of trade that is said to be the lot of many of her competitors.[16]

Table 23, which delineates the share of exports purchased by Nigeria's principal customers, is of more than academic interest. In less than ten years the Commonwealth's portion of the total decreased from more than three-quarters to less than one-half. And the trend appears to be continuing. During the decade, the six nations that make up the European Economic Community (EEC) increased their purchases almost sevenfold from 5.5 per cent to more than 37 per cent. This table also indicates that (1) Nigeria's trade is tied to the West, with the Communist Bloc never having taken 1 per cent; (2) Nigeria's trade with her African neighbors is negligible; and (3) as in the past, Nigeria ships the great majority of her exports to the leading industrial powers of the Northern Hemisphere.

Table 22

Total Value of Nigerian Merchandise Exports* (£ million)

Year	Produce of Na.	Re-exports	Total
1942	13.70	.83	14.53
1944	16.20	.99	17.19
1946	23.74	.89	24.63
1948	61.16	1.31	62.47
1950**	88.49	1.74	90.23
1951	116.61	3.45	120.06
1952	125.14	4.39	129.53
1953	120.89	3.34	124.23
1954	146.24	3.29	149.53
1955	129.82	2.72	132.54
1956	132.26	2.31	134.57
1957	124.18	3.36	127.54
1958	132.79	2.76	135.55
1959	160.62	3.00	163.62
1960	165.62	3.78	169.40
1961	170.07	3.42	173.49
1962	162.57	4.61	167.18
1963	184.87	4.83	189.70

* f.o.b.

**Sterling devalued by 30.5 per cent in September, 1949.

Sources: Nigeria, Department of Statistics, Trade Report: 1958 (Lagos: Federal Government Printer), p. 264; Nigeria, Nigeria Trade Journal (Lagos: Federal Ministry of Information, June, 1962), p. 77; Nigeria, Federal Office of Statistics, Nigeria Trade Summary, Vol. 46, No. 4 (Lagos: Federal Government Printer, April, 1961), p. 1; Vol. 47, No. 12, p. 4; and Vol. 48 (draft), No. 12, p. 5.

Table 23

Destination of Nigerian Merchandise Exports as a Percentage of Total Value of Domestic Exports*

	1953	1955	1957	1959	1961	1963
United Kingdom	75.4	70.0	63.0	51.2	44.2	39.9
Total Common-wealth	76.2	71.3	65.0	52.3	46.7	42.8
E.E.C.	5.5	17.1	25.9	34.6	34.0	37.5
U.S.A.	11.1	9.4	6.1	7.4	11.2	9.4
Africa	.4	.9	1.3	.9	1.3	2.2
Japan	-	-	.02	1.4	2.0	1.3
Communist Bloc	.2	.2	.2	.3	.4	.9

Notes: Commonwealth includes Ireland and South Africa; E.E.C. includes Trieste (with Italy), and E. Germany was incorporated in 1953 total.

*Excludes re-exports, parcel post, and ships' stores.

Sources: Nigeria, Department of Statistics, Trade Report: 1957 (Lagos: Federal Government Printer), p. 4; Nigeria, Nigeria Trade Journal (Lagos: Federal Ministry of Information, June, 1962), p. 77; Nigeria, Federal Office of Statistics, Annual Abstract of Statistics: 1960 (Lagos: Federal Government Printer, 1960), p. 25; Nigeria, Federal Office of Statistics, Nigeria Trade Summary, Vol. 45, No. 12 (Lagos: Federal Government Printer, December, 1960), p. 3, and Vol. 48 (draft), No. 12, Table 3.

It should be evident, then, that Nigeria must consider more than the political considerations involved in a limited association, if proffered, with the EEC. Just what the economic stakes are will now be considered.

Nigeria and the European Economic Community

In the spring of 1957 the overseas territories of the "Six"--then still colonies--were given, for at least five years and subject to renewal, a special associated status with the Common Market. Briefly, the products of the associated overseas territories were to benefit from a gradual lowering of import duties and restrictive quotas by the Six, and they were to have free access into the Common Market at the end of the EEC twelve-year transition period. Also, the preferential systems which still existed in overseas markets in favor of the *métropoles*, especially France, were to be gradually abandoned during this transition period to offer equal opportunities to the Six. Finally, a "Development Fund"--$580.25 million in the first five years--was established to finance economic development schemes and social establishments in the overseas territories. Reduced to simple terms, the Adjoining Acts meant that the eighteen associated territories such as Dahomey and the Ivory Coast (1) would not have to lower their import duties in favor of the Six--in fact, to protect developing industries and/or a deteriorating balance-of-payments position, they could increase their tariffs and quotas--and (2) at the end of the twelve-year period, would be able to export *all* their products to the Six without any tariff restrictions.

In late 1961 Britain announced her intention of seeking membership in the EEC. Nigerians then began debating whether or not to accept "association with" the Common Market. If the U.K. had been in the EEC the previous year, almost 75 per cent of Nigeria's exports would have been sold to the enlarged Common Market. Yet during the Commonwealth Prime Ministers' meeting in London in September, 1962, the year of agonizing over this question came to an end when Nigeria joined Ghana and Tanganyika in categorically stating that she would not seek associated status. Therefore, as far as Nigeria was concerned, it was anticlimactic when Britain's bid to join the EEC was rejected a few months later.

Nigeria's decision was primarily political. She desires to remain nonaligned and so outside the Cold War. How, she asks, can Nigeria be associated with the main continental NATO powers, receive economic aid and preferential treatment from them, and then remain neutral in the world forum? But economics cannot be forgotten. During October, 1962, in Brussels, the Fund's operation for the coming five years was worked out between the Six and the Eighteen Associated Members. (The latter are to receive $620 million in outright gifts plus an additional $110 million in the form of special advances and low-interest loans.)[17] Thus it was determined that the trial period at economic cooperation was to be continued for another five years. Moreover, the timetable was altered. The twelve-year span was shortened so that the EEC import duties on tropical products from the associated states in Africa will be abolished by January of 1965.

Specifically, at the insistence of the Germans and the Dutch, the tariff on cocoa has been reduced; and at the latter's behest, oilseeds will carry no duty in the Common Market.[18] Nigeria's increasing sales to the EEC, however, will be affected by tariffs of 5.4 per cent for cocoa, 9-14 per cent for palm oil, 5 per cent for logs, and 10 per cent for sawn timber.[19] Furthermore, should Nigeria begin to process cocoa, her cocoa butter and powder would face tariffs of 22 per cent and 27 per cent.

The picture is not as bleak today as it was in mid-1962, when a third of Nigeria's exports were to a large degree in jeopardy. Still, some barriers will be encountered, and her French-speaking neighbors are diversifying and receiving aid from a source that she does not In addition, processed materials and manufactures, e.g., tin metal as opposed to tin ores and concentrates, will meet stiff EEC duties. "Thus as the States of Europe struggle to unite, the arbitrary frontiers they left on the map of Africa bite deeper than ever."[20]

With the foregoing in mind, the Nigerian Government undertook informal contacts with the EEC during the winter of 1963-64. She hoped that a free trade area could be arranged. And by avoiding ties with the Development Fund she would avoid raising political passions at home. In mid-April, 1964, France alone vetoed the commencement of formal negotiations. This question, nevertheless, has arisen again. On June 2, 1964, France withdrew her veto when other members of the Six agreed to consider Spain's application for association.[21]

The prospective industrialist will perforce be affected by these negotiations. If Nigeria were to establish a link with the Common Market, pari passu, some sort of arrangement with her neighbors might be effectuated which would eventually result in an African customs union. This would, in turn, enlarge the "home" market in numbers, if not in significant purchasing power. Should this felicitous state of affairs be achieved, the businessman will find Nigeria a more favorable locale in which to conduct operations.

SUMMARY AND CONCLUSIONS

A visitor who travels to the major centers of Nigeria, who shops on the installment plan at Kingsway or Leventis, and who is subjected to local advertising in many media is apt to lose sight of the very underdeveloped state of the country.

Nigeria has been experiencing one continuous and accelerating period of economic activity since the start of World War II. Yet in 1960, the per capita share of national income was only $72.13. It has been suggested that a low level of income, about $6 per month, is a typical as well as an average phenomenon. Furthermore, an examination of the growth rates of population and GDP indicates that it will be a matter of at least two decades before Nigerians realize a $100 per capita share of GDP. Not surprisingly, 80 per cent of consumers' expenditures go for food, clothing, and housing. It follows that much of the manufacturing in Nigeria is in existence to supply these needs and that the composition of demand will not alter considerably in the coming years.

Many of the consumer goods are bought in relatively small units or quantities. For example, the women traders make sales of one cigarette at a time.

In a country of 40 million, the 30,000 non-Africans probably own at least one of three automobiles (see Chapter 3). It may well be that for many consumer goods, especially durables, one or two plants will be able to satisfy the Federation's demand for a product for some time. Indeed, the examination of the food canning factories in Chapter 7 indicates that two plants may be too many for the present state of demand.

Turning to channels of distribution: it has been seen that these vary from the African petty trader to the great expatriate trading firms, both of which seem well suited to the Nigerian scene. Industry will thus be able to meet the effective demand. But in order to sell their products, most manufacturers will have to continue using these traditional technical servicing facilities unless they are willing to take on the burden of a large overhead. This is necessary, because the limited market for many goods is also a widely scattered one. Therefore, technical service, in particular, is difficult to supply adequately in a country the size of Nigeria.

With respect to exports, 1964 finds Nigeria better positioned to deal with the vagaries of the international commodity markets than many underdeveloped nations, because her export list is diversified in makeup. No one item earns as much as one-fifth of the revenue received by international trade.

Nigeria's holdings of foreign exchange are earned by her exports, less than 1 per cent of which are manufactured goods. With this foreign exchange, Nigeria purchases the capital equipment she needs for economic development. But, somewhat paradoxically, the vulnerability of Nigeria's export sales has increased in parallel with the recent and extraordinary growth of her sales to the EEC. For, Nigeria is faced with the reality that many of her exports, from cocoa to palm oil, by 1965 will have to surmount tariff walls which such produce from her African competitors, like the Ivory Coast and the Congo, will not. In 1964, while working for a lowering of these prospective tariff duties, Nigeria apprehensively awaits the commencement of negotiations with the Common Market.

Footnotes to Chapter 5

1. Jackson and Okigbo, *op. cit.*, Table ED. IX. 4.

2. Stolper, *et al.*, Table ED. VI (4). All figures are at 1957 market prices.

3. See for instance, *Economic Survey of Nigeria*, *op. cit.*, p. 13.

4. Of course, much of the farmer's income is imputed.

5. As in most countries the distribution is likely to be positively skewed. This analysis has been simplified by neglecting to account for the greater degree of urbanization, education, and number of women engaged in trade in the south vis-à-vis the north.

Most manufacturers view Nigeria as a mass market; see for example the January 22, 1962, issue of the U.S. Department of Commerce's *Foreign Commerce Weekly*, pp. S-1 through S-7. Therefore, the writer believes this exposition of a national market is more meaningful than if the national income was allocated to the regions. (More specifically, the average incomes are highest in the West, and lowest in the North.)

6. This approach is suggested by the findings of an inquiry undertaken by the Department of Political Economy, University of Edinburgh, for the U.S. Department of Agriculture. "At the risk of compounding uncertainties, for neither the output series nor the population 'guesstimates' are wholly reliable, we can nevertheless advance the rather tentative opinion that real income per head has been rising only very slightly, if at all since 1954/55." (United States, Department of Agriculture, *Nigeria: Determinants of Projected Level of Demand, Supply, and Imports of Farm Products in 1965 and 1975*, a Report

by Ian G. Stewart, et al. for the Economic Research Service, ERS-Foreign-32 [Washington, D.C.: Department of Agriculture, August, 1962], p. 25.)

7. It should be emphasized that the above figures do not invite comparison with the U.S. standard of living. They are merely illustrative of the difficulties involved in selling many Western-type goods on a large scale in the next decade or so to Nigerians.

8. Nigeria, Federal Ministry of Commerce and Industry, Handbook of Commerce and Industry in Nigeria (5th ed.; Lagos: Federal Ministry of Information, September, 1962), p. 3.

9. Even full-time servants in European households are not, as a rule, provided with food as is customary in America.

10. Bauer, op. cit. Much of Bauer's exposition is still relevant.

11. A description of the establishment of the Lagos Kingsway Store is given in UAC's Statistical and Economic Review, op. cit., September, 1953.

12. Bernard Blankenheimer and J. C. O'Neill, Market for U.S. Products in Nigeria, U.S. Department of Commerce, Bureau of Foreign Commerce (Washington, D.C.: U.S. Government Printing Office, 1961), p. 8.

13. Indeed, the inverse is usually the case. The trading companies, prompted by political and economic considerations, are investing in manufacturing facilities that produce items they (used to) import, e.g., John Holt and Patterson,-Zochonis each have an interest in the asbestos-cement plant in Ikeja.

14. In 1961, the number of expatriate advertising agencies in Nigeria was seven, all British. (Interview with Mr. P H Harris, Manager of West African Publicity [Nigeria] Ltd. [Nigeria's only agency in 1955], September 8, 1961, Lagos.)

15. All governments have made these advances; the Federal Government provided a maximum of £1,200 to Members of Parliament. In the Eastern Region the maximum advance has been £950 for five years at 3 per cent which is below the bank rate. (Interview with Mr. H. Jaggi, UTC Motors Department, October 12, 1961, Enugu.) The situation has not changed although the unions are pressing for the abolition of these advances.

16. The balance-of-payments picture will be examined in Chapter 6.

17. Most importantly, $230 million of the total $730 million will be spent in diversifying the economies of those countries that are either dependent on a single cash crop, or on the present price privileges afforded by France--which will be liquidated in five years, i.e., by January 1, 1968.

18. _The Economist_ (London), January 18, 1964, p. 194. Also the 30 per cent duty on rubber has been reduced to zero.

19. In order to analyze the exact effects of these preferential duties on a non-Associate's exports to the EEC, it would be necessary to examine a host of factors. For instance, consumer preferences and internal taxation are particularly important with respect to coffee consumption in West Germany. Germany, traditionally, has purchased _arabica_ coffee from Latin America for the great majority of her coffee consumption. The 9.6 per cent coffee tariff facing coffee from nations outside the Association could (1) increase the rate of the relatively low but slowly increasing consumption of instant coffee from African _robusta_, and (2) aid the _arabica_ growing areas of East and Central Africa. Yet, it must be added, since coffee in Germany faces a high specific tax (D.M. per kilogram), the 9.6 per cent duty at the retail level would represent only a minor portion of the purchase price.

20. _The Economist_ (London), Nov. 25, 1961, p. 735.

21. "France Bars Nigeria" and "Fresh ECM Talks with Nigeria," front-page headlines, _Daily Times_ (Lagos), April 16, 1964, and June 3, 1964.

CHAPTER 6 FINANCING THE DEVELOPMENT OF INDUSTRY

As shown in the preceding chapter, a high proportion--about 85 per cent--of the national product is assigned to consumers' expenditures, primarily necessities. This is a result of the low per capita share of GNP. Thus, even though the total national income is sizable in contrast to the other nations of tropical Africa, private domestic savings cannot be counted upon to provide a substantial contribution to capital formation.

The material in this chapter suggests that the cost of industrial development will, in the main, have to be borne by the Nigerian public sector and foreign investment. And, further, due to the multifarious demands upon the Nigerian governments, most of the financing for industry will be sought abroad.

The governments are aware of the importance of providing incentives to draw foreign investment, mostly private, to Nigeria. Therefore, it should be worthwhile to examine the extent and efficacy of these inducements. This will be done subsequent to an examination of capital formation and industrial financing in Nigeria, both internal and external.

CAPITAL FORMATION

For the period 1950-60, Nigeria's gross capital formation (GCF) averaged 11.3 per cent of the GNP. Furthermore, during the past decade the trend has been steadily upward, and in 1960 the percentage rose to 15.4 (see Table 24 below).[1] This is all to the good, and will add to the economic base and the capacity for future growth. Of this fixed investment in 1960, as Table 25 indicates, plant and machinery accounted for £20.62 million, or 13 per cent.[2]

Table 24

Gross Capital Formation as a Percentage of GNP*

	GCF (£ mn)	GNP (£ mn)	%
1950	48.4	697.6	6.9
1951	59.7	750.7	8.0
1952	75.0	805.8	9.3
1953	79.9	826.3	9.6
1954	92.9	891.4	10.4
1955	102.6	918.3	11.1
1956	108.0	902.1	12.0
1957	113.0	943.6	12.0
1958	122.3	971.4	12.6
1959	136.7	986.0	13.9
1960	158.0	1,026.5	15.4

*At 1957 market prices.

Sources: E. F. Jackson and P. N. C. Okigbo, National Income of Nigeria for the Period 1950-1957 (Lagos: Federal Ministry of Economic Development, 1960) (Mimeo.); and W. Stolper, et al., Expenditures on Goods and Services (Lagos: Federal Ministry of Economic Development, 1961) (Mimeo.).

Perhaps of more significance is the figure for fixed investment net of depreciation, because this demonstrates what the country is adding to her plant above and beyond mere replacement.[3] For the fiscal year 1958-59, the Office of Statistics calculated that only £3 million of the GCF was assignable to manufacturing and processing.[4] If it is assumed that depreciation, on a replacement basis, was 50 per cent, then half of this amount, £1.5 million, was added to Nigeria's capacity to produce manufactured goods.[5] Probably, though, even this relatively low figure is overstated, because the £3 million total included such consumer durables as air conditioners and spare parts for passenger cars. Since independence, net investment in manufacturing facilities has increased, but the absolute value of net investment in manufacturing and processing remains quite low by any standard.

Table 25

Composition of Gross Capital Formation (£ '000)

	1957	1958	1959	1960
Vehicles	21,330	22,987	21,225	29,400
Plant and Machinery	18,040	14,106	20,000	20,620
Buildings and Civil Engineering Works	62,660	72,754	85,000	96,500
Mining Development	5,090	12,440	10,500	11,500
Total	107,120*	122,287	136,725	158,020

*This total disagrees with the corresponding figure in Table 24. In this total, the amount derived by the Federal Department of Statistics was used.

Source: W. Stolper, *et al*., *Government Expenditures on Goods and Services* (Lagos: Federal Ministry of Economic Development, 1961) (Mimeo.).

INTERNAL FINANCING

The funds accounted for in the federal and regional budgets play an important part in the Federation's economic progress. But since the major portion of the country's day-to-day, that is, recurrent costs have to be met by indirect taxation (chiefly duties on international trade), other devices have to be utilized for meeting all the developmental (capital) expenditures. These include marketing boards, development corporations, finance and housing corporations, the banking system, and even football pools. The commercial banks, the central bank, the stock exchange, the insurance companies, etc., are the institutions that make up the money market. Nigeria's money market, even if inchoate, is rapidly developing. As a backdrop to the government's part in financing, its institutions will be examined.

Financial Institutions: The Beginning of a Money Market

The Central Bank

In 1958, following the example of Ghana, Nigeria passed an ordinance establishing a central bank, wholly owned by the federal government, and possessing wide powers.[6] On July 1, 1959, the bank became the sole authority for the issue of currency, at par with sterling.[7] Prior to 1957, the four British West African colonies had maintained a common currency under the control of the West African Currency Board in London.

The bank has played an important part in the creation of a market for local securities by establishing a call money fund and by purchasing unsold treasury bills and government bonds. It has also established two clearing houses (for the Lagos and Kano banks), and a research department that is gathering basic monetary and financial information in cooperation with the Federal Office of Statistics.

The Commercial Banks

Barclays Bank D.C.O. and the Bank of [formerly, British] West Africa have, since before the last war, controlled the large share of banking in Nigeria. At the end of 1963, seventeen banks, with 218 branches and offices, held licenses granted by the Federal Ministry of Finance.[8] Of these, two are American (the Lagos branches of the Chase Manhattan Bank and the Bank of America), one is partially American (the Bankers Trust Company is one of the backers of the United Bank for Africa Ltd.), and three are, in effect, regional banks (the National Bank of Nigeria, wholly owned by the Western Region Government; the African Continental Bank, wholly owned by the Eastern Region Government, viz., one-quarter Eastern Nigeria Development Corporation and three-quarters Marketing Board; and the Bank of the North, more than 50 per cent owned by the Northern Region Government, i.e., Northern Nigeria Development Corporation and Marketing Board). The National and African Continental banks were party-run after the war until they got into financial difficulties, as did more than twenty African banks that either failed or went into voluntary liquidation between 1946 and 1952.

Part of the problem facing the prospective Nigerian entrepreneur has been his inability to obtain a line of credit from the European-operated commercial banks because either the expatriate managers suspect a "lack of underlying integrity on the part of the average trader in business dealing";[9] or the African is not able to supply the requisite collateral for a loan under the present system of land tenure wherein the tribe and not the individual is the owner. In response to the obvious need, Nigerians began to organize and administer their own banks. As pointed out above, these institutions have, unfortunately, had a precarious existence.

Table 26 demonstrates the rapid growth, from a very low base, of deposits during the 1950's.[10] Still, £47 million in time and savings deposits, equivalent to about $3.30 per capita, suggests that the savings habit is not as strong as the planners would like. Undoubtedly, many retain their savings in the form of cash.

On the asset side, total investments in Nigeria by these banks was £2.3 million at the end of 1963, and their loans and advances £89.5 million, of which £9.5 million was granted to borrowers engaged in manufacturing.[11]

Table 26

Deposits in Principal Commercial Banks of Nigeria* (£ '000)

Dec. 31	Demand	Time	Savings	Total
1950	13,190	1,762	1,450	16,402
1952	22,230	3,325	2,289	27,844
1954	32,870	4,289	3,445	40,604
1956	35,352	4,131	6,525	46,008
1958	40,266	6,645	11,145	58,056
1960	41,117	8,954	18,441	68,512
1961	41,658	14,068	21,188	76,914
1962	45,296	17,420	24,224	86,940
1963	48,773	18,948	28,187	95,908

*Since the fourth quarter of 1952 all banks completing returns under the Nigerian Banking Ordinance are included. (See Nigeria, The Laws of the Federation of Nigeria and Lagos, Chapter 19, Banking [Rev. ed.; Lagos: Government Printer, 1959].)

Sources: Nigeria, Annual Abstract of Statistics: 1960 (Lagos: Federal Office of Statistics, 1960), p. 12; and Nigeria, Economic and Financial Review, Vol. 2, No. 1, (Lagos: Central Bank, June, 1964), p. 29.

The Stock Exchange

On August 25, 1961, after several months of informal operation, the Lagos Stock Exchange--tropical Africa's second (after Nairobi)--was officially opened. Having agreed that it is fashionable today to have a stock exchange, one should add that it enables a portion of the public, lawyers, for example, to invest in the private sector of the economy. Moreover, this institution provides a medium for the purchase and sale of Nigerian Government securities.

The exchange was originally operated by the then major buyer and seller, the Investment Company of Nigeria (ICON). Subsequent to the transformation of ICON into the Nigerian Industrial Development Bank during January, 1964, John Holt (Nigeria) Ltd. took over this function. It deals in three categories of securities: stocks of the government and registered companies; stocks of overseas companies that conduct operations in Nigeria; and other overseas securities.[12]

The market in equity shares, as would be expected, is narrow. Government publicity, promotion by the banks, and listings in the local papers, have all been requested by the Federal Minister of Finance. With these measures in effect, turnover is picking up.[13]

Other Money Market Institutions
and Financial Intermediaries

In 1960, an acceptance house, Philip Hill (Nigeria) Ltd., commenced business as a merchant banker. It engages in bill finance thereby facilitating the financing of trade, especially exports. In 1961 Philip Hill undertook a 180-day bill-financing in London for the Northern Region Marketing Board, thus releasing working capital for other purposes. This arrangement was the precursor of the scheme whereby produce handled by the Northern and Western Region Marketing Boards is financed by commercial bills of exchange drawn on the Nigerian Produce Marketing Company Ltd., the company that acts as exporter for all the marketing boards. These bills, in turn, are discounted by the boards with participating commercial banks and the acceptance houses (and can be rediscounted at the central bank).

In May, 1962, Nigerian Acceptances Ltd., now 20 per cent owned by Bankers Trust, was set up by John Holt as the second merchant bank in Nigeria. Last of all, in 1964, Philip Hill's English parent sold 30 per cent shares to both Credit Lyonnaise and Banca Commerciale Italiana.

Most of the trading firms and large construction companies have provident and pension funds. The federal government is exerting great pressure on them to reinvest a portion of their holdings, now tied up in U.K. Government securities, in Nigerian development stocks. This will be further treated in the discussion below of the balance of payments.

The National Provident Fund, which began its operation in October, 1961, invests all its contributions in Nigerian Government securities. As of January 1, 1964, 390,646 workers, with cumulative contributions of £4.5 million, were covered.

Until after the last war, the British Royal Exchange Assurance Group was Nigeria's only insurance company. Today it still is primarily engaged in marine, fire, and automobile insurance with life and endowment policies of minor importance.[14] As with the pension funds, the insurance companies until recently have had most of their reserves invested in London.[15] So, though not yet important in the capital market, they provide local facilities which seem able to meet the insurance requirements of manufacturers in Nigeria.

Lastly, it will be recalled (see Chapter 5) that finance companies further the sale of consumer durables, especially automobiles.

The Budgets

The total budgeted revenue of the five governments, from all sources, is estimated to be £245.8 million in 1964-65. Table 27 breaks down this figure by government, and type of budget, i.e., recurrent or capital. The recurrent revenues, taking approximately 62 per cent of the total, are for the most part, at least before distribution to the regions, federally derived.[16] Of the £131.9 million total recurrent revenue received by the federal government, prior to any distribution, almost £95 million (72 per cent) is from the customs-and-excise category. Not only does international trade provide Nigeria with the wherewithal to purchase capital equipment for development, it also provides a major share of the funds to run the day-by-day activities of government. With a low level of average income, much of which is imputed, without the necessary

Table 27

Summary of Nigerian Budget Revenue Estimates, 1964-65 (£ million)

	Total Recurrent Revenue	Of Which From Fed. Gov't.	Capital Devel. Fund Receipts*	Total Revenue
NR	26.200	17.716	9.745	35.945
ER	23.514	14.453	9.415	32.929
WR	18.855	12.820	13.869	32.724
MWR	5.812	2.585	3.375	9.187
Fed	79.389**	--	55.665	135.054
Totals	153.770	47.571	92.069	245.839

* Excludes contributions from recurrent revenue and balance in consolidated revenue fund, but includes total 1964-65 recurrent surplus and internal borrowing.

**Excludes appropriations to the regions of £52.5 million (which is £5 million in excess of the estimates of the four regions).

Sources: Nigeria, Estimates of the Government of the Federal Republic of Nigeria: 1964-65 (Lagos: Ministry of Information Printing Division, 1964), pp. 13, 14, 329; Western Nigeria, Estimates: 1964-65 (Ibadan: Government Printer, 1964), pp. 13, 151; Northern Nigeria, Estimates of the Government of Northern Nigeria: 1964-65 (Kaduna: Government Printer, 1964), pp. 16, 162; Eastern Nigeria, Approved Estimates of Eastern Nigeria: 1964-65 (Enugu: Government Printer, O.D. 13/1964), pp. 16, 173; and Mid-Western Nigeria, Estimates: 1964-65 (Benin City: Ministry of Internal Affairs Printing Division, 1964), pp. 9, 10, 119.

technology and staff to manage a system of reporting and recording of incomes, and with few or no accountancy-trained businessmen, direct taxation has, of necessity, only a limited role in the scheme of things. The federal government expects to receive £6.1 million from the companies income tax and £2.1 million from the individual income tax. The £8.2 million expected from direct taxation represents 10.3 per cent of total federal recurrent revenue (after appropriations to the regions). The East expects to realize £4.3 million from such a (personal) tax, which is 18.3 per cent of its total recurrent revenue; the West hopes to receive £1.9 million (9.8 per cent); and the North £1.6 million (5.9 per cent), in 1964-65.

Table 28 lists some of the uses of the capital receipts. Only a bit more than 5 per cent has been allocated, in 1964-65, for investments in industrial ventures. The regional governments, however, primarily through their development corporations, have taken a more active participation than this budgetary figure would first indicate (see below). Also other governmental expenditures, for instance the development of industrial estates, are not included in the table. What is to be emphasized is the almost negligible use of the budgets to finance the establishment of industrial enterprises.

The recurrent budgets include the expenditure on the operations of the ministries of commerce/trade and industry. In the West, this includes the Industrial Promotions Commission, and a staff of 49, including watchmen and messengers, in the industries division; in the East, 9 men in the industrial laboratory division, and a 15-man industrial promotions and industries division; in the North, a 5-man industrial promotions section; and, at the federal level, a staff of 77 in the industrial division, 16 at the federal boatyard at Opobo, and 102 at the Federal Institute of Industrial Research. But commerce, not industry, still claims the greater part of money and effort in each of these ministries.

Table 28

Summary of Selected Nigerian Budget Capital Expenditure Estimates, 1964-65 (£ million)

	Buildings	Public Works*	Loans	Direct Industrial Investment	Total**
NR	2.905	2.439	1.625	.400	10.75[illegible]
ER	2.515	5.329	.375	1.303	11.88[illegible]
WR	4.797	6.735	.780	--	12.954
MWR	.200	1.000	1.000	--	3.335
Fed	13.104	21.378	6.139***	3.820	62.948
Totals	23.521	36.881	9.919	5.523	101.87[illegible]

* Consists of roads, bridges, runways, Niger Dam, and water supplies.

** Excludes probable underexpenditure and reserve provision.

***Includes subscription to African Development Bank.

Sources: Nigeria, Estimates of the Government of the Federal Republic of Nigeria: 1964-65 (Lagos: Ministry of Information Printing Division, 1964), p[illegible] 330-77; Eastern Nigeria, Approved Estimates of Eastern Nigeria: 1964-65 (Enugu: Government Printer, O.D. 13/1964), pp. 174-214; Northern Nigeria, Estimates of the Government of Northern Nigeria: 1964-65 (Kaduna: Government Printer, 1964), pp. 159, 166-88; Western Nigeria, Estimates: 1964-65 (Ibadan: Government Printer, 1964), pp. 152-94; and Mid-Western Nigeria, Estimates: 1964-65 (Benin City: Ministry of Internal Affairs Printing Division, 1964), p. 121.

Chapter 3 stressed the large recurrent expenditures on education. For 1964-65 the North has budgeted 23.8 per cent of recurrent revenue to the Ministry of Education, the East 30.9 per cent (versus 43.6 per cent in 1961-62), and the West 34.8 per cent.[17]

Health and welfare measures are to take in North, East, and West respectively another 17.3 per cent, 13.7 per cent, and 11.6 per cent of the regional recurrent revenues.[18]

Development Loans and Treasury Bills

In 1959, the year it commenced operations, the central bank issued a £2 million development loan (5 to 6 per cent). The proceeds were, in turn, lent to the Northern and Eastern governments. Though the interest rates were low, the issue was oversubscribed by £856,240. Patriotic motivation as well as the pressure on expatriate firms and banks to transfer some of their reserves held abroad to Nigeria probably had much to do with the favorable response. Banks, the post office, insurance companies, pension funds, sinking funds, marketing boards, and private individuals and companies, which were allotted £92,000 of the £2.355 million total, all played a part.

The Second Development Loan, a £10 million offering, was floated in the spring of 1961, but did not obtain the same gratifying results. The banks purchased £1.23 million, marketing boards £3.51 million, pension funds £1.23 million, corporations (public and private) £.20 million, and others £.16 million.[19] By inference, the central bank took up the remaining portion, again at 5-6 per cent. Since then the unsubscribed portion has been steadily distributed via the stock exchange. This points up the value of the developing money market. Institutions are more willing to purchase these obligations if they have a means of disposing of them before maturity. During 1961, £960,000 of the development stocks changed hands, or about a quarter of the stock in issue, via the central bank, and then after its establishment, via the Lagos Stock Exchange.[20]

In February, 1962, the central bank undertook the flotation of the Third Development Loan of £ 7 million at 5-6 per cent. This time the central bank subscribed to 34.8 per cent of the issue. The Fourth

Development Loan of £15 million was floated a year later at 5-5.75 per cent. Initially, the central bank took up 62 per cent of the stock. Fortunately, by year's end, it was able to dispose of some £6.8 million, thus leaving it with 16.7 per cent of the original issue. The largest internal loan of all, the Republic of Nigeria's First Development Loan of £20 million, was issued during January, 1964, and has met with a most disappointing reception to date. At the end of the first quarter, the central bank held more than 75 per cent of the issue. For the time being, the capital market for long-dated stock appears saturated. Moreover, should the central bank continue to underwrite such large percentages of government loans, inflationary pressures will be augmented.[21]

The Treasury Bills Ordinance was promulgated in 1959. The Federal Ministry of Finance was thus able to authorize the bank to issue bills so that the amount outstanding would be 10 per cent of the estimated current revenue of the federal government for that year. In April, 1961, the ordinance was changed to read 20 per cent, and in May, 1962, 40 per cent.

The first issue of 91-day bills took place on April 7, 1960, at a discount of 4.625 per cent (which was largely determined by the U.K. rate). This allowed the local banks, primarily expatriate, and the marketing boards to invest short-term balances locally. This mechanism can greatly help government, since "owing to the seasonal influence of the cocoa harvest, the banks and the Cocoa Marketing Board have liquid resources to spare, while on the other hand the Government is particularly short of funds."[22]

Bills have since been issued monthly, with the amount outstanding increasing gradually during the succeeding years. On April 1, 1964, £30 million in bills were outstanding. The central bank during 1961 took 17.4 per cent of the total amount issued versus 12.3 per cent in the preceding year. The bank then took 32.7 per cent in 1962 and 45.2 per cent in 1963. In addition, it stands by as a rediscount facility for holders who wish to dispose of their bills before maturity.[23]

National savings certificates, i.e., bonds of small denominations (up to £5), and stamps in three-pence and one-shilling denominations, were introduced at the end of 1962. In addition, premium bonds, whose interest is distributed quarterly via a lottery, were instituted. The amount outstanding after one month--December, 1962--was £11,000. The next year's results were also quite disappointing to the authorities. For at the end of November, 1963, the amount outstanding had reached only £59,000. Evidently, public demand for new, small-denomination government issues is far from strong.

Inflation

By raising the cost of living, the government could theoretically induce "forced saving" by the Nigerian people. Indeed, the continuing rise in prices in the main urban centers[24] for most of the past decade twice led the federal government, first in 1960, and then in 1964, to grant pay increases to all government employees. Since government sets the standard in this field, the effects are soon felt throughout the whole labor market.[25] But in a country where a sizable segment of the population is engaged in subsistence farming, where exports are sold in highly competitive markets, which is running a balance-of-payments deficit, and which is inviting foreign investment, it is dubious whether such a policy would be worthwhile. Nevertheless, Nigerians are having a taste of inflation.

Table 29, below, illustrates the nonintegrated character of the Nigerian economy: Lagos and Ibadan are 89 miles apart, yet the group index (10 per cent weight in the consumer price index) of the cost of Lagos accommodation in 1963 stood at 193, 72 points above that of Ibadan.[26] The five indexes all were lower in 1963 than in the preceding year. This may be attributed to the lower prices in 1963 of domestically produced food, which accounts for about half of the weight in the indexes, thus offsetting higher rents, clothing, transport, and other services.

Table 29

Consumer Price Indexes for Five Urban Areas*

Year	L	Ib	En	Kd	PH/Aba
1953	100	100	100	---	---
1955	108	108	105	---	---
1957	119	117	112	100	100
1959	124	112	119	109	107
1960	132	117	119	108	108
1961	139	127	122	115	122
1962	145	137	148	122	121
1963	144	128	144	119	116

*Yearly averages. Weights based on household budgets of a sample of laborers, artisans, and clerical workers whose basic earnings were no greater than £350-£400 when the inquiry was made: Lagos, 1952-53; Ibadan, 1955--adjusted to match Lagos; Enugu, 1954; Kaduna (and Zaria), 1955-56; and Port Harcourt/Aba, 1957.

Sources: Nigeria, Digest of Statistics, Vol. 10, No. 3 (Lagos: Federal Office of Statistics, July, 1961), pp. 75-79; ibid., Vol. 13, No. 1 (January, 1964), pp. 75-79; and Nigeria, Annual Report and Statement of Accounts: 1963 (Lagos: Central Bank, 1964), p. 13.

Another frequent harbinger of inflation is an increase in the money supply. In Nigeria the currency in circulation is now typically 63-65 per cent of the total money supply. The currency under the old West African Currency Board's operation was backed by the board's assets: more than 100 per cent [106-9 per cent] with sterling assets. The Nigerian pound is now backed by minimum external reserves of 40 per cent[27] of the aggregate of currency in circulation and the central bank's other demand liabilities. The replacement of external reserves with Nigerian securities permitted the introduction of a fiduciary element into the management of the currency. Thus, the government has raised funds by selling securities to the central bank. In the third quarter of 1961 the external reserves were 93 per cent of currency plus demand liabilities. By July 15, 1964, they had dropped to 54 per cent.

As shown in Table 30, from December 31, 1961, to December 31, 1963, the money supply[28] increased by more than 10 per cent. Evidently, inflationary pressures are making themselves felt. (This has occurred during a fairly slack period of business activity.) They are, however, partially obscured because, as we have seen, the consumer price indexes are not increasing in step.[29] But, as will be indicated in the section on balance of payments, foreign-exchange reserves have declined at a rapid rate. In effect, the governments' development programs plus the increased public demand due to the results of these programs have led to excessive demand. The price indexes probably would have increased had not imports "mopped-up" this excessive demand. Therefore, the inflationary pressures have been translated to the balance of payments.

Table 30

Nigerian Money Supply--1956-63 (£ '000)

Dec. 31	(a) Demand Deposits	(b) Currency in Circulation*	(c) Cash in Banks	(a)+(b)-(c) Money Supply
1956	35,352	67,130	6,810	95,672
1957	37,326	68,736	7,023	99,039
1958	40,266	67,821	6,653	101,434
1959	40,168	75,816	8,451	107,533
1960	41,117	87,209	7,967	120,359
1961	41,658	86,915	7,617	120,896
1962	45,296	87,327	7,547	125,076
1963	48,773	91,651	7,159	133,265

*Including coins.

Sources: Nigeria, Central Bank, 1st-5th Annual Reports (Lagos: Central Bank, 1960-64), and Economic and Financial Review, Vol. 2, No. 1 (Lagos: Central Bank, June, 1964), p. 24; and Nigeria, Annual Abstract of Statistics: 1963 (Lagos: Federal Office of Statistics, 1963), p. 38.

Marketing Boards and Development Corporations

Marketing Boards

Since 1954-55 each of the regions has had its own marketing board.[30] The laws that established them, in addition to their primary responsibility of purchasing and delivering export produce to the ports, call for the boards to promote "the development and prosperity of the producers and the areas of production."[31] So, by stabilizing producers' prices[32] at a level below the world prices, they accumulated reserves that have been used for economic development purposes. But in times of declining commodity prices, currently achieved reserves necessarily diminish, and indeed sometimes disappear.

The North has not had such a contribution in the 1960's, although in its first seven years of existence, the North's board loaned its government £6.8 million.

"With the exception of a short period from mid-March to mid-July 1959 the [Northern Nigeria] Board showed a continuous loss on its groundnut trading operations from December 1957 to October 1959."[33] In the period of, first, regional autonomy, and then, federal independence, it would not be politic to lower farmer incomes. A similar situation obtains in cotton, and benniseed producers have been subsidized. Thus, though the board made grants to agricultural research and development, e.g., £373,000 to the Samaru station, it has been unwilling to make grants for general (and industrial) development.[34]

The Western Region board has apparently made no direct loans or investments in industry, although loans of £10 million, £1.2 million, and £3 million to the Western Region's Government, Finance Corporation, and Development Corporation, respectively, were outstanding in late 1961.[35] Early in that year, cocoa prices hit an eleven-year low.[36] On August 30, 1961, the government of Western Nigeria was forced to institute a second cut over a short period in producer prices of cocoa: Grade one was lowered in two steps from £160 per ton to £100--a 37.5 per cent decrease.[37] The West has, therefore, often faced the prospect of being limited in its ability to turn to the board for financial help.

The West last received a capital contribution from its board in 1962-63 when £2 million was donated to the regional government. In addition to grants to various Western Region schemes and departments, from September, 1959, to May, 1962, the board made grants of £27.6 million--including the aforementioned £2 million--plus a loan of £10 million to the regional government. Indeed, by the latter date, it had to exist on overdrafts amounting to £2.5 million from the Bank of West Africa Ltd. This was one of the general findings in 1962 of the federal-government-appointed Coker Commission of Inquiry into the affairs of six Western Region statutory corporations.[38] The great proportion of these sums was, in all likelihood, not misused. (The region's development and finance corporations [discussed below] made unwise investments. But the main allegations of the commission--and they were accepted by the federal government--were that advances were made by three banks, including the National Bank [which made use of a £3 million loan from the marketing board], to the Action Group. Moreover, the Nigerian Investment and Properties Company was established "for the main purpose of providing funds for the Action Group.") Hopefully, these corporations are now being operated prudently and in the absence of political dictates.

In the East, the board earned profits of £9.3 million during the period from October, 1954, to December, 1959.[39] Loans have been made to the federal government and the Eastern Nigeria Development Corporation, plus grants to the latter and the University of Nigeria.[40] Yet, during the period grants were being made, producer prices for oil-palm produce were reduced from 15 to 19.5 per cent.

In 1964 the East's board is budgeted for a £2 million contribution to the region's capital development fund. Over the course of the development plan the government anticipates receiving £14 million from its board.

The Regional Development Corporations

Each of the regions has a development corporation which is an agency, like the marketing board, of that government. It is through these corporations that most of the governments' participation in industry is made.

The Northern Nigeria Development Corporation (NNDC) was established in 1956, taking over the assets, liabilities, and undertakings of the Production Development Board and the Development (Loans) Board. On October 1, 1961, it was placed under the authority of the Ministry of Economic Development. Today, the NNDC supports land settlement, agricultural-production development, the improvement of abattoirs, the development of communications and water supply, and industrial development, including investigations and estates, as well as making loans to native authorities and individuals. Among its largest investments/loans in industrial ventures, as of March 31, 1963, were £310,000 in the Nigerian Sugar Company Ltd., £450,000 in Kaduna Textiles Ltd., and £210,000 in another textile mill, Nortex (Nigeria) Ltd., located at Kaduna.[41] Additionally, by late 1961, £802,538 had been loaned to businessmen, many of whom were engaged in village and craft industries: sewing machines, rice mills, decorticators, etc.

Because the NNDC's staff was inadequate to supervise properly these small loans, which went as low as £100, probably 25 per cent of the funds disbursed were not spent on what was applied for. So the NNDC contemplated buying, and then providing, the capital equipment.[42] But, in this instance, no further such loans have since been made. This defect in the loans mechanism unfortunately appears to be universal.

The Western Nigeria Development Corporation (WNDC) replaced the old Production Development Board in 1959, but, unlike the other two regions, it did not incorporate the finance corporation, which maintains its autonomy. For the most part, its operations parallel those of the other two development corporations. As in the East, the corporation owns and operates a number of manufacturing and commercial enterprises. Among these are the Lafia Canning Factory (£579,624 expended), a rubber factory (£256,579), two Pepsi-Cola bottling plants (£470,306), and a rest-house (£133,148).[43] Included in its many industrial investments are £157,500 in an asbestos-cement plant, and £420,000 loan capital and £150,000 share capital in the textile mill at Ikeja.[44]

The corporation has received its funds from the marketing board and from government. In 1961 it did not appear to make investment decisions, acting only as an operational agency under the Ministry of Trade and Industry. The policy was set by government upon the recommendation of the fifteen-member Industrial Promotions Commission, the corporation having only one vote on this body.

The Eastern Nigeria Development Corporation (ENDC), in operation since 1955, is today under the control of the Ministries of Agriculture and Commerce. Likewise, it is divided into two divisions, each under the direction of a general-manager: the industrial and commercial, and the agricultural and plantation. Possibly as a result of this arrangement the dichotomy is not clean-cut; the former is still responsible for small agricultural loans, while the latter is in the industrial processing of agricultural produce, e.g., oil mills.

The corporation, in 1961, owned and operated 96 Pioneer oil mills,[45] a Pepsi-Cola bottling plant (£300,000), and the region's rest-houses; it maintains control of the African Continental Bank, and has since constructed two luxury hotels, a glass factory (£900,000), and a brewery (£950,000).[46] It has also invested in a cement clinker plant (£475,000),[47] and the Nkalagu cement plant.[48]

All three corporations claim that they are maintaining their investments "as a public trust," until such time as their citizens can purchase the equity shares. Actually, the decision to transfer the interests to the public eventually does not appear to have been made, even though the government officials pay lip service to the stated policy.[49]

Other Internal Sources of Funds for Development

In the Western Region there is a housing corporation (WRHC), established in 1958, which is developing, among other duties, the industrial estate at Ikeja. Its main function is to increase the availability of dwellings in the region. Deposits are made in units of at least £20[50] by individuals who hope eventually to build a house. Necessarily, the majority of would-be purchasers are executives and professionals. Consideration is being given to lowering this figure.

The West's finance corporation (WRFC) was created in 1955--and placed under the Ministry of Trade and Industry--to make loans, usually small ones, for agricultural and industrial applications. It made investments and loans totaling £5 million from 1955 to 1962.[51] In early 1964 it suspended operations because of organizational and policy problems as well as a lack of funds.

In making a loan during 1961 for industrial purposes, the corporation first decided whether the market would permit a new entrant. This policy seemed to be the result of the increasing number of defaults the corporation was encountering.[52] It was buttressed by a general feeling among the corporation's personnel that the dimensions of the economic pie are fixed. The 33 industrial loans granted during 1961-62 amounted to £68,670, mainly in amounts around £1,000. During the latter half of 1964, a newly created Agriculture Credit Corporation took over the supply of loans to this sector of the West from the WRFC.

The NNDC is set up to carry on a similar program in the North. When it will actually resume this activity is a moot point. In the East, the ENDC's engagement in small loans has been ended, for in April, 1963, the Fund for Agricultural and Industrial Development (FAID) was established and capitalized with

£200,000. Small-scale industry is scheduled to receive 40 per cent of some £1.5 million in loans over the plan period. As of June, 1964, FAID had made only two industrial loans--woodworking and shoemaking--totaling £4,000. In this case, stringent credit supervision may be the cause. For instance, strict rules regarding collateral deter many potential borrowers.

The Eastern Nigeria Housing Corporation, which is currently erecting relatively low-cost houses at Port Harcourt's Trans-Amadi Industrial Layout on a pilot basis, operates a savings-and-loans division. The government hopes to encourage the continued construction of low-cost housing, an endeavor that is to be financed by the peoples' savings.

At the federal level, in 1956 the Federal Loans Board was set up[53] to promote industrial development in Lagos and elsewhere. (It will not make loans in excess of £50,000, nor less than £10,000, for a regional project.) From its incorporation to June 30, 1962, the board approved forty-one loans totaling £344,776.[54] "Inadequate security" has often been given as the reason for an application's rejection. Again, this seems to be, at least in part, a result of an inability to appraise and supervise the loans. Many of the pounds have gone into homes and cars. A larger and more capable staff is required to make sure the loan goes to the right use.

The Post Office Savings Bank has been in operation since the early 1930's. By March 31, 1962, it had 295,517 accounts totaling £3,230,182. Two years later the latter figure had declined to £2,992,000, the lowest balance in fifteen years. Most of the investments originally were made overseas, but have since been brought home. None are in industry.[55]

The Nigerians' love of speculation has often competed with their desire to save. Formerly, they indulged their fondness for speculation by "playing" the football pools, all owned by overseas interests. But, since September 1, 1961, with the exception of the Nigerian National Pools Limited (Nigerpools), no

Nigerian has legally been able to take part in any foreign-owned football pool.[56] The federal government purchased a 51 per cent interest in Nigerpools so that Nigeria might retain much of the £3-£4 million that was leaving the country each year via this route. In a like vein, the Western Region Government in April, 1964, introduced a Casino (Licensing and Taxation) Bill so as to attract tourists. The government is to receive 12.5 per cent of the gross income of the proposed casinos. "From the monetary point of view [gambling is] . . . probably the only way to skim off purchasing power from the lowest income groups."[57]

EXTERNAL FINANCING

Financial aid from abroad is as old as Nigeria's railroad, the first of her great public works. Professor Frankel calculated that £75 million (both equity and loan) was invested in Nigeria from abroad during the period 1870-1936.[58] About £40 million of the total was private capital, the majority of which was investment by trading companies, who were followed by the tin-mining concerns.[59]

In March, 1962, Nigeria estimated the capital cost of the public sector of her 1962-68 six-year development plan at $1.895 billion.[60] During the preceding seven years, consumption and investment had exceeded GDP. And for the next six years Nigeria could hardly be able to discontinue her reliance on external financing if she were (and is) to fulfill the objectives of the plan. In fact, the United States promised £80 million; yet "it probably falls short of the amount Nigeria's planners were counting on."[61]

Private Investment

Official statistics that fully reveal the extent of overseas private investment in Nigerian manufacturing industry are not available. However, befitting a former British colony, most of the foreign investment is assignable to British companies.[62]

In his report to the shareholders in 1961, the chairman of Unilever Ltd. stated that Nigeria "is the country in which we have our greatest investment in Africa--£48.5 million."[63] This figure is the largest overseas company investment in Nigeria. The absolute amount allocated to manufacturing by UAC, Unilever's principal subsidiary in Africa, increased with the approach of independence. During 1959 and 1961 UAC placed more than 43 per cent and 47 per cent, respectively, of the year's capital expenditures in Nigeria in this category.[64]

The United States contributed negligibly to the acceleration in industrial development, supported by overseas investors and/or technical partners, which occurred with the approach of independence. At the end of 1960, the value of American direct investment in _all_ of West African manufacturing, excluding smelting, was approximately $1 million.[65]

Table 31 contains total figures for net overseas capital investment through 1961. According to the central bank, this figure declined to £10.4 million in 1962 and probably was even less in 1963. Interestingly, the bank attributes £5 million of the 1961 sum to manufacturing and processing, and £12 million--£1.6 million more than the total--to this activity in 1962. The paradox is explained by the redeployment of the financial assets of the major trading companies to other sectors, including manufacturing.[66]

Indicative of the commercial, noncompany, sources of industrial capital--though small-scale--available to Nigeria, are the private investment corporations.

Transoceanic-AOFC Ltd.,[67] an American source of private-venture capital, invested £25,000 in ICON. Now merged with the International Basic Economy Corporation (IBEC), it is proceeding, in cooperation with private Nigerian partners, with setting up the Nigerian Concrete Company in the Western Region.

Table 31

Net Overseas Capital Investment in Nigeria as a Percentage of GCF

	GCF £ mn	Net Overseas Capital Investment £ mn	Of which: UAC Capital Investment* £ mn	Overseas Capital Investment as % of GCF
1952	75.0	7.6	n.a.	10.1
1953	79.9	5.5	n.a.	6.9
1954	92.9	10.4	n.a.	11.2
1955	102.6	9.6	n.a.	9.4
1956	108.0	19.1	2.6 (.552)	17.7
1957	113.0	19.2	2.7 (.508)	17.0
1958	122.3	22.8	2.1 (.563)	18.6
1959	136.7	24.8	2.8 (1.224)	18.2
1960	158.0	28.0	2.3 (.736)	17.7
1961	162.9**	23.0	2.7 (1.267)	14.1

* Includes other Unilever associated companies. Figures in parentheses represent capital expenditures on industrial ventures.

**Provisional.

Sources: A. Rivkin et al., Report of the Special U.S. Economic Mission to Nigeria, U.S. Department of State (Washington, D.C.: Department of State, 1961), p. 61; E. F. Jackson and P. N. C. Okigbo, National Income of Nigeria for the Period 1950-57 (Lagos: Federal Ministry of Economic Development, 1960) (Mimeo.); W. Stolper et al., Government Expenditures on Goods and Services (Lagos: Federal Ministry of Economic Development, 1961) (Mimeo.); UAC, Statistical and Economic Review, Nos. 25 and 28 (London: UAC, 1961), p. 61, and p. 53; Nigeria, Economic and Financial Review, Vol. 2, No. 1 (Lagos: Central Bank, June, 1964), p. 13; and Nigeria, Digest of Statistics, Vol. 13, No. 1 (Lagos: Federal Office of Statistics, January, 1964), p. 85.

The Chase International Investment Corporation, a wholly-owned subsidiary of the Chase Manhattan Bank, was incorporated in 1930.[68] It expects its own investment to be at least $1 million in industrial projects. In addition to a $750,000 loan to the Embel Tin Smelting Company in Jos, it has had a major role in the financing of two large projects now in production: the Apapa flour mill and the Ikeja textile plant; and it has completed the financial planning of the Westinghouse-Koppers proposal for a steel mill.

Through John Holt Investment Company Ltd., the trading company of that name has invested in a number of industrial enterprises.[69] The Chemical Overseas Finance Company (a subsidiary of the Chemical Bank New York Trust Company), with a £25,000 investment in ICON, the Overseas Development Corporation of Barclays D.C.O., and the Nigerian Tobacco Company's Marina Investment Ltd. have also entered the field. The Bankers International Financing Company (a subsidiary of the Bankers Trust Company) anticipates doing the same.

Foreign Investments, Loans, and Capital Grants by Government and International Organizations

The United States

On December 12, 1961, the U.S. Department of State announced that a $225 million aid commitment had been made to Nigeria.[70] Prior to that, the Development Loan Fund (DLF) had made two loans: $3 million for track relaying in the North and $663,000 for a warehouse on the Apapa quay.

As of mid-1964, the Agency for International Development (AID), successor to the International Cooperation Administration (ICA) and DLF, had authorized six loans--for infrastructure and education projects--totaling $43.5 million. And a host of other applications were under review.

World Bank and its Affiliates

ICON, which has already been cited as the founder of the Lagos Stock Exchange, was set up in 1959 with a paid-up capital of £1 million. By the fall of 1961, three-quarters of these funds were committed to the stock exchange and twelve other ventures--ten of which were, or would be, engaged in manufacturing.

It was on this base that the International Finance Corporation (IFC) created the Nigerian Industrial Development Bank (NIDB) in January, 1964. The NIDB is designed to provide medium- and long-term financing for the industrial and mining sectors of Nigeria. It will also engage in underwriting operations in its effort to expand private participation in Nigerian industry.

NIDB has an authorized capital of £5 million, of which an initial £2 million has been paid in on ordinary shares and £250,000 on nonvoting preference shares. Fifty-one per cent of the ordinary shares have been designated as Class A shares and are reserved to Nigerian subscribers and the IFC. The central bank and the IFC have each acquired approximately £500,000. The federal government has, in addition, presented a £2 million interest-free loan to the new development bank. American shareholders include Chase International Investment Corporation, Bank of America, Irving International Financing Corporation, Bankers Trust, IBEC, Northwest International Bank, and Chemical Overseas Finance Corporation. In its first half-year of operation, the NIDB made loans totaling £300,000 to three companies, two of which are Nigerian. All told, NIDB itself may borrow up to three times its issued share capital, reserves, and subordinated borrowings.[71]

The World Bank (IBRD) made a $28 million loan toward the Bornu railway extension in 1958. This was drawn down in 1961, thus not counting as a portion of its contribution to the development plan. Since then, the IBRD loaned $13.5 million, in 1962, to the NPA for the Apapa quay extension, and, in 1964, $82 million to the Niger Dams Authority for the Kainji Dam and $30 million to the ECN for transmission lines and distribution facilities.

The World Bank's other affiliate, the International Development Association, has announced its interest in Nigeria's education needs. Financial assistance from this source should be forthcoming.

The United Kingdom

The Colonial Development Corporation (CDC) was established in 1948 by the U.K. Parliament with a statutory obligation to pay its own way. Its purpose was to help further economic development in the British colonies. Before October 1, 1960, the CDC had approved capital expenditures in twelve projects, including the Nigerian Cement Company, ICON, Ikeja industrial development, Northern Developments (Nigeria) Ltd. (NDNL), and the East's Industrial and Agricultural Company Ltd. (INDAG).

By the terms of its original legislation, CDC could not make further capital disbursements in Nigeria after the colony's independence. For a while it appeared that it would continue to operate in Nigeria only by using uncommitted funds, turning over old investments, and receiving grants from the Northern and Eastern Regions (in which it operated the two subsidiary development corporations).[72] Fortunately for Nigeria, the Commonwealth Development Act of 1963 restored its full powers of operation in the former colonies (and changed the CDC's name to Commonwealth Development Corporation).

INDAG, founded in 1959, and one-third-owned by the Eastern Nigeria Government, has invested in an aluminum-rolling mill and an asbestos-cement plant, and has loaned £30,000 to a Nigerian who is producing powdered clay, a substitute for Bentonite, for Shell-BP's oil drilling.[73]

NDNL was set up in November, 1959, with £1.25 million capital. By late 1961 it had invested £50,000 in a bottling plant, and a small amount in a tannery.[74] As with INDAG, it is a commercial operation. Consequently its limited funds so far have been allocated to industry slowly. This is particularly true in the North where management capacity and partnership money are not readily available.

During the spring of 1964 NDNL was reorganized as Northern Nigeria Investments Ltd. (NNIL). The total reserves of this company are now £4.6 million, shared equally by CDC and the NNDC. The latter is making up the majority of its share of the equity by transferring to NNIL investments in thirteen projects valued at £2 million.

The Commonwealth Development Finance Company (CDFC), which helps finance development undertaken by Commonwealth private enterprise, is 45 per cent controlled by the Bank of England and other Commonwealth central banks. CDFC was the main sponsor of ICON and organized the bulk of its capital subscription. It also loaned £1 million in 1960 for fifteen years to the Dunlop rubber plantation, and £400,000 to a cotton yarn-spinning mill in Kaduna on November 5, 1963, as well as making a number of other industrial investments (see Appendix).

Nigeria can no longer take advantage of the Colonial Development and Welfare grants which in the first fifteen postwar years amounted to nearly £25 million with education and infrastructure the chief beneficiaries.[75]

In honor of independence, the U.K. made a £5 million grant for the capital costs of higher education projects in early 1961. Since then, Britain has made a Commonwealth Assistance Loan of £10 million. This is in addition to a similar loan of $33.6 million made in 1960. Finally, through its Aid for Surplus Capacity Scheme, a 1963 loan of £1.5 million was made for rails.

United Nations

The U.N. Special Fund agreed in late 1960 to contribute $686,000 for the Niger Dam feasibility study. This was in addition to £350,000 for a federal teacher-training college, £188,000 for a Western Region fisheries survey, £517,000 for a Sokoto River Valley soil-and-water-resources survey, and £168,000 for vocational training.[76] By early 1964, projects worth $12 million were in hand, and many others were under active consideration. Of special interest is the Special Fund's assistance to the University of Lagos Engineering Faculty.

Others

West Germany agreed in September, 1961, to loan Nigeria $25 million for a new Lagos-mainland bridge, a training hospital in the North, and a technical school. Israel made an $8.4 million loan at the time of Nigeria's independence, all of which is being expended in the south at the Northern government's request. Italy is loaning $25.2 million toward the construction of the Niger Dam, and the Netherlands will probably finance some $3 million of commodities (not necessarily tied to Dutch goods).

Nigeria's first trade agreement with the Communist Bloc was initialed on September 23, 1961. It was agreed that Poland would construct a cement factory.[77] Three years later it appears doubtful that the project will go ahead. So far, no Bloc capital has been provided Nigeria.

Technical Assistance

This category differs from the preceding one in that services, not money, are supplied by the donor. For the most part they are aimed at developing Nigeria's human resources. Being of a nonrepayable nature, technical assistance releases Nigerian financial resources for other uses, and so falls within the subject of external financing.

United Nations Agencies

FAO, ILO, UNESCO, UNICEF, WHO, etc., have all been active in Nigeria. The majority of the funds expended under the supervision of the U.N. Technical Assistance Board, however, are channeled via the Expanded Program for Technical Assistance (EPTA) which, in turn, operates through the regular U.N. agencies. EPTA's combined budget for 1963 and 1964 is $1.9 million for technicians' services, such as statisticians working for the Federal Office of Statistics. For these same two years, the regular programs of these agencies totals $1.3 million.

The Economic Commission for Africa (ECA), whose secretariat is situated in Addis Ababa, has been functioning for four years. Eventually it may enter the field of regional economic planning on as important a scale as has ECLA in Latin America.

Commission for Technical Co-operation in Africa South of the Sahara

The CCTA, in recent years, with a Secrétariat Général in Lagos, has provided experts and instructors, trained personnel, and supplied equipment for training purposes through its Foundation for Mutual Assistance in Africa South of the Sahara (FAMA).[78] Also, its Inter-African Labour Institute was established to review and exchange information on all aspects of labor problems in tropical Africa.

Agency for International Development and the Peace Corps

The U.S. Peace Corps began sending volunteers to Nigeria during the second half of 1961. By the first quarter of 1962 it had placed 100 of them in the southern regions. Today the first batch has been replaced and the total number of Peace Corps volunteers is fast approaching the 500 mark. They are located throughout the Federation, and are mostly filling secondary teaching positions. A number of them are working as laboratory assistants and instructors at the university level.

Prior to the commencement of the plan period on April 1, 1962, ICA had obligated (and authorized) $22 million in technical assistance and grant aid. Since that date, and in addition to the loans cited above, AID had obligated another $46.5 million by June 30, 1964. These funds have been expended primarily in the fields of agriculture and education.[79]

Supplementing these activities, an industrial development center has been set up at Owerri in the East and is now programed for Zaria in the North. Advisory services are to be provided the managers of small industries--usually those with about ten employees--covering supervisory methods, production techniques, market and product development, financial control, and purchasing and inventory control. At Owerri there are demonstration shops in woodworking, leatherworking, and a number of others in the cottage-handicraft sector. Also, in late 1961 AID contracted with Arthur D. Little, Inc. (ADL)[80] for a series of studies to identify and evaluate specific opportunities for private investment in Nigerian industry. The scope of ADL's services has since been expanded to include an overseas promotional program, and advisory positions in the ministries of commerce/trade, and industry.

Others

In July, 1961, the Carnegie Corporation of New York donated £82,000 to the federal government so that it might more effectively coordinate overseas aid to Nigerian education.

The African-American Institute, with headquarters in New York, maintains a field office in Lagos. It is principally concerned with teacher placement in Africa and with awarding scholarships to Nigerian students for study in the United States.

The Ford Foundation commenced operations in Nigeria during 1958. Since then it has made grants of $6.2 million to Nigeria (forty grants to Nigerian institutions--twenty-three to the federal government, including seventeen to the University of Ibadan--and one to the West African Examinations Council), plus twenty-one foundation-administered grants at a cost of approximately $2.5 million.[81]

The West African Program (Ghana and Nigeria) of the Rockefeller Brothers Fund (RBF) was inaugurated in 1959 and specifically concerned itself with increasing the national output through the establishment of productive enterprises, chiefly manufacturing industry. By paying for feasibility studies on specific enterprises it hoped to create partnerships between Nigerian entrepreneurs and Free World private enterprise. RBF also acted the part of a catalyst by utilizing its unique position to disseminate information on the Nigerian economic scene to all comers, from Nigerian labor leaders to IBRD missions.[82] With the pre-emption of this field by ADL, RBF closed down its operation in 1963.

Through the Special Commonwealth Aid to Africa Programme (SCAAP), Britain spent $184,000 in equipment and experts in 1963. This is only one of various means by which the U.K. is channeling technical-assistance funds to Nigeria at a rate that may be approaching £1 million a year. Canada, too, uses SCAAP for its technical-assistance program, which for the past several years has been averaging about $1.6 million a year. Topographical mapping is the largest Canadian endeavor.

Many other nations, from Japan to Switzerland, are doing their part too. One universal means of assistance appears to be the offering of scholarships (and subsistence) to Nigerian students, usually post-secondary, in the donor country. And, of course, many voluntary agencies are engaged in worthwhile activities in all parts of the Federation.

The Balance of Payments

Since 1955, consumption and investment have exceeded Nigeria's gross domestic production, and the value of imports has exceeded exports (see Tables 32 and 33). Necessarily, Nigeria's foreign-exchange reserves have been continually drawn down, and a deficit in her over-all balance of payments has appeared.

Even if the figures are not completely accurate,[83] they do point up a disquieting trend. This is especially so when the inability of Nigeria to supply her own consumption and investment needs is presented against a background of incipient inflation.[84]

Table 31 listed the net overseas capital investment in Nigeria. It will be noted that, in 1960, the investment in Nigeria from abroad of £28 million filled only 39 per cent of the gap between GDP and total consumption plus investment. Most of the remainder was supplied by drawing down Nigeria's foreign-exchange assets (see Table 34).

Table 32

Consumption and Investment versus GDP*
(£ million)

	GDP	Expenditures by Consumers	Expenditures by Gov't.	Investment	Balance
1951	755.2	650.2	26.8	59.7	18.5
1953	829.5	717.3	29.7	79.9	2.6
1955	918.9	805.5	42.6	102.6	- 31.8
1957	938.4	815.5	47.3	113.0	- 37.4
1959	987.7	830.0	70.0	136.7	- 49.0
1960	1,023.0	870.0	77.0	158.0	- 72.0

*At 1957 market prices.

Sources: Stolper, et al., Government Expenditures on Goods and Services (Lagos: Federal Ministry of Economic Development, 1961) (Mimeo.), and E. F. Jackson and P. N. C. Okigbo, National Income of Nigeria for the Period 1950-57 (Lagos: Federal Ministry of Economic Development, 1960) (Mimeo.).

The two largest Nigerian sources of capital for industry, the marketing boards and the development corporations, in a period of less than seven years, reduced their overseas reserves from £87 million to £0.9 million. After accounting for the transference of funds from British to Nigerian securities, and after examining the state of the international commodity markets, it is patently evident that infusion of further large amounts of capital into the Nigerian economy by these two bodies cannot again be anticipated during the foreseeable future.

Table 33

Value of Nigeria's External Trade and Visible Balance (£ million)

	Imports	Exports*	Balance
1951	84.6	120.0	35.4
1953	108.3	124.1	15.8
1955	136.1	132.5	- 3.6
1957	152.5	127.6	- 24.9
1959	178.2	163.5	- 14.7
1960	215.9	169.7	- 46.2
1961	222.4	173.4	- 49.0
1962	203.0	168.6	- 34.4
1963	207.5	189.6	- 17.9

*Includes re-exports and parcel post. Figures are rounded.

Sources: Nigeria, Annual Abstract of Statistics: 1960 (Lagos: Federal Office of Statistics, 1960), p. 18; Nigeria, Digest of Statistics, Vol. 10, No. 3 (Lagos: Federal Office of Statistics, July, 1961), p. 19; Nigeria, Nigeria Trade Journal (Lagos: Federal Office of Information, June, 1962), p. 77; and Nigeria, Review of External Trade: 1963 (Lagos: Federal Office of Statistics, 1964), p. 2.

Of the £86.8 million official and banking reserves that Nigeria held overseas on March 31, 1964, about £32.4 million must be maintained under present law as backing for the currency in circulation and the demand liabilities of the central bank.[85] Furthermore, Nigeria will need to maintain reserves to finance near-term imports if she is not to find herself more dependent on current export earnings than is desirable. Nigeria's imports seem to be running at an annual rate of more than £200 million (see Table 33). If reserves are kept for four months' imports, then another £67 million will be needed. (This exposition ignores the fact that, in effect, some sterilization of reserves is taking place.) Thus, of total reserves, we have accounted for £99.4 million, or 114 per cent.[86]

Nigerian Official and Banking System Overseas
Financial Assets (£ million)

	3/31/55	12/31/57	12/31/59	12/31/61	3/31/64
Federal Government	47.3	56.0	29.6	27.1	9.5
Regional Governments	23.2	33.8	31.6	19.5	7.0
Local Governments	3.1	3.5	3.5	3.9	--
Regional Development Corporations	13.0	8.0	5.3	1.3	*
Marketing Boards	74.0	40.3	35.2	- 0.4	4.3
Other Semi-Official*	19.5	11.3	11.2	9.4	7.0
West African Currency Board**	54.0	77.0	27.4	6.8	--
Central Bank	--	--	57.5	75.7	57.9
Post Office Savings Bank	4.7	4.4	3.0	1.6	--
Commercial Banks	24.3	8.8	12.2	6.1	1.1
Totals	263.1	243.1	216.5	151.0	86.8

* Includes statutory corporations, universities, and institutes, as well as development corporations in 1964.

**Since July 1, 1959, represents estimated West African Currency Board currency circulating in Nigeria.

Sources: Nigeria, Digest of Statistics, Vol. 10, No. 3, and Vol. 13, No. 1 (Lagos: Federal Office of Statistics, July, 1961, and January, 1964), p. 16; p. 16; and Nigeria, *Economic and Financial Review* (Lagos: Central Bank, June, 1964), p. 40.

Nigeria has available another $55 million (£19.6 million), which is the International Monetary Fund's (IMF) total tranche position for her as of June, 1964. For an agreed period, and under specified conditions, this sum may be provided as a "drawing" on the IMF. This would increase Nigeria's foreign-exchange reserves to £106.4 million. Further, should reserves be kept for only three months' imports, and reduced to 25 per cent backing for the currency and demand liabilities of the central bank, then Nigeria would have a cushion of about £36 million.

All of the foregoing is of especial importance to all foreign private enterprise that is considering establishing manufacturing facilities in Nigeria. For some time, Nigeria has had to conserve foreign exchange. This explains why Nigerians are prohibited from taking part in foreign football pools, and why, in part, treasury bills and development loans have been instituted.

But Nigeria's foreign-exchange reserves are evidently reaching a critical level. IMF drawings and lowering the amount of reserves needed to back the currency and near-term imports are stop-gap measures. Nigeria raised her tariffs in August, 1964, for the second time in three years. Her deteriorating balance-of-payments position was the prime mover for this step. Some countries have gone further and have introduced stringent exchange controls. These can lead to a misallocation of resources and constitute a heavy burden on the government's administrative capacity. And too often these have led to bribery and corruption as importers bid for the necessary, scarce authorizations for foreign exchange.

With such restrictions placed on imports, the "mopping up" of excessive demand will diminish, and prices, especially of consumer goods, will rise. The next step often is capital flight as investors seek to avoid losses incurred when an exchange devaluation takes place. Thus, all the efforts of government to create a salubrious investment climate, discussed below, can be more than offset.

Steps may be taken to increase taxes, to mobilize savings, and to cut administrative expenses more effectively. Should these fail to rectify the situation, any of three occurrences will necessarily take place: Reserves will continue to fall, or inflation will take place, or the development plan will be retarded. If Nigeria is to live within her means--including overseas private investment and aid--the third course is the preferable one. To be sure, government is becoming aware of this.

Of course, the key to the problem is increased exports. Nonetheless, time is a factor. In the meanwhile, the manufacturer will have to keep a weather eye on the over-all economic scene since Nigeria has entered a period of difficulty. For some time, government will be entering into economic decision-making more often than heretofore.

Part and parcel of the search for funds for development is the drive to require investment of specified assets in Nigeria rather than overseas.

> In the proposed Income Tax legislation [since enacted] . . . provision has been made that, if such [pension] funds are to enjoy favoured treatment under the Income Tax laws, as they do at present, it will be the requirement in the case of existing funds which have been approved by the Federal Board of Internal Revenue that their investment income shall only continue to be exempt if by the 1st of April, 1963, one-third of the income is derived from Nigerian securities. The legislation will also provide that no new pension or provident funds shall be approved for income tax exemption unless a minimum of one-half of their investment income is derived from Nigerian securities. . . . I do not regard these [percentages] as maximum limits.[87]

These steps suggest that Nigeria will encourage industry that either earns foreign exchange, or, by substituting for imports, saves foreign exchange. An accurate figure for these "savings" in the latter instance, however, is next to impossible to determine. Indeed, the savings may be a mirage. To calculate the savings it would be necessary to know the cost of the imported capital equipment for the domestic plants, the decrease in foreign-exchange earnings brought about by the diversion of the raw material to the domestic market, e.g., cotton to indigenous textile mills, the added imports produced by the wage-earners of these factories, and so forth. In any case, government seems to be encouraging production of items that loom large on the country's import list rather than those manufactures that can compete in the world market.

Because Nigeria's reserves are widely held, even within the official category, and because the central bank was unaware of what is really happening with respect to private capital flows,[88] the Exchange Control Act was put into effect in July, 1962. So far it has been used primarily to channel funds from abroad through the banking system.[89] At the present time, in mid-1964, no substantive limitation on the repatriation of capital, profits, and interest has been publicly anticipated.[90] The new exchange control law did set up the apparatus whereby such limitations can be instituted.

In the matter of balance-of-payments difficulties as in others, prudent decisions are not always made. During October, 1961, Nigeria converted £7 million of her sterling balances into gold and £3.5 million into U.S. dollars. But, gold earns no interest, and the yields in London were much higher than in New York. Therefore, the exchange meant a loss of "close on £500,000 in foreign exchange earnings."[91]

Government and the Foreign Investor

All Nigerian governments have set themselves the task of furthering Nigerian industrial growth. To attract foreign private investment of £200 million[92] over the six-year-plan period, Nigeria is relying on four major fiscal incentives. These fall within the domain of the federal government. The all-important investment climate, however, cannot be allocated among the governments; all are jointly accountable.

Import Duties

Until 1962, "the Nigerian customs tariff [was] constructed on the principle that basic raw materials attract no duty, semifinished products 10 per cent, and finished products 20 per cent."[93] At that time, and again in August, 1964, the tariff schedule was revised. Today, to protect industries and to bolster her balance-of-payments position, Nigeria has raised tariffs to as high as 66.7 per cent for many items. Indeed, the standard rate of 20 per cent is now 33.3 per cent. So far, no preferential duties exist, the rates applying equally to all countries. Nigeria uses these duties on imports in two ways as inducements to the expatriate or indigenous industrial investor: first, as a protective tariff, and second, as a means of granting relief from duties on the import of industrial materials.

The existence of an import duty can, in itself, act as an inducement for industry. Among the advantages UAC foresaw for its Apapa Bedford truck assembly plant was the lower amount of import duty payable on the unassembled vehicles.[94] Since both the vehicle parts and the assembled vehicles are assessed on an *ad valorem* basis, the former, with a lower ex-factory cost in the U.K. bear a lower import duty in Nigeria. But the duty, to function as an inducement, must, under most circumstances, provide special treatment.

A protective tariff, if it were really effective, would result in a partial lowering of Nigeria's main source of revenue. Also, the government seems to realize that once protection is given, it is next to impossible to remove it. For these reasons, and because the civil servants cannot determine which "infants" will grow up, government has been chary in applying this blunt instrument, although, in the years since independence, import duties have increased on many goods manufactured in Nigeria.[95]

The tariff inducement that the government promotes more actively is that of import-duty relief. This allows the repayment of duties on materials imported for use in manufacturing if it can be shown that the domestically produced good cannot compete with the imported product.[96] By March 31, 1961, £155,747 had been repaid to manufacturers of singlets, tarpaulins, rubber-soled shoes, groundnut decorticators, prestressed concrete products, terrazzo tile, metal products, and plastic water piping.[97] Of more than a hundred applications received to that date, forty-four were still under consideration while eleven approvals had been made in eight industries. A rebate was claimed for the plastic piping under section five of the ordinance, which provides relief if the imported article bears a lower proportion of import duty than the materials imported to manufacture the same article in Nigeria. In this instance, the tubing came in duty-free while the polythene granules were subject to a duty of 20 per cent.

The relief granted may be limited as to the amount of annual refund, or the period of relief, the maximum being ten years.[98] But a restructuring of the duties on plastics would, in the case cited, have obviated the need for the application of this ordinance and would have been more compatible with the desire to encourage industrial development.

<u>The Company Income Tax</u>

The federal income tax on companies is eight shillings per pound of net income, or 40 per cent, and is collected by the Federal Board of Inland Revenue.[99] In addition to double-taxation relief, which is subject to arrangements with foreign countries,[100] industrial firms may qualify for either or both of the domestic income tax reliefs: accelerated depreciation of capital assets, and a tax holiday.

Under The Income Tax (Amendment) Ordinance, 1952, and as extended under the Companies Income Tax Act, 1961, expenditures on industrial buildings and plant, machinery, and equipment, if they qualify, will receive initial allowances of 20 and 40 per cent, respectively. These write-downs may be obtained by any company that operates in Nigeria.

The primary incentive Nigeria offers to a prospective industrial concern is that of pioneer status. In accordance with The Income Tax Relief Ordinance,[101] a tax holiday of up to five years will be provided a pioneer company. The stated period will be extended on a year-by-year basis for each year during the original period a loss was sustained. Also, losses may be offset against tax liabilities after the holiday has ended.

The first step is for government to declare an industry "pioneer," for example, the processing of oil seeds or the manufacture of textiles. By mid-1963 more than fifty industries had been so designated. The individual company has to be granted a pioneer certificate; not all companies in the industry receive a certificate.[102] Finally, the certificate is good for only stated pioneer products. Thus, within the pioneer industry of textile manufacturing, a company might have a tax holiday only on the production of towels and blankets.

The pioneer certificate is granted only in cases where "it is expedient in the public interest to encourage the development of industry in Nigeria."[103] This ordinance, not surprisingly, has not been easy to administer. The Federal Ministry of Commerce and Industry is in the position of choosing between rival projects, often located in different regions. "We came upon cases where these political difficulties had led to delays of many months in reaching decisions."[104] The ministry also chooses among complementary products. Kano's Nigerian Metal Fabricating Company received a certificate for aluminum hollowware in March, 1961. Management then asked for an extension to include aluminum castings; seven months later they had not received a reply.[105]

Government appears to be torn between wanting new industry and not wanting to lose any revenue, even temporarily; indeed, government has difficulty in making up its mind how much it wants to concede to get what it wants. In part, this indecision is due to ignorance of the effects of the inducement. Chas. Pfizer and Company, the American pharmaceutical manufacturer, established itself in Aba without submitting an application for pioneer status.[106] Such occurrences lead Nigerians to question the need for the granting of any privileges. Pfizer may have made the judgment that the special status was not worth the compulsory disclosure of profitability to the Ministry of Commerce and Industry.[107] On the other hand, the backers of the Ikeja asbestos-cement plant would not have come to Nigeria were it not for the tax holiday.[108]

Because the government is giving up revenue, it probably would find it worthwhile to tie a proportion of the tax forgiveness to a required reinvestment of profits. The ploughing back of profits by the Nkalagu cement mill, described in Chapter 7, is an exception and not the rule. Moreover, it would seem advisable to grant pioneer certificates automatically to all new plants in a pioneer industry. This would serve as a welcoming gesture on the part of the Nigerian Government, it would save the time and effort now absorbed by drawn-out negotiations, and it would to some degree exclude politics, since an exclusive privilege would no longer be a sought-after prize.

Land for Industry

Only in the Federal District of Lagos may a non-Nigerian own land. And practically all the industrial plots there have been accounted for. Outside the Federal Territory, due to the present state of land registration in the regions, title is often the subject of prolonged legal conflict. Therefore, all regional governments have established, or have planned for, industrial estates in most of the major urban centers. With government approval, leases of up to ninety-nine years may be acquired.

One of the most ambitious of these estates is Port Harcourt's Trans-Amadi Industrial Layout. Of the total 2,450 acres, 1,520 have been set aside for industrial use. Subject to revision,[109] the rent per acre per annum was £307/10*s*./-*d*. in 1962. This includes a premium, or development charge, for roads, storm-water drains, electricity, railroad sidings, and water. The Eastern Region Executive Council may since have decided whether or not to include gas in this package of services.

The land for this and most of the other estates is state land owned by the government.[110] In fact, all land in the Northern Region, including the capital district of Kaduna, is state land.[111] Government is thus in the position of setting rents, and approving and administering the leases. This relieves the industrialist of dealing with individuals whose title may be questionable. It also requires the industrialist to negotiate with government even if he wants no import duty or income-tax relief.

In general, land acquisition for industry appears to present no barriers to industrial development.[112] But some large companies, like Shell-BP, believing they can save in the process, have negotiated their own leaseholds.

The lack of residential housing for plant management is a barrier to expatriate industry in many areas. Government would like expatriate housing to be leased from local builders. Yet quite often housing is insufficient and extremely costly. "Expatriate companies often found themselves forced into a position where they could be and were held up to ransom."[113]

Trans-Amadi's residential area was planned in 1958. In late 1960 a Ford Foundation team reported that "residential building is in fact not being made available."[114] It was not until September 27, 1961, that a low-density government residential area at Diobu was finally approved.[115]

Immigration of Expatriate Management

The Chief Federal Immigration Officer authorizes the entry of expatriates who intend to work in Nigeria. In setting up an industry, negotiations concerning the expatriate quota may involve considerable wrangling with the immigration authorities, the regional governments, and the Federal Ministry of Commerce and Industry. Discussions with the latter are usually carried on simultaneously with the company registration procedure.[116] In one 1960 case an American asked for ten non-Africans, was offered a quota of four, and finally received an allotment of six. In mid-1961 a request for six more was pending. "There's no limit on the time for Nigerianization, but a request for more [expatriates] brings questions up."[117]

Nigerians, as was illustrated in Chapter 3, lack many technical and management skills. The foreign enterprise, though, wants to Nigerianize as rapidly as possible. In fact, while discussing the present limitations on a more rapid flow of private American investment to Africa, an officer of Trans-Oceanic testified "The difficulty and expense of getting qualified American managers and technicians to work in tropical Africa can be a critical deterrent to launching a new enterprise."[118]

Promotional Activities

All four Nigerian governments have, in recent years, actively promoted the industrial possibilities that exist in Nigeria.

The federal government has issued many publications, including five editions of the Handbook of Commerce and Industry, which is kept up to date by the quarterly Nigeria Trade Journal. It has opened Trade and Industry sections in New York and London,[119] published Sunday supplements in New York newspapers,[120] and organized the Nigeria Exhibition on Victoria Island, Lagos, October 1-22, 1960, which included displays of more than 110 manufacturers. In addition, Nigeria was the only African exhibitor at the U.S. World Trade Fair in New York City's Coliseum, May 3-13, 1961. Its exhibit, including the showing of two films in color, was one of the highlights of the fair. From October 27 to November 18, 1962, Victoria Island was once again the site of a fair, this time an international trade fair.[121] Finally, in September, 1964, Nigeria was represented at the San Francisco and Brno trade fairs.

The regions have also been energetic in this field. Each has issued many publications, notably the *Industrialists Guide to Northern Nigeria* (1960), *The Industrial Potentialities of Northern Nigeria* (1963), *Investment Opportunities in Eastern Nigeria* (1960), and *A Directory of Industries and Allied Trades in the Western Region of Nigeria* (1960), and has emulated the federal government by dispatching investment-seeking missions on worldwide trips. It may be added that the West has established a formal Industrial Promotions Commission, and the East, through the New York public relations firm of Barnet and Reef Associates, Inc., distributes the *Eastern Nigeria Newsletter* monthly to American readers.

The Federal Institute of Industrial Research

Upon the recommendation of the IBRD, the federal government in 1955 started the conversion of an RAF World War II signal station at Oshodi, near Lagos, into the Institute of Applied Technical Research. In 1958, permanent buildings were erected and the institute was renamed the Federal Institute of Industrial Research (F.I.I.R.).

The aim of F.I.I.R. is to adapt fundamental research carried out elsewhere--for example, by the United Kingdom Department of Scientific and Industrial Research--to new industries in Nigeria as quickly as possible. The Institute's work in the period 1961-64 included the production of coir fiber (for mattresses) from coconut husks, fish drying, mechanized gari production using freshly dug cassava roots, the fortification of gari with proteins, the substitution of conophor oil for linseed oil in paints, the use of cashew-nut shell oil for plastic manufacture, and the evaluation of the potentialities of local materials for pulping and making paper.[122]

In the future, F.I.I.R. expects to investigate the tanning of hides and skins, the production of building board from waste materials, the manufacture of rubberized coir mats, the making of smokeless briquettes from coal, and the producing of chemicals from coal tar. The government's efforts in this direction have, however, been somewhat thwarted by an inability to fill the full complement of staff. Thus, money continuously remains unspent from recurrent appropriations.[123]

The Investment Climate

The "investment climate" refers to the feeling that foreign investors bear toward a particular country. If the investment climate is considered good, this is tantamount to a statement of confidence. Domestic political stability and international politics both have an effect on the climate: "A certain degree of Soviet influence will suddenly and completely kill off overseas investor confidence and all possibility of further private investment inflow."[12] Most important of all, however, is the wish of foreign businessmen to be told that they are welcome and will be treated fairly.

Nigeria speaks with many voices. With five governments, a proliferation of agencies engaged in economic development, and four major political parties, as well as youth groups, labor unions, and newspapers, this is to be expected. It is stated government policy that Nigeria has no plans to nationalize industry beyond the extent to which public utilities are already nationalized. "Nevertheless . . . should this occur, then fair compensation, assessed by independent arbitration, would be paid."[125] The regional premiers and the Federal Minister of Finance reiterate this policy every time a contrary point of view is evoked.[126]

Events other than the threat of nationalization also shake investor confidence. On Monday, February 20, 1961, the main article on the editorial page of the Wall Street Journal was entitled "The Lumumba Myth: It Grows Rapidly in Africa, Was Used by Local Communists in Nigerian Riots."[127] On August 19, 1961, the leader of the minor Dynamic Party, Dr. Chike Obi, was quoted as saying, "The American teachers sent to Nigeria were spies for the American Government."[128] These two outbursts may be attributed to irresponsible elements of the population. But when the government newspaper headlines, as it did on April 4, 1964, "Minister Blasts Foreign Firms,"[129] the prospects for continued private capital inflow are diminished.

In 1957, the government issued a pamphlet entitled Our War Against Bribery and Corruption.[130] Seven years later, letters to the editor of West Africa on this subject still appear. In truth, Nigeria is probably no better and no worse than most of the countries of the world when it comes to the taking of "dash."

In 1964, threats to private foreign investment are more apparent than real. No foreign investor has been driven out of Nigerian industry, nor is one likely to be in the near future. Nigeria's energies so far have been turned into the channel outlined by the economic-development program.

Exchange controls may be gradually tightened. Therefore, it would behoove the federal government to sign investment guarantee agreements with the European nations--as it has done with the U.S.--guaranteeing that private capital investment in Nigeria, and local currency receipts from such investments, will remain convertible into francs, marks, etc. This guarantee would supplement the Nigerian promise that profits and capital may be freely expatriated.[131]

SUMMARY AND CONCLUSIONS

In 1960, the year Nigeria achieved independence, the net fixed investment in manufacturing and processing by corporations and major companies was less than £1.5 million, or about 2 per cent of the total net capital formation. This was parallel to the 1.5 per cent share of the GNP that was contributed by modern manufacturing in that year.

Nigeria wishes to increase the rate of investment in industry. "Since the individual accumulation is so difficult, we must turn to public enterprise."[132] This statement is borne out by the discussion on savings: On a per capita basis, time and savings deposits equaled $3.30 in 1963. To this end the governments of the federation, especially the regional, have established a host of agencies that are involved in the financing of industrial development. With the budgets contributing almost nothing to the establishment of industrial enterprises, these agencies have relied on the surpluses built up by the marketing boards in the postwar years. The organization of a money market in Lagos made these reserves more available for development purposes, foreign securities being exchanged for Nigerian development loans and treasury bills. But, the reserves have been rapidly depleted.

Nigeria is also threatened by inflationary pressures, which have been building up. Adding to the mixed price situation in the international commodity markets of late, inflation would balk Nigeria's development efforts. Moreover, inflation would further encourage real-estate speculation at the expense of industrial development: Lagos rents are already very high, and still rising.

In sum, as a result of falling foreign-exchange proceeds and an increasing rate of expenditures on development, Nigeria has drawn down her foreign reserves. They are at a level where they can no longer satisfy the demands made upon them by the development agencies, as was the case during the 1950's. Therefore, because Nigeria cannot finance current consumption and investment from her own resources and export earnings, she has sought foreign aid and investment.

Foreign loans, grants, and technical assistance are important because they release internal funds for development as they upgrade the quality of Nigeria's infrastructure and human resources.

Private foreign investment, particularly by British companies led by UAC, increased absolutely in the 1950's, although remaining fairly constant as a percentage of GCF. Since then the investment picture has not been so sanguine. As the trading firms leave more and more commercial activities to the

Nigerians, they have invested increasingly in manufacturing facilities. Yet over-all new foreign investment has diminished. There are also other sources of private industrial capital in Nigeria, but these are comparatively small.

Sixty-one per cent of the gap between GDP and total consumption plus investment remained in 1960 after £28 million was invested in Nigeria from abroad. Two years later Nigeria was reckoning that foreign investment in industry and plantations would total £33.3 million per year during 1962-68. But, during each of the first two plan years, less than one-third of this target was realized. To attract such a magnitude of external financing, the federal government has held out to the prospective foreign investor in Nigerian industry four major fiscal incentives: relief from income tax, exemption from certain import duties, accelerated depreciation, and the possible imposition of a protective tariff. The regional governments have done much in the way of providing sites for industry, although they have lagged when it comes to residential housing for expatriate management. The federal government has undertaken research to find further industrial uses for Nigerian resources, and all governments have actively promoted their desire for foreign investment in Nigerian industry.

Yet profitability remains the ultimate test. A survey of British overseas direct investments in 1962 revealed that U.K. firms were gaining a return of 23.4 per cent on their investments in West Germany, 14 per cent in Malaya, and 1.2 per cent in Nigeria.[133] These figures should be treated charily. However, the comparisons are suggestive of the competition Nigeria faces in luring overseas private investment to her shores. Furthermore, incentives are offset if they are doled out overcautiously and hence slowly.[134]

When examining the so-called investment climate, warning signs, such as riots and calls for nationalization, occasionally crop up. In comparison, however, to many underdeveloped lands the world over, and to the majority in Africa, Nigeria's investment climate remains favorable to the would-be foreign investor. In recent years, Nigeria has introduced exchange controls, at first only to channel capital movements to and from abroad through the banking system. Exchange controls of a more restrictive nature would augment the nation's administrative overhead, and could lead to abuses. Of greater importance, should restrictions on the repatriation of foreign capital, profits and/or interest be instituted, Nigeria will risk frightening away the foreign investment she so evidently requires. (The foregoing excludes a possible near-term, dramatic upswing in oil revenues.)

Footnotes to Chapter 6

1. These figures are a matter of definition, and as a result understate the "true" capital formation. A portion of recurrent expenditures on education could theoretically be incorporated, as could improvement on the land made by the farmer.

2. Including plant and machinery for agriculture, communications, etc. Plant and machinery averaged 13.9 per cent of GCF for the period 1957-60.

3. Because cost of replacement is more relevant than the accountants' original cost, the result would be more meaningful if the effect of inflation could be estimated. To date, the lack of data does not make this possible.

4. Nigeria, Federal Office of Statistics, *Estimates of Capital Formation: 1958-59* (Lagos, 1960), p. 1 (Mimeo.).

5. Jackson and Okigbo calculated that depreciation amounted to 47.7 per cent in 1956 and 52.5 per cent in 1957. (*Op. cit.*, Table ED. IX. 4.) And, for the first time, in 1960, the Department of Statistics estimated net capital formation of corporations and major companies. The resulting figures in the category of manufacturing and processing were £1,551,000 for major companies and *minus* £131,000 for corporations (*Ibid.*) The £1,420,000 difference supports the assumption of 50 per cent for depreciation.

6. See Nigeria, "The Laws of the Federation of Nigeria and Lagos," Central Bank of Nigeria (rev. ed.; Lagos: Government Printer, 1959), Chapter 30. The ordinance was based on the recommendations of J. B. Loynes in his Report on the Establishment of a Nigerian Central Bank, the Introduction of a Nigerian Currency, and Other Associated Matters (Lagos: Government Printer, 1957).

7. Ibid., Section 17.

8. Nigeria, Central Bank, Annual Reports and Statements of Accounts for the Period Ended 31st December 1962 and 1963 (Lagos: Central Bank, 1963 and 1964), pp. 24 and 18.

9. Interview with Manager of Bank X, Nigeria. The same suspicion is directed toward the Nigerian industrial entrepreneur who wishes to obtain short-term financing from the commercial banks.

10. It will be noted that the time and savings deposits have been increasing faster than the demand deposits. Probably, this is mainly due to the recent rapid growth of commercial bank branches that will accept such deposits. Also, the Post Office Savings Bank, beset by poor customer relations, has lost some of its deposits to the commercial banks.

11. Nigeria, Central Bank, Economic and Financial Review, Vol. 2, No. 1 (Lagos: Central Bank, June, 1964), pp. 29-30. Commerce and agriculture are the main recipients of these loans and advances.

12. On July 8, 1964, the Daily Official List of the exchange contained fourteen entries under Nigerian Government Securities, eighteen under Nigerian industrial and commercial securities, and twelve from the London Stock Exchange. The first public issue of company shares took place in Nigeria in February, 1959, when the Nigerian Cement Company Ltd. offered 174,898 shares of £1 each at par.

13. From its June, 1961, informal opening to August 25, 1961, the volume of trade handled by the

four brokers (including ICON) amounted to approximately £250,000, 90 per cent of which was in governments (West Africa [London], September 2, 1961, p. 978). Total activity for the year was £760,152, £710,440 being transactions in government stocks. (Central Bank, Annual Report for 1961, p. 23.) By 1963 the annual value of transactions had grown to £5.2 million, including £323,100 worth of industrials. (Central Bank, Annual Report for 1963, p. 33.)

14. After the release of the 1963 census, it is possible that mortality statistics will be improved. The present state of these statistics is a major barrier to the establishment of life insurance companies. The Royal Exchange Assurance Group insures Africans up to age 65. They pay premiums until they die; therefore, "whole-life" policies are not available to them. The company started insuring Africans in 1960--only to age 55 then--on a sworn certificate of age, since birth certificates usually are not available. Europeans now pay the same rates as obtain in the U.K., that is, there no longer is "tropical loading." (Interview with John Chutter, Royal Exchange Assurance, Lagos, May 5, 1964.)

15. The Insurance (Miscellaneous Provisions) Bill was gazetted on March 3, 1964. In brief, it requires that life and endowment policies issued in Nigeria be issued by a Nigerian company and denominated in Nigerian pounds; that 25 per cent of statutory investments be held in Nigerian Government securities; and that assets held against endowment policies, plus 40 per cent of the gross premium income received on other Nigerian risks, be invested in Nigerian securities. From the individual's point of view, he may deduct the premium from his income when computing his personal income tax if the policy is issued in Nigeria. Otherwise, he may deduct only one-third of the premium.

16. The division of royalties on crude oil production (before the creation of the Mid-West Region) illustrates the allocation of this distributable recurrent revenue: 50 per cent to the region of origin, 20 per cent to the federal government, and

30 per cent to the distributive pool. Of the latter 30 per cent, 40 per cent is given to the Northern Region, 24 per cent to the Western Region, and 31 per cent to the Eastern Region (the Southern Cameroons used to receive 5 per cent). The distributive pool formula was suggested in 1958 by Sir J. Raisman's Fiscal Commission. Their report was accepted practically _in toto_ by the 1958 Constitutional Conference. See U.K., Colonial Office, _Nigeria: Report of the Fiscal Commission_, Cmnd. 481 (London: Her Majesty's Stationery Office, 1958). With the loss of the Southern Cameroons the denominator became 95 instead of 100. Then, when the Mid-West broke off from the West, the latter's share was divided on a population basis of 3:1. The current allocations of the distributable pool are: North, 40/95; East, 31/95; West, 18/95; and Mid-West, 6/95. K. J. Binns of Tasmania is now reviewing the Nigerian tax situation. It is likely that the foregoing will be altered sometime in 1965.

17. The federal government has budgeted £6.3 million to university grants and to the Federal Ministry of Education under recurrent expenditures in 1964-65. These percentages would be increased if other education expenditures were consolidated with the ministries of education, e.g., training and extension services of the ministries of agriculture. Also under the capital budgets the amounts apportioned to the ministries of education for buildings are omitted.

18. Including category, Pensions and Gratuities. The federal government expects to expend £6.1 million in these categories. (With respect to the public welfare, the federal government has budgeted £6.2 million for police expenditures and £7.2 million on defense. These two heads account for 16.9 per cent of recurrent revenues in 1964-65.)

19. Interview with J. Beach, Deputy General Manager, Central Bank, August 28, 1961, Lagos.

20. Nigeria, _Annual Report and Statement of Accounts for the Period Ended 31st December 1961_ (Lagos: Central Bank, 1962), p. 200.

21. Central Bank, Annual Reports for 1962 and 1963, pp. 36 and 31; and Economic and Financial Review, p. 37. The 1964-65 federal budget calls for another development loan--£15 million--during 1964. According to the Federal Minister of Finance, the central bank has agreed to provide up to £40 million in long-term finance over the plan period (1962-68) through the purchase of long-term federal government stocks. (Nigeria, Estimates of the Government of the Federal Republic of Nigeria: 1964-65 [Lagos: Ministry of Information Printing Division, 1964], pp. 296 and 313.)

22. E. E. Jucker-Fleetwood, The Monetary and Financial Position in Ghana and Nigeria, Series A: No. 29 (Basle: Centre for Economic and Financial Research, 1960), p. 11. The produce marketing boards have been superseded by regional boards.

23. Central Bank, Annual Reports for 1962 and 1963, pp. 34 and 30. On May 1, 1964, the central bank held £18 million of federal government securities and included among its assets £8.9 million of rediscounts and advances. Total assets were £84.9 million. (Economic and Financial Review, pp. 20 and 22.)

24. Determination of the cost of living for the whole of Nigeria is not yet possible, though consumer price indexes are now computed by the Federal Office of Statistics for Lagos, Ibadan, Enugu, Kaduna, and Port Harcourt/Aba.

25. See Nigeria, Review of Salaries and Wages, Report of the Mbanefo Commission (Lagos: Federal Government Printer, 1959). In 1960 most of the established staff received a 15 per cent raise. See also Nigeria, Report of the [Morgan] Commission on the Review of Wages, Salary and Conditions of Service of the Junior Employees of the Governments of the Federation and in Private Establishments (Lagos: Federal Ministry of Information Printing Division, 1964), and Nigeria, Conclusion of the Federal Government on the Report of the Morgan Commission (Lagos: Federal Ministry of Information Printing Division, S.P. 5/1964). In the event, the actual wage rise was between the

structures set forth in these two documents. Chapter 3 has a brief discussion of the national strike that accompanied the negotiations.

26. The base year used is 1953 in both cases. The recent slum-clearance operations, the relatively large expatriate population in Lagos, and the constant immigration of Nigerians to Lagos account for much of the difference.

27. See _Central Bank of Nigeria (Amendment) Act, 1962_ (Act No. 17 of 1962), §4. "The value of the reserve of external assets shall be not less than forty _per centum_ of the total demand liabilities of the Bank." This replaces provisions of Central Bank of Nigeria Act §26, which reads: "The value of the reserve . . . shall--(a) for a period of five years from [Bank's taking over currency issue from WACB] . . . be not less than the aggregate of an amount representing sixty per cent of the Bank's notes and coins in circulation together with an amount representing thirty-five per cent of the Bank's other demand liabilities; (b) after five years . . . be not less than forty per cent of the aggregate of the Bank's notes and coins in circulation and other demand liabilities."

28. On March 31, 1964, the total money supply equaled £129.6 million. The period June-August sees the end of the decline in the seasonal demand.

29. The Joint Planning Committee of the National Economic Council established a Committee on Statistics which, in 1961, was considering the possibility of devising a wholesale price index. (Interview with M. Rice, U.S. Federal Reserve System adviser to the Central Bank, August 28, 1961, Lagos.) Today, it remains a problem of implementing this suggestion.

30. These replaced the Cocoa, Oil Palm Produce, Groundnut, and Cotton Marketing Boards. Each board is under the jurisdiction of a different ministry, the Ministry of Agriculture in the East, the Ministry of Economic Planning in the North (from September 1, 1961), and the Ministry of Trade and Industry in the West.

31. *Handbook of Commerce and Industry*, p. 133.

32. Producers' incomes are *not* stabilized. It will be noted that they are government agencies, not producers' organizations; that the members are appointed, not elected.

33. Northern Nigeria, Marketing Board, *Sixth Annual Report: 1st November 1959-31st October, 1960* (Kano: Marketing Board, 1961), p. 17. In late 1961 the price paid to producers was reduced by 10 per cent. For the financial year, the board showed a trading deficit of £887,818. (*Seventh Annual Report*, p. 21.)

34. An £800,000 loan (plus £150,000 in equity) to Kaduna Textiles Ltd. is one of several nongovernment loans outstanding.

35. Western Nigeria, Western Region Marketing Board, *Seventh Annual Report: 1st October 1960-30th* September 1961 (Ibadan: Marketing Board, S.P. #2/1962), p. 52.

36. *New York Times*, March 5, 1961, p. F 1.

37. *Times* (Lagos), August 31, 1961, p. 1. In 1955-56 the price paid to producers was £200 per ton.

38. See Nigeria, *Report of the Coker Commission of Inquiry into the affairs of Certain Statutory Corportations in Western Nigeria* (4 vols.; Lagos: Ministry of Information Printing Division, 1962); and Nigeria, *Comments of the Federal Government on the Report of the Coker Commission. . .* (Lagos: Ministry of Information Printing Division, S.P. 4/1962). This inquiry was an outgrowth of the declaration of a state of emergency in the Western Region by the federal government in May, 1962.

39. Moore, *et al*., *op. cit*., p. 87.

40. The board's "commitment" to the University of Nigeria in 1962 was stated to be £5 million. (Eastern Nigeria, Marketing Board, *Seventh Annual*

Report: 1st January, 1961-31st December, 1961 [Port Harcourt: Marketing Board, 1963], p. 51.)

41. Northern Nigeria, Development Corporation, Eighth Annual Report: 1962/63 (Kaduna: NNDC, 1963), p. 9 and Appendix 13.

42. Interview with R. J. Osborne, Chief Project Manager, [then] NRDC, October 23, 1961, Kaduna.

43. Equivalent to an American motel.

44. Western Nigeria, Development Corporation, Annual Report: 1961/62 (Ibadan: WNDC, 1963), pp. 59-62.

45. It sold twenty, primarily to cooperatives. (Interview with Hugh DeB. Brock, General-Manager, ENDC Agriculture and Plantation Division, October 20, 1961, Enugu.)

46. Interview with James T. Daniel, General-Manager, ENDC Industrial and Commercial Division, October 10, 1961, Enugu.

47. The £100,000 debenture portion may have been written off (see Chapter 7).

48. The ENDC holds approximately 47 per cent of the equity which it purchased from the federal government, so that it would not "get into the hands of foreign investors and speculators." (Daniel, *loc. cit.*)

49. "With respect to government ownership, no philosophy has been developed yet--it is all *ad hoc*." (Interview with R. L. Claringbould, New Projects and Industrial Manager, WNDC, September 27, 1961, Ibadan). [Mr. Claringbould has since returned to Australia; the writer will not quote other officials who still are in the three governments.]

50. Western Nigeria, Western Region Housing Corporation, Annual Report and Accounts for the Year Ended 31st March, 1962 (Ibadan: Government Printer,

O.D. 4/63). It is an agency of the Ministry of Lands and Housing.

51. Western Nigeria, Western Region Finance Corporation, Seventh Annual Report: 1961-62 (Ibadan: Government Printer, O.D. 7/1963). Government apportioned the investments between the WNDC and the WRFC.

52. "This makes sure that competition won't prevent our getting the money back." (Interview with E. O. Otitoju, Senior Assistant Secretary, Western Region Finance Corporation, in the Corporation's new skyscraper, September 20, 1961, Ibadan.) In each of the first five annual reports there was a statement to the effect that there was a need for supervised credit in due course. See also Report of the Coker Commission, Vol. 2, p. 44, and Vol. 4, pp. 90-91. Of five large investments, only one, a hotel, was yielding a return sufficient to cover the interest charge.

53. See Industrial Loans (Lagos and Federation) Ordinance, April 21, 1956 (No. 17 of 1956). The Board is the responsibility of the Federal Ministry of Commerce and Industry.

54. Nigeria, Federal Loans Board, Sixth Annual Report: 1st July, 1961 to 30th June, 1962 (Lagos: Ministry of Information Printing Division, 1963), p. 4. Initially capitalized with £300,000, the board received another £139,000 in 1960. It is budgeted for an additional £500,000 over the plan period. This entity is distinct from the Revolving Loans Fund for Industry which was established in August, 1959, with £200,000 from U.K. counterpart funds made available to Britain under America's European Co-operation Administration. (West African Pilot [Lagos], August 18, 1959.) Evidently, both the fund and board are presently fully loaned up.

55. Nigeria, Federal Ministry of Communications, Annual Report of the Nigeria Post Office Savings Bank: 1959-60 (Lagos: Ministry of Information Printing Division, 1963), p. 12; Nigeria, Annual Abstract of Statistics: 1963, p. 40; and Nigeria, Central Bank, Economic and Financial Review, p. 38.

56. Sunday Post (Lagos), September 3, 1961, p. 1. Nigerpools' slogan is "For Security and Profit."

57. E. E. Jucker-Fleetwood, Monetary and Financial Problems of Certain New Countries in Africa, Series A: No. 34 (Basle: Centre for Economic and Financial Research, 1961), p. 15.

58. S. H. Frankel, Capital Investment in Africa: Its Course and Effects (London: Oxford University Press, 1938), p. 158. This figure includes a 5 per cent estimate of nonlisted capital.

59. Regarding industry, in 1936 fifteen European nonmining firms were engaged in some sort of manufacturing activity, with only seven solely in this field. (J. Mars, "Extra-Territorial Enterprises," Mining, Commerce, and Finance in Nigeria, Vol. II of The Economics of a Tropical Dependency, ed. M. Perham [London: Faber and Faber, 1948], p. 50.) During this period there were no restrictions on foreign private investment.

60. New York Times, March 29, 1962, p. 6.

61. West Africa (London), January 27, 1962, p. 85.

62. In 1950, "the book value of the U.S. direct investments in the whole of British West Africa amounted to no more than $10.5 million" (primarily distribution facilities of petroleum companies). (Blankenheimer, op. cit., p. 19.) In 1957 the U.S. investment in Nigeria was $15 million and in 1959, $16 million. (S. Pizer and F. Cutler, U.S. Business Investments in Foreign Countries, U.S. Department of Commerce, Office of Business Statistics [Washington, D.C.: U.S. Government Printing Office, 1960], p. 92.) According to a partial survey carried out by the central bank in 1962, the net flow of foreign capital into Nigeria (exclusive of banks, air transport, shipping companies, and insurance firms) amounted to £23.0 million in 1961 and £10.4 million in 1962. The corresponding American figures were £5.1 million and

£5.4 million, a majority of which went into manufacturing. (Nigeria, Central Bank, Economic and Financial Review, pp. 10-14.)

63. The Economist (London), April 29, 1961, p. 479.

64. UAC, Statistical and Economic Review, No. 28, p. 53.

65. U.S. Department of Commerce, Office of Business Economics, Survey of Current Business, Vol. 41, No. 8 (August, 1961), p. 22. According to the survey cited in footnote 62 above, U.S. investment in fixed assets reached £15 million in 1962.

66. Ibid. The rationale for this transformation is discussed in UAC, Statistical and Economic Review. Partially as a result of this redeployment, the company suffered "a substantial loss . . . in Nigeria" during 1962. (The Economist [London], August 18, 1962, p. 638.)

67. The American Overseas Finance Co. was consolidated with the Transoceanic Development Corporation on January 20, 1960, and merged into the (Rockefeller) International Basic Economy Corporation in May, 1962.

68. Under the "Edge Law," as was Transoceanic-AOFC. This amendment to the Federal Reserve Act provides for federal incorporation of institutions organized for the purpose of carrying on international or foreign banking and other financial operations.

69. Formerly known as the Guinea Coast Holding Co., the company has an authorized capital of £600,000, most of which has been issued. It was established in 1960, the year of Nigeria's independence, "To achieve a real and effective partnership with the Nigerian people, and to meet the changing pattern of commerce in the future. . . ." (Paragraph 1 of "Reason for the Offer," Offer for Sale [Lagos], July 21, 1960.)

70. New York Times, December 13, 1961. Loans, including those of the Export-Import Bank, capital grants, and technical assistance comprise the total commitment.

71. Forty-two Lagos and fifty overseas subscribers made up the list of ICON shareholders on August 11, 1961. The latter contributed more than 80 per cent of the total. (Interview with R. L. Powell, Managing-Director, ICON, Lagos, September 4, 1961.) A general outline of NIDB's reserves, purpose, etc., is to be found in Nigeria, Nigerian Industrial Development Bank, Explanatory Memorandum and Guide to Applicants (Lagos: NIDB, 1964).

IFC's involvement in NIDB is described in IFC Press Release No. 64/4, Washington, D.C., January 22, 1964. In general, the NIDB will make fully secured loans in the range of £10,000 - £200,000, over a period of up to fifteen years. The IFC has also made an investment of £250,000 in a Kaduna textile mill: £117,000 in capital shares and £133,000 in loans.

72. The Eastern Region Government had a 32 per cent equity interest in INDAG, and the Northern Region Government a 40 per cent equity interest in NDNL. In Nigeria, CDC had invested £2,590,000, made loans of £1,543,625, and was committed to loan an additional £2,625,000. (Interview with A. F. Cooper, Director, West African Division, Colonial Development Corporation, Lagos, September 8, 1961.) By 1964, the CDC had about £11 million worth of interests in Nigerian ventures.

73. Interview with P. G. Nelson, Manager, INDAG, Enugu, October 11, 1961. With Shell-BP ready to take the product, their first indigenous loan seemed to be incurring a minimum supervisory cost. In 1964, new investments totaling £400,000 are to become effective. (U.K., Commonwealth Development Corporation, Report and Accounts: 1963 [London: CDC, 1964], p. 115.)

74. Interview with J. C. Brown, Acting Manager, NDNL, Kaduna, October 25, 1961.

75. U.K., Commonwealth Economic Committee, Commonwealth Development and its Financing (London: Her Majesty's Stationery Office, 1963), Vol. 5 (Nigeria), p. 16.

76. Times (Lagos), October 24, 1961, p. 5.

77. The site was not named in Times (Lagos), September 24, 1961, p. 1.

78. Funds used to be supplied largely by Britain, France, and Belgium. Now the organization is completely an African venture. Possibly it will be tied to the Organization of African Unity (OAU) as an economic arm.

79. The U.S. AID Mission to Nigeria maintains headquarters staffs in each of four capitals, with additional experts--direct hire and on contract--located in the field, and assigned to government ministries.

80. Originally a two-year project, costing the Agency $1.9 million, this is AID's first such program in tropical Africa. It is an outgrowth of a Private Enterprise Program for Nigeria prepared by Charles L. Terrel, Chief of the Private Enterprise and Industrial Development Division, USOM/Nigeria, January 16, 1961.. (Mimeo.)

81. This sum represents 80 per cent of the figure for Nigerian and Ghana combined. Ford Foundation, Annual Report: October 1, 1962 to September 30, 1963 (New York: Ford Foundation, 1964). The Foundation has a staff in Lagos that supervises this expenditure.

82. By October, 1961, nineteen Nigerian feasibility studies were completed, and the total number of projects had reached fifty-six. (The writer was a guest in the Lagos RBF office for nine weeks during the summer of 1961.)

83. The Federal Office of Statistics estimated that (provisionally) the net credit balance for 1960 was £76.87 million. (Lagos, July 1, 1961.) (Mimeo.)

84. "Inflation is more apt to increase expenditures than revenues" (Rivkin, *et al.*, *op. cit.*, p. 80), because as exports are deterred, and imports reduced by a lack of foreign exchange, government revenue from taxes on international trade will be reduced.

85. *Economic and Financial Review*, p. 22. Forty per cent of £81.2 million. (See footnote 27.)

86. This account does not consider a continuing rise in the level of imports, nor an expansion of the money supply.

87. Nigeria, *The Sovereignty Budget* (Budget Speech by Chief The Honorable Festus Sam Okotie-Eboh, Federal Minister of Finance, April 6, 1961 [Lagos: Federal Ministry of Information, 1961]), p. 14.

88. UAC, for one, transfers millions of pounds a year for its own financing.

89. This step was under consideration for some time prior to the introduction of the legislation. "If development proceeds at the rate which is expected, probably some measure of exchange controls--only capital movements--will be necessary." (Interview with P. S. N. Prasad, economic adviser to the federal government [Prime Minister's Office], Lagos, September 15, 1961.)

90. "Investors who are resident in Nigeria and are not controlled by bodies outside the country are free to invest without asking for approved status and they can also issue or transfer shares provided the transferees are not resident in non-scheduled territories [e.g., U.S., Canada, France, Italy, etc.]." (Akintola Williams, "Taxation and Exchange Control," Paper read before an investment seminar, Lagos, February 25, 1964.)

91. *Economist* (London), October 21, 1961, p. 280. Nigeria was the fourth biggest buyer of gold from the U.S. in the final quarter of 1961. (*West Africa* [London], March 17, 1962, p. 301.)

92. IMF, International Financial News Survey (Washington, D.C.), Vol. 14, No. 7 (February 23, 1962), p. 57. This amount supplements the $1.895 billion cost of the federal and regional programs during the period 1962-68.

93. Federation of British Industries, Nigeria: An Industrial Reconnaissance (Report of the FBI Delegation to the Industrial Development Conference, Lagos, January, 1961 [London: FBI, February, 1961]), p. 37.

94. UAC, Statistical and Economic Review, No. 23, p. 26.

95. Excise duties have also been imposed on locally produced paint, shirts, singlets, sugar confectionary, and nails, and raised on footwear and matches. To keep the same margin of protection, import duties have been increased accordingly.

96. Nigeria, Industrial Development (Import Duty Relief) Ordinance, 1957 (Lagos: Federal Government Printer, #27/1957), pp. A 103-6.

97. Nigeria, Federal Ministry of Commerce and Industry, Annual Reports, 1958-59, 1959-60, and 1960-61 (Lagos: Federal Government Printer, 1960, and Ministry of Information Printing Division, 1963), pp. 30, 35, and 19.

98. Nigeria, Handbook of Commerce and Industry, p. 54.

99. See Section 32 of Nigeria, Companies Income Tax Act, 1961 (Lagos: Federal Government Printer, #22/1961), pp. A 157-214. Assuming a 50 per cent U.S. rate, an American company would have to pay 10 per cent more to the U.S. at the time it repatriates its profits.

100. For example, such arrangements have been concluded with the United States and Commonwealth nations. A new bilateral agreement is being negotiated with the United Kingdom. Nigeria hopes it will

include a waiver of British taxes on income exempt from taxation under Nigerian pioneer-industry tax legislation.

101. Nigeria, Industrial Development (Income Tax Relief) Ordinance, 1958 (Lagos: Federal Government Printer, #8/1958), pp. A 43-54. A company must be a public company and must be incorporated in Nigeria.

102. During the first three years of operation, thirty-nine certificates were issued or approved, and thirty-three remained under consideration. (Federal Ministry of Commerce and Industry, Annual Reports, 1959-60 and 1960-61, pp. 34-35 and 18.)

103. Income Tax Relief Ordinance, p. A 44.

104. FBI's Industrial Reconnaissance, p. 36. I. F. E. Myers, Senior Industrial Officer of the Ministry of Commerce and Industry, told the writer on August 2, 1961, that the average time for a decision had been improved to two-and-a-half months.

105. Interview with George Jabre, Manager, Nigerian Metal Fabricating Co., Kano, October 30, 1961. Mr. Jabre's request for pioneer status for the production of mirrors was refused. It might be noted that the import duties on both glass and mirrors were 20 per cent.

106. Interview with Professor B. Lewis of Oberlin, adviser to the Federal Ministry of Commerce and Industry, Lagos, August 4, 1961. The plant as established was not eligible, since it is a wholly owned subsidiary of the American company.

107. As required by the legislation. With respect to its first plant, Pfizer now has to reveal its profits only to the Board of Inland Revenue.

108. Interview with C. F. Delsaux, Company Manager, Asbestos Cement Products (Nigeria) Ltd., Ikeja, August 8, 1961.

109. Rental revision may take place every decade, supposedly equal to the average rise in the value of the land.

110. An exception is Enugu's industrial area at Emene, which is Railway land. (Interview with Y. Elon, Eastern Region Town Planning Adviser, Enugu, October 11, 1961). In the south, land can be gazetted as state land, with compensation given to the owners. Before October 1, 1963, state land was known as crown land.

111. Interview with O. W. Attoe, Assistant Town Planning Officer, Northern Region Ministry of Lands and Survey, Kaduna South, October 21, 1961.

112. As for Lagos, plots are now available in the Western Region estates of Ikeja and Mushin. Within the Territory, consideration is being given to the reclaiming of more land in the Ijora area.

113. FBI's Industrial Reconnaissance, p. 39.

114. F. Moore, et al., op. cit., p. 72.

115. Interview with F. Kennedy, Port Harcourt Provincial Secretary, Port Harcourt, October 5, 1961. (See text, p. 177, on the Eastern Nigeria Housing Corporation.)

116. "If there is no Nigerian on the Board of Directors, you will wait forever. . . . Get a local solicitor." (Advice from Mr. Y., a Lagos businessman with many years of experience.)

117. Interview with Mr. Z., Lagos, August, 1961. The situation appears to be the same three years later. During 1960-61, the Federal Ministry of Commerce and Industry processed requests for permission to employ 1,301 expatriates. Of these, 926 expatriates were approved. (Federal Ministry of Commerce and Industry, Annual Report: 1960-61, p. 19.)

118. Statement by E. Kennedy Langstaff, Assistant Vice-President, Transoceanic-AOFC, Ltd., _Hearings Before the Subcommittee on Africa_, p. 90.

119. In the former, it joined with many American companies in 1960 to form the Nigerian-American Chamber of Commerce.

120. Supplements prepared by the African Research and Development Co., Inc., of New York City appeared in the _New York Times_, October 2, 1960, and the _New York Herald Tribune_, October 29, 1961. Also the international edition of the former on February 28, 1964, carried a full-page advertisement, "An Invitation to Invest," placed by ADL.

121. Because of the expenditures involved in this fair, Nigeria was unable to participate in the New York World's Fair of 1964-65. Eighty-three U.S. firms exhibited their wares.

122. _Nigeria Trade Journal_ (March, 1962), pp. 22-26; Federal Institute of Industrial Research, _Progress Report: January-March, 1961_ (Oshodi, May 29, 1961), Mimeo.; and Nigeria, Lagos Chamber of Commerce, _Commerce in Nigeria_, Vol. 5 (1963), p. 44.

123. "We're 50 per cent understaffed, especially on the research side." (Interview with A. S. Cook, Director, F.I.I.R., Oshodi, August 30, 1961. The situation was the same on March 31, 1964. Nigeria, _Annual Report of the Federal Institute of Industrial Research: 1963-64_ (Lagos: Ministry of Information Printing Division, 1964), p. 13.

124. F. Taylor Ostrander, "Conditions for Private Investment," _Current_ (March, 1961), p. 15.

125. One of many such statements, this one appeared in Nigeria, Federal Ministry of Information, _Investment Opportunities in Nigeria_ (Lagos: Ministry of Information, 1961), p. 6. Subsequently, the airline and the shipping line were nationalized. Full compensation was paid.

126. In September, 1961, the Vice-Chairman of the Port Harcourt Chamber of Commerce called on the government to nationalize foreign banks. On September 16, via press and radio, the Federal Minister of Finance reaffirmed that it had no intention of nationalizing any bank in Nigeria. On September 29, 1961, the Parliamentary Secretary to the Federal Minister of Mines and Power told miners in the tin fields that the "Federal Government had no intention of nationalising any foreign company at the moment [italics mine] as such a move would . . . adversely affect the economy." Times (Lagos). On October 27, 1961, the Federal Minister of Finance warned that "those advocating nationalisation of foreign industries . . . create an unhealthy climate for foreign investors." Times (Lagos), p. 1. On November 16, 1961, a motion was introduced calling the House of Representatives to approve in principle the nationalization of basic industries. On November 17, the Federal Minister of Economic Development said, "the imperialists would try to safeguard their financial interests." Information Sheet, No. 3034/264/61 (New York: Information Division, Nigerian Consulate General, November, 1961). And, on November 29, the House rejected the motion by 132 to 42. The motion had been tabled by Chief Awolowo, Action Group leader and Head of the Opposition. On the occasion, the Federal Finance Minister this time said the "Federal Government . . . did not believe in indiscriminate nationalisation." Information Sheet, No. 3034/274/61 (December, 1961). On April 11, 1964, several years later, the Times (Lagos) carried the following headline: "No Nationalisation Plan, Says Balewa."

127. " A particularly ugly note was the anti-white . . . character the demonstration assumed." Wall Street Journal, February 20, 1961.

128. Daily Express (Lagos), August 19, 1961.

129. Morning Post (Lagos), April 4, 1964, p. 1.

130. J. K. Ladipo, Our War Against Bribery and Corruption ("Crownbird Series No. 12" [Lagos: Federal Information Service, 1957]).

131. AID has been urged to expand the investment guaranty provision of the Mutual Security Act to include coverage of losses sustained by Americans due to a host of nonbusiness risks: e.g., revolution, insurrection, and civil strife. See Ralph I. Straus, Expanding Private Investment for Free World Economic Growth (Washington, D.C.: Department of State, April, 1959), pp. 19-22. At the present time, AID is able to extend insurance to American investors, for projects approved by both governments, against nonconvertibility of capital and annual returns, and against losses due to expropriation.

132. K. D. S. Baldwin, Some Problems of Autochthonous Capital Formation in British West Africa (with particular reference to Western Nigeria) (Paris: Ministère De La France D'Outre-Mer, 1957), p. 58.

133. The Economist (London), November 23, 1963, p. 789.

134. For a list of criticisms of the Nigerian authorities, see West Africa (London), November 30, 1963, p. 1363.

PART III

THE ESTABLISHMENT OF MANUFACTURING

CHAPTER 7 MANUFACTURING IN NIGERIA: ITS ORIENTATION

Part II, in setting the industrial scene, determined the place of modern manufacturing industry in the Nigerian economy. A comprehension of the quality and quantity of the inputs, of the external economies, and of the markets is necessary to ascertain what types of manufacturing activity are suitable for a country, like Nigeria, that is embarking on industrial development. This judgment may be tempered and modified by a knowledge of the government's attitudes and influences, which, particularly in a developing nation, can materially retard or induce the process of industrialization.

Part III will be concerned with manufacturing itself, concluding with an examination of the role of manufacturing in the Nigerian economy, now and in the not-so-distant future. This chapter will present eight case studies--mainly written in early 1962--that represent revealing examples of the opportunities and limitations inherent in the establishing of a manufacturing facility in Nigeria during the 1960's.

THE NATURE OF INDUSTRY

The basic system of classification that will be used to deal with the extent of the existing types of industry (such as textiles and cigarette manufacture) is the one of major locational orientation. Professor Hance in a review of West African industry,[1] having excluded African crafts, classified the location of modern industry by determining whether they were primarily attracted to (1) raw materials, (2) sources of low-cost power, (3) an unusual labor supply, or (4) a specific market. The writer believes that this is a meaningful framework for discussing an economy where manufacturing accounts for so little of the GNP. It is an arrangement that is structured to indicate the nature and *raison d'être* of the relatively little modern manufacturing that is present and to disclose the potentials for manufacturing in Nigeria. A system that divides production goods into, for example, consumer and industrial would not be nearly so suitable or advantageous.

Labor in Nigeria is not the barrier to industry that some may believe it to be (see Chapter 3). But, on the other hand, it is neither the possessor of some unusual skill, nor is it low cost. Therefore, *no* industry has been attracted to Nigeria to base itself specifically on this factor of production as it has in, say, Puerto Rico.

Likewise, a second of the four classes cited above, that of power-oriented industries, so far claims only one Nigerian candidate. Until the end of the decade, when the Niger Dam is completed (see Chapter 4), low-cost power will be restricted to the delta area of the south, a section where natural gas is available. In greater Port Harcourt, the gas has already been used to fuel the ECN's gas-turbine plant at Afam, and a glass plant has been constructed at a site on the Trans-Amadi Industrial Estate. Other factors, including the availability of raw materials and transport facilities, contributed to the decision to locate at Port Harcourt, but the presence of gas was the determining factor.

So it may be stated that, through 1964, the location of manufacturing plants in Nigeria was *primarily* determined either by the (anticipated) existence of a nearby domestic market of sufficient size to consume the plant's production, or by the pull of raw materials to a particular geographical site. However, it is realized that *every* industry requires a market, whether it be at home or abroad. A raw-material-oriented industry like an abattoir may serve a portion of the domestic market, while one such as a tin smelter produces especially for customers overseas.

others in this category--for example, cotton gins--produce for consumers both within <u>and</u> without Nigeria. Thus, though Part III discusses and explains <u>where</u> the various industries exist in Nigeria explicitly, it casts light on <u>why</u> they exist at all in this West African nation.

It was mentioned in Chapter 1 that in 1960 modern manufacturing industry contributed 1.5 per cent (£15.65 million) to the national output. Table 35 supplies a breakdown of this figure, but unfortunately the value added by a few of the categories is not available. They have been estimated for 1957 and, perhaps surprisingly, 52.6 per cent of the universal total for manufacturing falls within the class of market-oriented industry.[2]

POWER-ORIENTED INDUSTRY

The only Nigerian industry, in operation or building, that falls within this class is the Port Harcourt glass plant.

It is the general consensus that the Eastern Region's glass sands are not now suitable for flint glass applications (see Chapter 2). This immediately excludes the pressed or blown glassware and flat (plate) glass sections of the industry from consideration, leaving the third, containers. The users of bottles, especially breweries, do not find the coloring, caused by the metallic oxides present in these sands, objectionable.

In the East, with its natural gas and coal, its glass sands, and the Federation's largest consumption of beer,[3] a ground-breaking ceremony was held at Port Harcourt, on October 21, 1961, for the ENDC's glass container plant. With capital costs of £900,000, the plant commenced operations with a capacity of 12,000 tons per year and 500 employees.[4] This appears to be the best location for the container factory; whether or not it is premature is another question.

Table 35

Value Added by Manufacturing Industries
at 1957 Factor Prices (£ '000)

	1957	1960
Market-Oriented:		
Bakeries	210.0	316.0
Beer and soft drinks	1,683.7	2,800.0
Tobacco	2,100.6	2,190.0
Textiles	377.0	613.0
Perfumes	160.7	n.a.
Plastics	9.2	n.a.
Tire retreading	43.7	n.a.
Furniture and fittings	275.8	n.a.
Cement	372.4	1,160.0
Pre-stressed concrete	41.1	n.a.
Metal products	476.7	n.a.
	5,750.9	
Raw Material-Oriented:		
Oil milling	2,161.6	2,610.0
Canning	12.6	n.a.
Margarine	18.2	18.2
Meat preparation	50.8	n.a.
Soap	662.5	n.a.
Tanning	39.2	40.5
Saw milling	1,531.4	1,809.0
Boat building	102.7	n.a.
Rubber processing	594.8	1,378.0
	5,173.8	
Total	10,924.7	15,650.0

Source: W. Stolper, *et al.*, *Government Expenditures on Goods and Services* (Lagos: Federal Ministry of Economic Development, 1961) (Mimeo.).

In early 1962, total domestic brewing capacity was 5.5 million gallons per year, with another 6-7 million gallons per year under construction or proposed. During 1960, beer imports totaled 7,191,929 gallons;[5] and in 1961, 7,142,000 gallons.[6] If it were assumed that new domestic production would substitute for most of the imported beverage,[7] then Nigerian consumption would continue at a rate of 13 million gallons or 104 million (pint) bottles per year. "The exact number of times a bottle is reused in Nigeria is not known but it may easily be ten times (one-third of the United Kingdom figure)."[8] Thus, it could be argued that so long as Nigeria imported 10 per cent of her beer, she had no need for a glass container industry. "In order to produce bottles locally at a price comparable with that of imported bottles, a plant with a minimum annual output of about fifty million bottles would probably be required."[9]

On June 22, 1961, the New York Times reported that the WNDC and the Amkor Corporation of New York had signed an agreement whereby the latter would construct a $6 million brewery and glass plant in the Western Region. The East, which had been conducting tests on its sands, reacted immediately: Obviously at this stage there was no room in Nigeria for two glass container plants. Because no private enterprise was then ready to join in partnership,[10] it was decided that the ENDC would proceed on a 100 per cent ownership basis. By the time Amkor's bankruptcy became known, it was too late to alter the course of events.[11]

The decision to build a glass container plant having been made, the most appropriate site was selected. The Port Harcourt/Afam sands lie beneath soft, noncompacted soil; the Enugu sands are under a hard, deep overburden. Although both are on the rail line, Port Harcourt is in a better position to serve the Western Region, and any possible export markets in neighboring West African countries. Moreover, imported raw materials, particularly soda ash, are cheaper in Port Harcourt.

The decisive factor, though, was the choice of natural gas over producer gas from Enugu's coal. In manufacturing glass, sand is mixed with lime and soda ash, and heated to 2500-3000° F. to form a homogeneous and noncrystalline mass. Fuel is also required for the feeders (to the bottle-forming machines) and the annealing lehrs. A British engineering firm calculated that the utilization of natural gas would save the plant £23,000 annually.[12]

A German supplier, which made no investment in the plant, has completed an equipment sale, under seemingly liberal terms. To be sure, no reputable private enterprise was willing to invest in a glass manufacturing facility in 1961. If it were not for regional rivalry, neither the West nor the East would have committed themselves to what may prove to be a premature effort.

Postscript: In April, 1964, the plant's general manager appealed to the federal government for a protective tariff on imported bottles--his operation was heavily in the red. Then, during the national strike of June, 1964, the supply of natural gas was shut off by Shell-BP. As a result, the plant's two furnaces froze. It will be a costly job to get them working once more.

RAW-MATERIAL-ORIENTED INDUSTRY

Approximately half of all manufacturing in Nigeria may be placed in the category of raw-material-oriented industry; this section will examine four of these industries: oil-seed milling, tin smelting, soap manufacture, and food canning. The list ranges from the abattoirs in the Northern Region, which engage in meat packing, to the processing of timber in the south.[13] The outstanding example of the latter is UAC's African Timber and Plywood Company, whose sawmill and plywood/veneer plant at Sapele is one of West Africa's largest industrial enterprises.

Both the meat-packing plant and the sawmill were established near the raw material in order to lower transportation costs by reducing bulk and weight. For example, in being converted to a more suitable form, half the weight of a log is lost. By locating the mill near the forest, "it pays to use small inferior trees and less popular species whose value as logs would not support the cost of transporting them to a [more] distant sawmill."[14]

Another factor militating for location of a plant near the supply of raw materials is that of perishability. A typical case in West Africa is the processing of palm fruit. Of course, this eliminates the export of waste matter. But, most importantly, extraction of the oil locally is made necessary by the rise in the percentage of free fatty acid once the fruit has been cut from the tree.[15]

Much of Nigeria's industry is raw-material-oriented because up to 55 per cent of Nigeria's exports of primary products require some processing, prior to overseas shipment (see Table 21, Chapter 5). Since independence, tin smelting at Jos has been introduced; a sugar refinery is being erected near Jebba; and a petroleum refinery is near completion in the Port Harcourt area. Not only will the value added accrue to Nigeria rather than to one of the industrial nations of the North Atlantic, but each enterprise, hopefully, will eventually earn foreign exchange.

Oil Seed Milling

Table 2 of Chapter 2 listed eight crops grown primarily for export. Of these, groundnuts, palm produce, soya beans, and benniseed are particularly valuable for the vegetable oils obtained from them. And 15 per cent or more of the value of the cotton crop may be allocated to its seed (see Table 21, Chapter 5). In 1962 there was no commercial milling of palm kernels, soya beans, cotton seed, or benniseed in Nigeria. Besides palm-oil extraction, only groundnuts were processed locally on a commercial basis--in four Kano mills, and one in Zaria.

The family of oil seeds does not fit any of the usual criteria for raw materials processed *in situ*.

For example, "The mere process of converting decorticated groundnuts into oil and cake does not result in any reduction of quantity. Apart from an insignificant process loss, the whole nut is converted into oil and cake."[16] And this, in turn, leads to new transport problems. For one, the NRC will have to provide tank cars if milling in the North is to develop on a large scale. Otherwise, the current and cumbersome practice of shipping the oil in 44-gallon drums to the ports, where it is stored in bulk-oil plants and then pumped into ocean-going vessels, will have to suffice.[17]

The picture with respect to the criterion of weight-saving would change, of course, if a local market for the cake existed. At present, the demand for animal feeds, of which the cake could be an important ingredient, is negligible. This, in addition to the technical problems involved, has so far prohibited the introduction of a palm-kernel processing plant in the south; and also has inhibited the expansion of the groundnut milling industry in the north.

The Northern Region Government is especially anxious to introduce groundnut cake into the cattle diet for a couple of reasons: (1) "We lose 80,000 tons of phosphates from the soil each year. Groundnut cake as a feed would help."[18] (2) "The country is carrying about as many cattle as it can. The biggest change required is to put more weight on the existing cattle."[19]

Another local end use for the groundnut oil mill's high-protein residue is groundnut flour. Zaria's Northern Oilseeds Processing and Development Mill in 1960, on an experimental basis, supplied flour at cost to UNICEF in Vom (near Jos). The flour was mixed in the proportion of three-to-one with dried milk powder, and supplied to babies and pregnant women. Since then, a commercial concern, U.K.'s Cow and Gate, has taken over the Vom operation, and joined a plant in Mushin (near Lagos) as a manufacturer of a groundnut flour-based baby food.[20]

With respect to the overseas market, the large, high-pressure, modern mills in Europe and America can more effectively compete in the world market than can the lower-pressure Kano expellers. This is because the former have been designed to receive oil seeds the year round. Thus, they can switch from one oil seed, such as soya beans, to another, such as copra, within wide limits.[21]

In addition to the size of the market, and supply of labor and capital, the North faces a special problem in its drive to enlarge this industry. It is one that has been raised in Chapter 4: the limited availability of water. A plant that processes 20,000 tons per year of decorticated nuts uses approximately 500,000 tons per year of water.[22]

It is against this background that the North expected a £3 million new investment in oilseed crushing during the period 1962-68. The Northern Region Government was to provide 20 per cent of the capital required for plants to be erected in Maiduguri, Gusau, Makurdi, Zaria, and perhaps Gombe.[23] The government anticipated that 25 per cent of the groundnuts produced would be processed on a commercial basis in 1962. Five years hence the percentage would rise to 42 per cent of a larger crop. Likewise, 40 per cent of the North's soya beans and 70 per cent of its cotton seed would be crushed locally by 1967.[24]

This case, in summary, represents the retarding effect of an insufficient demand for by-products of an industry. Also, it is a reminder that an adequate supply of water near the raw material cannot be taken for granted, explicitly in the Northern Region.

<u>Tin Smelting</u>

From the early part of this century, when the Jos tin fields were first exploited, the mining companies have operated ore treatment plants. The washing and dressing operations enable tin concentrates of 74 per cent tin, after drying, to be bagged and shipped to Wales and Liverpool for smelting.[25] But until March 24, 1961, the ultimate reduction in weight and bulk was not achieved, for no tin smelting was conducted in Nigeria. Due to the inadequate power and the long distance from the Enugu coal, which was required for smelting and/or power, this was always considered to be uneconomic.

In 1960, the appraisal changed when a Portuguese, who held a patent for an electrometallurgical process and who had successfully operated plants in Portugal and Brazil, announced that he would set up Nigeria Embel Tin Smelting Company in Jos. Shortly thereafter, the announcement was issued that the Makeri Smelting Company, which is associated with Consolidated Tin Smelters in the U.K., was coming to Jos too. The basic question that arose was whether or not there was sufficient raw material output to supply the furnaces of the two smelters. In the case of Embel, a subsidiary power problem also developed.

Embel with an initial capital investment of £250,000 had by November 1, 1961, installed three of eight furnaces, each capable of a monthly consumption rate of 180 tons of ore when working three shifts per day, seven days per week. Each furnace required a power capacity of 250 kw. With NESCO, despite its new dams, barely able to fulfill its contractual obligations to the mines field due to a shortage of water, Embel was able to obtain only enough electricity for one furnace.[26]

Makeri invested £500,000 in its coal-using plant, which started in early 1962. Each of its two furnaces, one being a spare, could handle 20 tons of ore per day or 600 tons per month. At full production Makeri needed only 100 kw. of power capacity.

With Makeri shipping to Liverpool and Embel to New York, it would appear that all, including the Nigerian Government which collected royalties of £1/13s./-d. per ton of metal,[27] would have been satisfied.

If it is assumed that Embel could obtain the necessary electricity, then six of its eight furnaces would need (180 x 12 x 6) 12,960 tons of ore a year. Makeri eventually planned to have three furnaces in operation requiring (600 x 12 x 3) 21,600 tons per year. But, Nigeria's total annual production seldom exceeded 12,000 tons!

Embel could, with its two remaining furnaces, resmelt the slag to obtain all but 2 per cent of the original 74 per cent, and produce tin with a minimum purity of 99.9 per cent. Makeri could not match these standards.[28]

In an industrial competition, strange to the Nigerian scene, the seemingly more efficient process might stumble. Jos is the correct site for a cassiterite-oriented industry; but it does not offer either sufficient raw material for the total plant capacity, or the secondary attraction of plentiful, steady power.

Postscript: Embel closed down in January, 1963, declaring itself bankrupt.

Soap Manufacturing

For centuries, soap, made in the villages from palm oil and wood-ash, has been known to Nigeria. "On 11th April, 1923, the first soap factory to be built in Nigeria was founded by a subsidiary of Lever Brothers, known as the West African Soap Company, on the site at Apapa, Lagos, which it still occupies."[29] By 1950 this plant was one of Africa's largest soap works.[30]

Soap manufacturing, like food canning, is an agricultural, raw-material-oriented industry that is not limited to just the first stage of processing, the usual case in Nigeria. The canning operations, though, have not been nearly as successful as have the large manufacturers of soap in Kano, Aba, and Apapa (see below).

Aba is situated on the railroad in the center of the palm-oil area, is the center of a road distribution area, and has plentiful labor. It is at Aba, adjacent to a river that supplies extremely soft water, that Lever Brothers started construction of its second Nigerian soap plant in 1956. Manufacturing soap only since April, 1958, this plant's annual production of 10,000 tons now usually exceeds the Apapa plant by 43 per cent.[31]

In the East, Lever Brothers was faced with high pressure competition from Paterson, Zochonis and Company's (P,Z) Associated Industries, formerly Alagbon Industries, and P. B. Nicholas'[32] International Equitable Association, who together produced about 7,000 tons per year. Parenthetically, it might be noted that besides Lever's Apapa Plant, the Paterson, Zochonis plant is the only other one in Nigeria operating a palm-kernel expeller unit. Also, within a 50-mile radius of Aba, there were dozens of small backyard soap makers who produced a few hundred cases per month.

Lever Brothers dealt with a wholesaler plus two to three African distributors in every major town. And it had a "marketing mix" that included newspaper and screen advertising, and demonstration vans in the village markets. So Lever Brothers felt it was able to meet competition from Paterson, Zochonis and from Nicholas. It was primarily concerned about its backyard competitors who underpriced the major companies.

Among the many ingredients the major soap companies import are perfumes, colors, salt, and, most important of all, caustic soda, which is also required by the small producers. For years, a 10 per cent excise tax had been levied on all soap production. But, as a practical matter, only the big producers had to bear this ex works cost. This was the situation in late 1961 when the federal government abolished the excise and in its stead instituted a £35 per ton (about 150 per cent _ad valorem_) import duty on caustic soda.[33] Thus, the government expected to come out even, while the import duty was spread on all. Lever Brothers had every reason to be pleased. With economies of scale in its favor, supplemented by the export of 82 per cent glycerol (crude glycerine), a by-product, to the U.K., Lever Brothers would probably be able to do better than most of its competition, especially the smaller enterprises. In fact, it lowered prices in the second half of 1961.

Government appeared to be aiding modern expatriate industry rather than indigenous rural industry. This is a case, then, of government, and not the market place, determining which producers would be the beneficiary of the consumer preference for a low-price, bar soap.

Food Canning

The genesis of Ibadan's cannery is associated with cocoa. In 1944 a cocoa farm survey in the Western Region revealed that 10 per cent of the trees had been damaged by swollen shoot disease, a virus transmitted by the mealy bug. It was decided to attack the problem by cutting down the affected trees. Failure of the cutting program led, in 1950, to "a determined attempt . . . to close off the area of mass infection, 479,000 acres."[34]

As a substitute cash crop the government suggested that the farmers in the affected area grow citrus trees. During World War I they had been planted in the West. But with no orchards, and no marketing arrangements, the farmers, who practiced shifting cultivation, left them behind when they moved on. This time, in the 1950's, the government hoped the outcome would be different. To obtain the cooperation of the farmers, it agreed to provide a market for the fruit, the market being a wholly-owned WNDC cannery.

So it was that Ibadan's Lafia Canning Factory opened in 1954 at a fixed investment of £450,000,[35] and with an annual capacity of 20,000 tons of fruit per year. Production exceeded 3,000 tons in only one year, and in recent years even this seemed unobtainable:

1957-58	2,000 tons
1958-59	1,400 tons
1959-60	3,000 tons
1960-61	1,500 tons
1961-62	less than 1,500 tons.[36]

This poor showing is a result of two factors. First, from an input standpoint, the factory was erected too soon. Most of the orchards that were planted in the 1950's were not to mature until 1964-65. A similar situation held for pineapple (juice, pieces, and slices), which had been added to the line. Thus, the raw-material supply was not assured. Second, the farmers were provided with a market, but not Lafia. The Nigerian home market appeared to be insufficiently large to absorb more than 5 per cent of the total plant capacity.[37] And in the international market, Nigeria did not seem able to compete with the United States, Australia, Israel, South Africa, etc. These countries had home consumption rates that exceeded 70 per cent and could afford to lower prices for export.[38] Furthermore, Nigeria had to import her cans and sugar, thereby paying freight twice.[39]

This white elephant might eventually see better times. Cans, labels, gum, and sugar will be available in Nigeria; and mangoes, guava (jelly, shells, and cheese), and gooseberries will be additions to the product mix. Moreover, the supply picture could straighten out; and the home market will increase. Yet the future remains clouded. In 1958 South Africa offered large quantities of citrus on the world market. This led to the abandonment of many of the Western Region's trees. The orchards could be re-opened in two or three years, but history might very well repeat itself. Nigeria's pineapples and grapefruits appear to have a more favorable reception abroad than do her oranges and lemons. The latter, according to U.K. soft-drink firms, suffer a loss of flavor in processing.[40] Finally, the Western Region Government may lack the necessary initiative to seize opportunities as they come. For instance, a request by the factory manager in 1959 for equipment to emboss "Made in Nigeria" on the cans, as required by some prospective customers, had not been complied with in late 1961. Even more inexplicably, the adjacent WNDC-owned-and-operated Pepsi-Cola plant, maker of Mirinda orange soda, imports all its orange concentrates from the United States.[41]

The canning of meat by Nigeria Canning Company, Ltd., of Kano was also encountering difficulties. The plant opened in 1955 with an investment of £100,000. Corned beef, jollof rice with beef, groundnut soup, and groundnut stew with guinea fowl were packed and sold under the "Crescent" label. The jollof rice seemed to be well-liked in the North, but is a "dead loss." "It's not what they like, but what they can afford."[42]

A substantial volume of business had been obtained with the Nigerian Police Force, and the Nigerian and Ghanaian armies. But in September, 1961, Ghana cut off all imports from the cannery. The situation was further complicated by a strike, and an apparent shortage of beef. Word had reached the Fulani herdsmen that a Texan was going to fly meat to Lagos (see Chapter 4) with the result that shipments to the abattoirs were being held back as they waited for the price to rise. Management hoped to weather the storm. Soluble extracts were being supplied to Oxo for gravy concentrates; and soups, mixed vegetables, tomatoes, etc., were being canned on a trial basis.

Food canning is a raw-material industry that has no intermediary processing: There is only one step to the finished product. Still, in the food-canning industry, manufacturing costs were raised because the factories were established in Nigeria before the complementary industries. Also, raw-material supply and consumer demand--domestic and foreign--present difficult hurdles to successful operation. The former has been variable, and the latter ineffectual.

MARKET-ORIENTED INDUSTRY

If raw-material-oriented industries have accounted for approximately half of all manufacturing in Nigeria, the same can be said for market-oriented industry. Market-oriented industries cover the gamut from the two asbestos-cement plants at Ikeja and Emene to the Nigerian Tobacco Company's three cigarette factories at Ibadan, Zaria, and Port Harcourt. The list is a lengthy one because it includes a multitude of assembly plants: for bicycles, motor vehicle bodies, radios and television sets, umbrellas, etc.

Often the rationale for locating near the population conurbations is the inverse of that governing the siting of raw-material-processing facilities. Bakeries produce a product that is more perishable after manufacturing, furniture is more bulky than sawn timber, and bottling plants add liquid weight to a fragile container.

The sawmill and the tin smelter industries are export industries based on the raw material: forests and tin ores. The waste is removed prior to transport. On the other hand, many market-oriented industries are selected from a country's import list. Not gainsaying perishability, bread is more bulky than flour, and thus would encounter higher transportation costs than the raw material. Assembly operations may be carried on near the market for the same reason. Also, as with the petroleum refinery, any value added in Nigeria will accrue to her, and foreign exchange might be saved.

Another consideration, which cannot be ignored, is one enacted by government. Import duties and quotas may affect the ultimate decision of whether or not to establish a manufacturing facility.[43]

The two market-oriented industries that will be discussed require, among other factors, large inputs of capital. Cement milling and textile manufacturing involve, necessarily, a large portion of the funds available to Nigeria for industrial investment.

Cement Milling

Portland cement is mainly made from limestone and clay, to a lesser extent gypsum, and the by-products of other industries--such as slag from a steel mill.[44]

Assuming that a suitable deposit of limestone is available within a reasonable distance, due to cement's low value per unit weight, there is a strong desire to produce it in, or near, the market. Also, since a very large amount of large equipment is required to achieve the necessary economies of scale to make this undertaking feasible, the adequacy of the domestic market is essential. The rated capacity of a single kiln of Nkalagu (near Enugu) equals the "annual imports [of cement] into the four territories of Commonwealth West Africa"[45] prior to the last war. Thus it was not until 1956, when cement imports had reached 488,600 tons, that a Nigerian cement factory commenced operations. This was NEMCO's cement clinker[46] plant in Port Harcourt, which shut down after producing only 300 tons.[47]

NEMCO imported everything: clinker, bags, and gypsum. Therefore, it fell to the Nigerian Cement Company, Ltd., whose mill opened on December 20, 1957, at Nkalagu, to be the first domestically based cement factory. The company's capital structure consisted of £1.75 million equity and £0.5 million in debentures. Of the £2.25 million total, the Eastern Region and federal governments contributed 75.5 per cent. Operating twenty-four hours per day, seven days per week, the first 330-foot long rotary kiln was able to produce 100,000 tons per year, or about 20 per cent of Nigeria's 1957 import of this product.[48]

This is a case of raw material, fuel, and a large segment of the market all being juxtaposed. Coal comes from Enugu 32 miles away, power from the Oji River Station 60 miles distant, limestone deposits are at Nkalagu, and 8-mile branches to the main Enugu-Abakaliki road and Port Harcourt-Kaduna rail line, which connect the mill with the Eastern Region and much of the Northern Region markets, have been constructed.

During 1960 the capacity of the plant was more than doubled to 230,000 tons at a cost of £1.5 million, all financed out of profits. And at the end of 1961 the decision was made by the board of directors to once again double output. By mid-1965 the plant's four kilns will be able to turn out 450,000 tons per year. The third kiln, at least, was to be financed out of retained earnings.[49]

In late 1961, the mill was shipping 40 per cent of its output, all by rail, to the Northern Region.[50] Part of this figure could be attributed to the re-opening of the NEMCO clinker plant in Port Harcourt under new management. Producing 35,000-40,000 tons per year, it was able to undersell Nkalagu's "Niger-cem" not only in Port Harcourt, but also in the area north to Aba.[51]

Neither NEMCO nor Nkalagu is able to supply the large Lagos-Western Region market. The void has been filled by the West African Portland Cement Company, Ltd.'s[52] £4.5 million mill at Ewekoro on the Abeokuta-Lagos road. The site is adjacent to raw material deposits, near several large markets to which it is connected by road and rail, and 50 miles from Lagos' Ijora Power Station. Using an advanced, more expensive design than Nkalagu, the Company hoped to cut its fuel-oil requirements by a third. The single kiln was rated at 200,000 tons per year, but in 1961 fell 25 per cent short of this due to technical difficulties that arose subsequent to the December 4, 1960, opening.

In addition to a 1960 domestic production of 160,000 tons of cement, Nigeria imported 626,486 tons.[53] The corresponding quantities for 1961 were approximately 415,000 tons, and 477,000 tons.[54] Although imports decreased by 150,000 tons, total consumption increased by more than 11 per cent.

If it was assumed that the number of construction contracts let at the time of independence was unusually high, an annual growth rate of 10 per cent might have been hypothesized for cement consumption. Then, consumption of 1,306,000 tons in 1965 was to exceed domestic capacity, planned as of 1962, by about 600,000 tons.

The North consumed 17-19 per cent of the 1960 total, or 150,000 tons.[55] Assuming that the North maintained this proportion of the total, after subtracting 40 per cent of Nkalagu's production, the Northern Region would face a deficit of 55,000 tons in 1965. The Sardauna of Sokoto had, in many public statements, promised his people a cement mill. What on the surface looked like an example of regional metooism could be economically justified, especially if a Northern mill with a capacity of 100,000 tons per year were able to supply some of the requirements of the Niger Dam project.[56]

As was stated in Chapter 2, good cement-type limestone deposits exist in the Northern Region at Sokoto, Ashaka, Igumale, and Jakura. Igumale is a continuation of the Nkalagu seam. Jakura, at least prior to the completion of the Niger Dam, is not well situated with respect to power, fuel, and markets, and no road or rail line connects it to centers of population. The choice of site thus devolved upon either Sokoto's or Ashaka's limestone. The market should determine the actual plant location. Yet it was announced in late 1962 that the mill would be constructed near Sokoto. More than economic considerations seemed to have been involved.

Besides a hand-loom center and two small tanneries, Sokoto has no industry. Furthermore, it is not on the railroad, being 136 miles to the northwest of Gusau. Although Ashaka is on the railroad's Maiduguri extension, it does not serve a market of sufficient size at this time either. The mill should (1) serve the leading industrial centers of Kaduna, Kano, and Jos, and the developing industries of the northeast, (2) supply cement to the Niger Dam project, and (3) have reasonable access to coal. Selection of a site near Kafanchan, the junction of the Port Harcourt-Kaduna rail line and the northeast rail extension, would probably have been the most advantageous one.

Cement manufacture from local limestone has been extremely successful in the Eastern Region, and appears destined for good fortune in the West and North too. In this case, regional rivalry is leading to the rapid development of a major industry in many sections of the nation; fortunately, there have been sound economic justifications for this expansion.

Postscript: Supplier-financed cement clinker plants at Koko and Calabar will soon join the two in operation at Apapa. Whether the former are so justified is now being debated.

Textile Manufacturing

In 1954, a factory with 1,620 spindles and 60 looms in Mushin (near Lagos) was the only spinning mill in Nigeria. At that time a 50-loom mill in Kano used imported yarn.[57] Eight years later, in each region, large integrated mills were in operation, under construction, or proposed. An industry that is traditionally associated with industrial development was taking root in all sections of Nigeria.

In some respects, namely, raw-material supply and market potential, textile manufacturing seems ideally suited to Nigeria. During the early 1960's 5 per cent of her export earnings could be attributed to raw cotton shipments; and 7.4 per cent of Nigeria's consumer expenditures in 1960 were for clothing, exclusive of footwear (see Chapter 5). On the other hand, although low wages are typical, output per capita is too. Therefore, considering the supervision required, labor costs are not low. Presumably, this situation will improve as the many training schemes make their impress (see Chapter 3).

Nigeria imported 211 million sq. yds. of cotton fabrics during 1960, and 245 million sq. yds. in 1961.[58] In the latter year, domestic capacity of the mills at Mushin, Kano, and Kaduna amounted to 28 million sq. yds., only about 10 per cent of imports plus Nigerian capacity. This great dependence on imports was rapidly changing. The Kaduna mill's expansion to 41.6 million sq. yds. was scheduled for completion in April, 1962, and the Ikeja mill, near Lagos, was to open in mid-1962 with an annual capacity of 18 million sq. yds. In addition, arrangements were completed by the Eastern Region Government for a 7.5 million sq. yd. mill in Aba and a 20 million sq. yd. mill in Onitsha; and the North anticipated two new mills in Kaduna by 1965 with a total capacity of

15 million sq. yds. Thus, total Nigerian capacity in that year was forecast for 102 million sq. yds., almost a fourfold increase in just four years. This import substitution[59] made available about 8,000 jobs in the industrial sector.

The first large-scale spinning and weaving plant opened with Nigerian capital at Mushin in 1948. This was the Nigerian Spinning Company's mill. A few years later the Northern Region Ministry of Trade and Industry set up and administered the Kano Citizens Trading Company as a pilot scheme. In 1959 the Kano weaving mill was transferred to the control of the NNDC. Both the Mushin and Kano mills produce drills, and the latter also weaves cords--in part from Nigerian yarn.[60]

In November, 1957, Kaduna Textiles Ltd. started production under the technical management of David Whitehead and Sons (Nigeria) Ltd., a subsidiary of a well-established Lancashire company. Through 1961 the mill concentrated on spinning and weaving baft, an unbleached cloth, 90 per cent of which it sold to the northern market.[61] Although baft was sold in the south, primarily to northerners who have moved there, and for maps and pocketing too, it appeared that the market for baft lay in the Northern Region.

The Ikeja mill (owned by the Nigerian Textile Mills Ltd.) was to commence production in 1962 of a variety of cotton goods, varying from bafts to printed piece goods.[62] Unlike the Kaduna mill, which gained five years of experience in the relatively simple spinning and weaving of baft before proceeding with bleaching and finishing operations, the Ikeja mill was to make finished shirtings and prints immediately. The nature of the difficulties that would be encountered will be treated below. The Kano and Mushin mills had bleached and dyed their fabrics, but heretofore no printing had been done in Nigeria. Since the Kaduna mill satisfied most of the North's needs for baft, the Ikeja mill, presumably, found it necessary to carry its production through the more complicated operations. Training problems aside, this was compatible with its location in an area that customarily purchases prints.

That greater skills are involved in the establishment of a printing facility, which require a longer period of training, was evident to Scheur Textile Consultants, Inc., of New York, which was acting in an advisory capacity to South Carolina's Indian Head Mills, Inc. In conjunction with the Eastern Region Government, Indian Head was scheduled to start construction of an integrated mill in Aba during 1962. The Scheur report[63] recommended that the plant should commence with the spinning and weaving of grey baft and drills. Then, following a step-by-step approach, the plant would progress to printing and dyeing, but not until after some experience had been gained with the basic operations of spinning and weaving. The Eastern Region Government retorted that there was a very limited market for bafts, which the Kaduna and Ikeja mills could meet. The result was that the Indian Head proposal had to be reworked to include capability for bleaching, finishing, dyeing, and printing.

Besides the labor difficulties involved, the integrated mill engaged in printing would have to deal with two other major problems. First, it was not certain that the Dutch wax prints favored in the south, especially in the Eastern Region, could then be produced from the length of staple and quality of cotton grown in Nigeria. Second, the prints are very susceptible to changes in style. It could be a case of either not having enough if the design is a good one, or maintaining an unwanted inventory if the print does not catch the public's fancy. Because the wax blocks used in this process produce a blurred result, they are often considered to be bad prints outside of West Africa. Therefore, these designs cannot readily be disposed of elsewhere.[64]

While discussions were carried on with the American group, the East was simultaneously negotiating with a British-Dutch group. It was decided that the Onitsha plant would also have a printworks. The four member firms that comprise the international textile group known as A.D.A.T.I.G.[65] had many years of experience in the techniques of producing for, and marketing prints to, Nigerians. Soon A.D.A.T.I.G.

announced that it would begin by importing unbleached cloth for bleaching and printing.[66] By use of this whipsaw tactic, whereby the Europeans and Americans were played off one against the other, the Eastern Region will get two fully integrated mills. It is not unlikely that each group thought it would be the only mill in the region.[67]

Postscript: Both mills are under construction in 1964.

A mere citation of Nigerian capacity for the manufacture of cotton piece goods, vis-a-vis imports, masks the pitfalls that face a new mill that would try to do too much too soon. Government in its haste to encourage industrial development should neither overlook, nor obscure, these dangers. With respect to the Eastern Region textile development it is possible that this is what has occurred. For the present case calls attention to the risk of introducing technology beyond the capability of the plant's labor force.

THE MULTI-ORIENTED STEEL MILL

"It is the conviction of the Federation of Nigeria that the establishment of an integrated iron-steel plant would provide the optimum launching pad for the economic development of the nation."[68] The steel mill is a subject that is broached with the same fervor by Nigerians as the dam across the Niger. More than prestige seems to be involved; it is a matter of self-reliance, of self-realization on a national scale. Nigeria will get a steel mill as she has a dam.[69] What the total cost will be cannot yet be determined, although the steel facility is the third biggest single item of expenditure, after the Niger Dam and roads, in Nigeria's six-year development plan.[70]

Steel manufacture is dependent on so many permissive factors, from availability of suitable ore and fuel to the size and structure of the market, that it is not possible to place this complex industry in a specific orientational category. Therefore, it is being treated separately.

Normally, when one thinks of iron and steel, a blast furnace comes to mind. To manufacture one ton of pig iron, the furnace receives two tons of iron ore, a half-ton of limestone, and one ton of coke, i.e., bituminous coal after the volatile matter has been driven off. Nigeria has suitable limestone at Itobe on the Niger River, 89 miles north of Onitsha,[71] extensive medium-grade iron deposits on the Agbaja Plateau in Kabba Province, 28 miles from Lokoja, and low quality, sub-bituminous coal at Enugu (see Chapter 2). The ostensible lack of a coking-quality coal has until lately seemed to preclude the manufacture of steel in Nigeria. But recent technological advances in the field of metallurgy may have altered this conclusion.

Before examining the two smelting processes under consideration, it might be well to note the extent of the market in Nigeria for fabricated steel products. Table 36 below is a tabulation of most of the iron and steel manufactured goods imported by Nigeria in 1960 and 1962. Two points stand out. First, the total annual use of iron and steel in 1962 was less than half the output of a modern blast furnace in America. Second, with the exception of corrugated galvanized sheets, the list is spread over many shapes, sizes, and forms. The large item, railway rails and accessories, may be accounted for by the Maiduguri railway extension, which, together with the track relaying programs, will be completed in 1965.

If railroad accessories and rails are excluded, the consumption growth rate in 1961 and 1962 averaged approximately 2 per cent. Assuming a greater annual growth rate of 4 per cent in 1963 and following years, an increase of 30 per cent (from 1960) in Nigeria's use of iron and steel products would be attained by 1968. Even this increment would lead to only a relatively small total. Still, in 1961 prices, imports of 192,000 tons of iron and steel products would entail the expenditure of about £14.5 million in foreign exchange.

Table 36

Nigerian Imports of Manufactured Iron and Steel Intermediate Goods* (tons)

	1960	1962
Joists, girders, angles, shapes, etc.	44,089	40,152
Pipes, tubes, and fittings	21,629	28,298
Corrugated sheets, galvanized	37,987	29,625
Other sheets and plates	6,035	15,378
Rods, bar, strip, frames, etc.	5,474	12,324
Railway rails and accessories	18,584	16,894
Miscellaneous, e.g., cables, structural parts, etc.	14,313	8,642
Total	148,111	151,513

*Excludes nails, bolts, screws, tools, safes, axes, household utensils, containers, etc.

Sources: Nigeria Trade Summary (Lagos: Federal Government Printer, December, 1960, and December, 1962), pp. 15-19 and pp. 95-102.

The Westinghouse report recommends Onitsha as the site for a steel mill. Located on the Niger River, it is situated on the border between the Eastern and Mid-Western Regions. From a resource standpoint Onitsha is 66 miles to the west of Enugu's collieries, 120 miles to the north of the Afam gas field, and 12 miles to the east of Nigeria's main lignite deposit to which it will shortly be connected by the bridge across the Niger. The limestone and iron ore are both situated near the river, so comparatively cheap river transport may be utilized. And, finally, Onitsha has both plentiful water and labor.

In 1959, an analysis of the regional destination of 80 per cent of the imported iron and steel products was made. Only 10 per cent of the sales were made in the North, while 33 per cent were made to the Eastern Region, and the remainder to Lagos plus the Western Region.[72] Since then the demand in the East has continued to increase. In 1960, Williams and Williams, fabricator of steel door and window frames, and venetian blinds, commenced operations in Port Harcourt. And, in 1961, construction started on the Nigersteel Company's rolling mill at Emene (near Enugu). For the present, this mill is dependent on scrap.

As with cement, the availability of raw materials dictates a general area in which the proposed steel mill may be located. In this instance, the size of the market and the location of the raw materials determine that no more than one mill may be economically constructed. Since the northern market will be accessible via the Niger River and the railroad spur at Baro, and Lagos and its hinterland will be connected by water transport, Onitsha appears to be fairly well positioned from a market point of view.

Two questions remain: What type of plant is suitable for Nigeria's resources and market? How much will it cost, and how will it be financed? In early 1962 the National Economic Council was considering the Westinghouse proposal, while the Eastern Region was continuing negotiations with West Germany's industrial group of Didier-Ferrostaal.

Westinghouse, et al. proposed the use of the Strategic-Udy Process, which they claim can produce good pig iron from almost any ore containing more than 33 per cent iron. Furthermore, neither scrap nor coke is required. The total plant is to include a 12-foot diameter by 350-foot long rotary kiln to remove impurities, two 34-foot diameter electric reduction furnaces, a basic oxygen furnace to convert the pig to steel, a continuous casting machine to form billets and slabs for subsequent rolling, and two 25,000 kw. turbine generators. Capable of producing 97,000 tons in 1967 and 143,000 tons per year by 1972, the layout, exclusive of housing, training, and mining operations, would require an investment of $72.5 million.[73] Two factors stand out: (1) $64 million in foreign exchange would be required for the steel mill alone; and (2) the Strategic-Udy Process had not been commercially operated.[74]

The Ferrostaal proposal envisaged a small blast furnace at Enugu, about 10 feet in diameter, that would have an annual output of 100,000 tons. Steel would be made by the oxygen top blowing process with L.D. converters. The capital costs for the foregoing, plus a rolling mill, power station, coking plant, and lime kilns, was estimated to be $63.25 million.[75] Besides the use of coke, this plant would require the importation of refractory materials, and coking additives. The scheme presupposed that nearby coal could be transformed into metallurgical coke by the addition of pitch, an oil refinery product.

In January, 1960, the British coke-oven builder, Simon-Carves, Ltd., and the Shelton Iron and Steel Company had begun eighteen months of testing three charges of Ekulu coal. The final report to the Nigerian Coal Corporation stated, "While the general quality of the coke is inferior to that normally used in blast furnace practice, it is considered that a blast furnace could be operated with this coke. . . . Some improvement in the quality of the coke will be expected using a blend containing freshly mined coal."[76] The report makes no mention of costs.[77]

Nigeria, sooner or later, will become a steel producer. But a precipitate decision could be costly in more ways than one. It would not seem advisable for Nigeria to be the first to test a new process, since she is more vulnerable than many to any difficulties that might occur.

Nigerian attitudes toward development dictate that a steel mill will be constructed in their country, probably in the second half of this decade. Whether it is an appropriate choice for so large an expenditure of scarce development funds seems doubtful. But more specific information, in the realm of both costs and technology, is required before such a determination can intelligently be made.

SUMMARY AND CONCLUSIONS

In determining the nature of the modern manufacturing extant in the Federation of Nigeria, it was found that about half of the total falls within the classification of (domestic) market-oriented, and about half within the classification of raw-material-oriented, industry. This breakdown excludes the proposed multi-oriented steel mill and the power-oriented glass plant. As it turns out, because of the present status of Nigeria's labor force and sources of power, the industries that are serving foreign markets are associated with raw materials. However, the converse does not hold. For example, margarine, wooden boats, soap, and processed meat--all raw-material-oriented manufactures--are purchased by Nigerians.

The eight cases and supporting material that have been presented in this chapter point up some of the problems that exist in establishing industry in Nigeria during the 1960's. The industries considered were chosen because they depict each of three categories that are represented by modern manufacturing, because they are located in different sections of Nigeria, and because they illustrate the major obstacles that must be overcome, while at the same time pointing up the basic attractions that led, or will lead, to their establishment.

The problems range from a lack of demand for the industry's by-product (oil seed mills), to a lack of demand for the main product under consideration (food canning); from insufficient raw material supply (tin smelter), to an inability to meet the price and quality of the imported item (glass bottle plant). Concomitantly, advantages also stand out. These include raw materials located near the market (cement kilns and steel mill), and raw materials domestically available (soap manufacture, textile mills, and steel mill).

Even in the positive instances danger has either narrowly been skirted or remains in the background. Government is the prime mover behind the steel mill project, vide, the development plan; and it entered the picture with vital effect in the soap case by helping the large expatriate plants. Obversely, the textile case pointed up the ill effect of government pressure on the over-eager investor; the Aba mill's labor force may well be overextended. The Northern Region's cement kiln is a result of regional rivalry. This is a competition that may not always have sanguinary results, witness the East's glass plant. Furthermore, economic factors alone do not appear to account for the cement plant's location near Sokoto. Finally, equipment sales made by means of supplier financing will bring smokestacks to Nigeria; they often will not, unfortunately, further industrial--and hence economic--development.

Footnotes to Chapter 7

1. William A. Hance, "West African Industry: An Analysis of Locational Orientation," Journal of International Affairs, Vol. 15, No. 1 (1961), pp. 29-41.

2. It will be noted that the washing, sorting, and concentrating of mineral ores, viz., cassiterite and coal, is excluded from the list. If they were included, the tables would have been turned.

3. "Easterners are drinking most of the beer in Nigeria." (Interview with H. Hansel, Technical Manager, Nigerian Breweries, Aba.)

4. Interview with James T. Daniel, General Manager, Industrial and Commercial Division, ENDC, Aba.

5. Nigeria Trade Summary (December, 1960), p. 8.

6. Digest of Statistics, p. 32.

7. The predominantly Moslem federal government will probably further increase the tariff or impose a quota on beer imports to conserve foreign exchange.

8. UAC, Statistical and Economic Review (September, 1959), p. 37.

9. Ibid. This analysis has been simplified by omitting the lesser demand for bottles (of a different size) by the soft-drink bottling plants.

10. Ball Brothers Co., Inc., of Muncie, Indiana, wanted more time to search for a silica satisfactory to produce flint glass.

11. Arrangements had been concluded with a West German firm for machinery credits and technical assistance in setting up the plant and a brewery.

12. A. G. Eadie, Report on the Establishment of a Glass Container Industry in Eastern Nigeria, prepared by Industrial and Process Engineering Consultants, London, July, 1961.

13. The reader will note that the Appendix comprises a listing--including where possible, the capitalization, number of employees, and output/capacity--of Nigeria's major modern manufacturing facilities that were in operation, under construction, or proposed as of September, 1964.

14. UAC, Statistical and Economic Review, p. 14.

15. The grade of the oil is inversely proportional to the free fatty acid (F.F.A.) content. Too much F.F.A. will make the oil inedible.

16. J. C. Gardner, Oilseed Processing in Nigeria, A Report to the Government of Nigeria and the Nigerian Groundnut Marketing Board (November 29, 1952), p. 11.

17. Oil and cake cannot be stored with the ease of the groundnuts in the tarpaulin-covered pyramids at Kano.

18. Interview with A. C. MacKellar, Acting Deputy Permanent Secretary, Northern Region Ministry of Agriculture, Kaduna, October 25, 1961. Cotton seed is less valuable than palm kernel or groundnut cake. Benniseed food can be given to animals only in small amounts since it has a laxative effect.

19. Interview with D. E. MacGregor, Deputy Chief Veterinary Officer, Northern Region Ministry of Animal Health and Forestry, Kaduna, October 25, 1961.

20. The by-products of this industry are virtually endless. For instance, in addition to its edible uses, the cotton-seed meal may be used as a technical protein, e.g., for plywood glue, and as a filling agent in the manufacture of phenolic plastics. Going back a step, the husks of the cotton plant can be used as a fuel for the cotton-seed crushing plant. Also they can be added as roughage to animal feeding stuffs, used as soil conditioners to build up humus content, and may enter into the manufacture of plastic fillers, insulating materials, cellulose, potash, tannins, fibreboards, furfural, etc. (Cited in a private report, Enquiry Into the Economics of Cotton-seed Crushing in Northern Nigeria, prepared by L. H. Manderstan and Partners, Consulting Engineers, London, for George Calil, March, 1956.)

21. Senegal is in a different position as long as arrangements continue with France for an assured market.

22. Gardner, op. cit., p. 42. Dakar can use sea water.

23. Northern Nigeria, Ministry of Trade and Industry, The Industrial Development of Northern Nigeria (Kaduna, October, 1961), pp. 3 and 6 (Mimeo.)

24. Ibid., p. 4. In 1954, the IBRD recommended, "There should be no restriction on the quantity of nuts which may be purchased from the [marketing] board for processing." (IBRD, op. cit., p. 239.) In 1960, the quota remained in effect. (Northern Nigeria, Northern Region Marketing Board, Sixth Annual Report, p. 14.)

25. In the mines, .75 lb. cassiterite is yielded per cubic yard of dirt and gravel. (Interview with F. A. Cassidy, Deputy Chief Inspector, Federal Department of Mines, Jos, October 27, 1961.)

26. Interview with F. Dos Santos, Enbel's managing director, and son of the furnace inventor.

27. Every morning the collector visited the smelters.

28. Using coal and fuel oil, Makeri is unable to reach the temperatures necessary for slag reduction.

29. Nigeria, "Soap Manufacturing in Nigeria," Nigeria Trade Journal, Vol. 8, No. 3 (Lagos: Federal Ministry of Information, September, 1960), pp. 103-7.

30. In 1955, the company changed its name to Lever Brothers (Nigeria) Ltd. Like UAC, Lever Bros. is an offshoot of the British-Dutch Unilever group. With 570 employees, the Apapa plant manufactures eight brands of soap including Life Buoy and Lux, cooking fat, margarine, baking oil, pomades, and talcum powders.

31. The plant's 270 employees make four brands of bar soap: Key, Pale, Umbrella, and Magnet, plus one wrapped tablet, Sunlight. (Interview with A. G. Davis, Technical Manager.) When the demand for margarine equals Apapa's capacity, Lever Bros. will consider its production at Aba.

32. He sold Alagbon to Paterson, Zochonis and Company, Ltd.

33. Legal Notices No. 116 and 117 of 1961, published in the Supplement to the Federation of Nigeria Official Gazette, Nos. 66 and 67, Vol. 48, September 14 and 21, 1961.

34. IBRD, op. cit., p. 136.

35. Western Nigeria, Ministry of Trade and Industry, Schedule of Industries Operating in Western Nigeria (Ibadan, 1960), p. 14 (Mimeo.). By March 31, 1960, total capital invested in the plant by the Western Region amounted to £572,039. (Western Nigeria, WNDC Annual Report: 1959/60, p. 13.)

36. Interview with J. M. Gregory, Manager, Lafia Canning Factory, Ibadan, September 22, 1961.

37. Ibid.

38. The factory often found itself charging more at the factory gate for its product (without insurance) than the going price for a similar product in the U.K. which included a 5 per cent commission.

39. The factory paid a 20 per cent duty on imported packaging materials.

40. In 1960, 90 per cent of the fresh lemons were thrown away by the factory.

41. It also imports its kolanuts from the West Indies.

42. Interview with T. W. Gooday, Director and General Manager, Nigeria Canning Co., Kano, October 30, 1961. Liebig, a world-wide organization, and John Holt and Co. are NNDC's technical and commercial partners.

43. In 1960, Nigeria imported 1,619,556 machetes (Nigeria Trade Summary [December, 1961], p. 18), 90 per cent of which were destined for use in the Western Region cocoa and Eastern Region palm areas. The UAC's "Crocodile" brand controls about 82 per cent of the market. (Stephenson-Walsh and Associates, Inc., The Economic and Technical Feasibility of a Machete Manufacturing Plant for Nigeria, A Report Prepared for RBF [York, Pennsylvania: Stephenson-Walsh, November, 1960], 57 pp.) Because of the existing low price for a machete of good quality (the average unit import price was 38.1¢ in 1960), and because "there is no existing protective tariff for this product . . . the manufacture of machetes . . . in Nigeria is not feasible." (Ibid., p. 2.)

44. Concrete consists of cement, plus sand, broken stones, etc.

45. UAC, Statistical and Economic Review, No. 23, p. 28.

46. The raw materials are ground, mixed, and heated near the fusion point. As the mixture cools, it forms a clinker, which when ground or pulverized is ready for use.

47. The IBRD had recommended Apapa as the site. (IBRD, *op. cit.*, p. 255.) Beset by maintenance problems, and without trained labor and sufficient technical advice, the Nigerian entrepreneur suffered a nervous breakdown.

48. "Nigercem: The Story of Nigeria's New Cement Factory at Nkalagu," *Nigeria Trade Journal* (June, 1958).

49. In 1960 and 1961, ex-factory price cuts of 5/- per ton and 10/- per ton were made, and dividends were raised in the latter year to 10 per cent of the increased capital. For the five-year period through December, 1962, the company paid no taxes under the *Industrial Development (Income Tax Relief) Ordinance*, discussed above. (Nigeria Cement Co., Ltd., *Report of the Directors . . . for the Year Ended 31st March 1961* [Nkalagu, October 5, 1961], p. 8.) Moreover, imported cement was charged a duty of 28/- per ton. 1964 capacity is 500,000 tons per year.

50. Interview with M. L. Bisset, Secretary and Chief Accountant, Nigeria Cement Co., Nkalagu, October 21, 1961.

51. Interview with H. M. Bosch, Chief Engineer, Port Harcourt Cement Co., Ltd., October 4, 1961.

52. Associated Portland Cement Manufacturers Ltd. (51 per cent), WNDC (39 per cent), and UAC (10 per cent). (Capacity in 1964 is 450,000 tons.)

53. *Nigeria Trade Summary* (December, 1960), p. 15.

54. *Nigeria Trade Journal* (June, 1963), p. 78.

55. Stanley Engineering (Nigeria) Ltd., Feasibility Report on Cement Manufacturing Industry in the Northern Region of the Federation of Nigeria, a Report Prepared for RBF (Lagos: Stanley Engineering, June, 1961). This report does not take into account the Nkalagu expansion, but at the same time uses lower consumption rates than the writer.

56. Estimated at 50,000 tons in 1964, 110,000 tons in 1965, 100,000 tons in 1966, and 70,000 tons in 1967. (Ibid.) This project is usually considered to fall outside the normal demands of the economy.

57. IBRD, op. cit., p. 248.

58. Nigeria Trade Summary (June, 1963), p. 78.

59. In 1961 prices, 102 million sq. yds. cost Nigeria about £10.75 million. (Nigeria Trade Summary [June, 1961], pp. 12-13.) See Chapter 6 for a discussion on the difficulty of ascertaining an accurate figure for the "saving" of foreign exchange.

60. Yarn is made by spinning loose fibers, and cloth is produced by weaving (interlacing of yarn at right angles).

61. Interview with R. A. Mortimer, Commercial Manager, Kaduna Textiles Ltd.

62. The share capital was taken up by Arcturus Investment and Development Ltd. (a subsidiary of Chase International Investment Corp.), the Italian-Swiss Amenital Holding Trust, and the WNDC.

63. See Scheur Textile Consultants, Inc., Feasibility Report on Integrated Textile Mill in the Eastern Region of the Federation of Nigeria, a Report Prepared for RBF (New York, March, 1961).

64. Styles popular in Ghana do not sell in Nigeria, and vice versa.

65. Ankersmits of Holland, Calico Printers' Association of Great Britain, van Vlissingens of Holland, and UAC. West Africa (December 30, 1961), p. 1455.

66. *Ibid*.

67. Since 1962, many new textile schemes have been announced, four of which are under construction: (1) Arewa Textiles Ltd. in Kaduna (8.5 million sq. yds.); (2) Norspin Ltd. in Kaduna (5.25 million lb. yarn); (3) Nortex (Nigeria) Ltd. in Kaduna (12 million sq. yds.); and (4) Zamfara Textile Industries Ltd. in Gusau (10 million sq. yds.).

68. An American paraphrase of a prevalent Nigerian sentiment. (Westinghouse Electric International Co., Koppers International, C.A., United Engineering and Foundry Company, Chase International Investment Corporation, and Bechtel Corporation, *Report on the Feasibility of Establishing an Integrated Steel Mill in Nigeria*, Prepared for the Federation of Nigeria [New York: Westinghouse, *et al*., July, 1961], Foreword.)

69. Political leaders in both the Northern Region and the Eastern Region made public vows that it would be located in their region.

70. *West Africa* (London), (February 17, 1962), p. 170.

71. The proportion of magnesia in this deposit (13.37 per cent) is too high for cement manufacture.

72. P. E. Management Group, *op. cit*., Part 1, p. 5.

73. Pricing of the product mix is based on selling prices equal to C.I.F. Lagos prices of imported materials plus port charges and applicable duties. (Westinghouse, *et al*., *op. cit*., p. 11.)

74. New York's Strategic Materials Corp. has operated a pilot plant at Niagara Falls, Ontario. Koppers Co. has the rights to engineer plants using the Udy Process. (*Time*, April 7, 1961, p. 90.) In 1964, Koppers is obtaining its first commercial data for this process from its operation in Venezuela.

75. Summary of a Report on the Erection of an Integrated Iron and Steel Works by Eisenbau G.M.B.H.-Essen, May, 1961. (Mimeo.)

76. C. W. Wood and L. Alderman, Production of Metallurgical Coke Using Pitch Blending (Large Scale Tests), Report to the Nigerian Coal Corporation (CWD Ref. No. R/45/3/2), September 27, 1961, pp. 9-10 (Mimeo.) It is the writer's understanding that the residue from Nigerian oil is too waxy for this method.

77. The chairman of the NCC told the writer that it can be done "economically." (Interview with C. C. E. Onoh.)

CHAPTER 8 MANUFACTURING IN NIGERIA: ITS EXTENT, ROLE, AND PROSPECTS

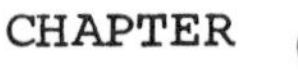

THE EXTENT OF INDUSTRY

Chapter 7 explored the nature of manufacturing in existence, or scheduled for introduction in the near future. Industry was categorized in terms of its attraction to the domestic market, the raw material, or the source of power. The study of the location and types of existing industry reveals that, if the multi-oriented steel mill and the power-oriented glass plant are excluded, manufacturing is divided nearly equally into market-oriented and raw-material-oriented industries.

Both the the major categories are represented in each of the original three regions as well as in the Federal Territory of Lagos. The Northern Region has raw-material-oriented abattoirs, cotton ginneries, mineral-concentrating facilities, oil-seed milling, soap manufacture, tanneries, tin smelters, and a cannery; a sugar refinery is under construction. The Eastern Region has a coal-sorting, washing, and concentrating plant, rice mills, soap manufacturing, palm-oil mills, and rubber processing. Petroleum refining will be soon added to its list. Lagos has a factory that produces both margarine and soap, and the Western Region possesses a cannery, rubber processing plants, sawmills, and may soon introduce a cocoa-processing plant.

Turning to a more lengthy itemization of market-oriented industries, examples include the cement plants in the East and the West (and under construction in the North), and the bicycle-assembly, bitumen-processing, and asbestos-cement plants located in both the East and the West. Additionally, factories for bakery products, textiles, brewing, boat building, cigarettes, furniture, metal fabrication, soft-drink bottling, industrial gas production, printing, tire production and/or retreading, the production of toilet preparations, and the assembly of umbrellas are established in all regions. Lagos alone has a wheat-flour mill, a motor vehicle assembly plant, and the assembly of electric appliances. Other market-oriented industries, including plastics, shoe manufacture, prestressed concrete, pharmaceuticals, paints, pressing of phonograph records, candy, bedding, dairying, and enamelware, are situated in one or more of Nigeria's major political subdivisions.

For a nation that was a colony until late 1960 this may appear to be an imposing enumeration. But, because many of the raw-material-oriented industries are located in or near the major urban areas, a visitor whose itinerary avoids the "bush" receives an exaggerated impression of the extent of Nigerian industry.

Indeed, manufacturing remains only a very minor contributor to the national product and a relatively negligible employer of labor. At constant (1957 factor) prices, the value added by manufacturing and processing rose fivefold in less than a decade: from £3.1 million in 1951 to £10.9 million in 1957 and to £15.7 million in 1960. Yet, the percentages these represent are respectively 0.41, 1.16, and 1.53 per cent of the total.[1] Moreover, in 1959, a total of 45,206 were employed in manufacturing and processing, only 0.5 per cent of the male labor force in that year.[2]

Reality casts a pall on the assertions that industry will soon serve as the smooth and straight road to "economic freedom" for Nigeria. The path to the realization of Nigeria's industrial potential may be charted, but it will not be an easy one to hew.

THE ROLE OF MANUFACTURING IN THE NIGERIAN ECONOMY

In 1964, it will be recalled, the governments of the Federation of Nigeria are implementing their first coordinated economic-development plan, the largest of its kind in tropical Africa. How well Nigeria does in strengthening her economy during this six-year period will, in all likelihood, determine the outcome of an experiment of the first magnitude. In the four years since Nigeria received her independence from Britain, the most populous of all African nations has been assaying the practicability of a federal form of government that permits the exercise of strong regional powers. This has been accompanied by the maintenance of domestic political stability in a democratic framework, the manifestation of a moderate posture in her international dealings, and the almost complete absence of racialism.

Nigerians have an especially strong desire to enlarge their relatively limited industrial sector. Often, Nigerian politicians put forth rapid, large-scale industrialization as the panacea for Nigeria's economic ills in general, and for her unemployment, in particular. Thus, in addition to its attestation as a demonstration of her economic independence, and its importance as a symbol of national distinction, industrialization has a leading role to play with respect to internal politics.

Although it is doubtful that the establishment of additional modern industry will solve the nation's unemployment problem, more manufacturing facilities will provide new jobs. The production of tapioca, varnishes, salt, glue, starch, electric storage batteries, alcohol, ammonia-based fertilizers, paper and paperboard, new kinds of plastics, air-conditioners, and produce bags,[3] among others, may be anticipated. As a supplement to these industries, there will be opportunities created in other sectors of the economy. For instance, the steel mill is expected to entail the opening of an iron mine at Lokoja, a limestone quarry at Itobe, and either the expansion of production in the Enugu coalfields or the exploitation of lignite at Asaba. Construction, transportation, and other service industries would also benefit by the introduction of this facility. Thus, the creation of some thousands of new industrial jobs during these six years will have greater ramifications on the over-all employment situation than would at first be indicated.

With the growth of Nigerian industry the country will profit by the introduction of skills now foreign to the majority of both labor and indigenous management. Moreover, the provision of administrative jobs outside the civil service will assist in the development of a professional class. Indeed, it probably will be from these industrial practitioners, rather than from those now engaged in commerce and construction, that the manufacturing entrepreneurs of tomorrow will arise.

Industry acts as a vehicle to bring new jobs and skills to Nigeria; concomitantly, it diversifies and strengthens her economy. Nigeria is (or soon will be) supplying an ever-increasing proportion of the domestic demand for such commodities as cotton, sugar, tobacco, and rice and the products derived from them. Furthermore, she is exporting higher grade produce, augmenting her export list, and progressing beyond the early stages of the processing of her raw materials. There may not be an over-all net saving in foreign exchange, but that exchange that is earned and saved will better enable Nigeria to meet the evolving demands of her people and some of the capital costs of development.

In expanding, industry is also serving other purposes. It is improving the general level of nutrition. The growing dairy industry in Vom and Lagos, for example, will soon benefit many of the country's children. It is spurring economic development throughout the Federation as is demonstrated in the cement case study. And it is evidencing a psychological impact. An internal "demonstration effect," as it were, is making itself felt. A continuing, visible, and dynamic proof of progress may very well contribute much to the sustenance of Nigeria's youthful democratic institutions and promote the maintenance of her political stability.

It is thus evident that Nigerian industry has many functions to perform, with society as the beneficiary. The performance of this role, however, is affected by numerous influences. It is to these factors that the discussion will now be directed.

FACTORS DETERMINING THE DEVELOPMENT OF INDUSTRY

Nigeria's industrial prospects are closely related to things she can utilize, such as her natural resources, to things she cannot alter, for example, her climate, and to things she can further develop, like her infrastructure. An assessment of the prospects of industry in Nigeria during the latter 1960's starts from an examination of these factors.

Natural Resources

The heavy dependence of the Nigerian economy on primary production is one of the more significant, pervasive problems affecting the development of industry. Including livestock management, forestry, and fishing, primary production accounted for three-fifths of the gross domestic product in 1960. But despite the importance of this sector, and notwithstanding the prevailing low standard of nutrition, Nigeria has no coordinated and integrated agricultural policy. In fact, the 1962-68 development plan attracts no more than 13.6 per cent of its expenditure in this direction, primarily because sufficient information for investment decisions is not available.

The primary sector also supplies more than four-fifths of Nigeria's foreign exchange earnings. Even though no one export regularly provides as much as 25 per cent of the total receipts. Nigeria's commodity terms of trade have declined in recent years.

As the world prices of tropical products have fallen from the peaks of the early 1950's, the gap between the prices of tropical agricultural products and industrial equipment has grown wider. Increasing output and improving quality has only partially offset the effects of the downward movement in prices. This situation is compounded by the growing threat presented by synthetics, e.g., the stereo rubbers.[4]

The majority of Nigeria's raw-material-oriented industries, from abattoirs to oil-seed mills, are dependent on tree and field crops, as well as livestock. Therefore, the export situation aside, further improvement of quality, erection of storage facilities, use of pesticides and fertilizers, introduction of new crops, and improved veterinary procedures should benefit Nigeria's incipient secondary industry.

From the standpoint of mineral resources, Nigeria is well suited for the establishment of industry, with two major exceptions. A lack of commercial quantities of basic chemicals, such as sulphur, brine, phosphates, and potash, will inhibit the introduction of a heavy chemical industry and will make more costly the institution of allied chemical facilities and chemical processing. The second exception is of a more general nature, and also falls within the category of infrastructure. Unless, and until, the water reserves of the Northern Region are proved to be available on an assured basis, the continued growth of industry in Kano, Jos, Zaria, and Kaduna, as well as the development of manufacturing in Sokoto and Maiduguri, will be jeopardized. Moreover, expansion in the agricultural sphere will be greatly inhibited. The Northern Region Government has heretofore done little to ascertain the extent of its water supply. But now it is beginning the time-consuming task of appraisal.[5]

More auspiciously, Nigeria has varying amounts and grades of tin, columbite, coal and lignite, lead, zinc, glass sands, ceramic clays, and zircon. It is, however, the petroleum, natural gas, limestone, and iron that will have the greatest impact on the development of modern industry. Already the dieselization of the railroad is decreasing the demand for Enugu's coal, and now, hydroelectricity and natural gas are rapidly making their presence felt too.

Nigeria's natural resources can contribute to the development of the economy in general, and industry in particular. Yet, overenthusiasm on the part of politicians, government officials, and industrial promoters may actually thwart this development. The North, for example, does have the resources and the market to support a single-kiln cement mill. It did not, however, have the tin ore to meet the requirements of the two smelters in Jos. Neither has Ibadan's cannery had a consistent supply of fruit. In sum, Nigeria has the natural resources to sustain her manufacturing, but unwise decision can only inhibit her domestic industry from using them.

Infrastructure

Generally speaking, Nigeria's transportation facilities, communications media, and electricity supply may be considered to be some of the brightest constituents of her economy. With the exception of water supply in parts of the North, Nigeria's infrastructure appears to be adequate for additional industrial undertakings in the Federation's major urban centers. Furthermore, the main roads are being surfaced, the railroad extended to the northeast, television stations erected, electric generating capacity expanded, inland water navigation improved, and water works constructed.

More specifically, Lagos, Ibadan, Kaduna, and Enugu, plus Kano and the Port Harcourt/Aba conurbation, are the sites of most of Nigeria's industry, both market- and raw-material-oriented. All, in common, are well connected to their surrounding areas by road, are served by Nigerian Airways, are on the rail line, and have, at least for the present, electricity and water sufficient to meet all their needs. As other towns offer comparable external economies to prospective industrialists they too will appear on the Nigerian map of manufacturing. For instance, Gombe will soon have both electricity and a railroad; Jebba will have electricity and a Niger River navigable for most of the year; and Onitsha will benefit from a bridge connection to the Mid-Western Region. But in many other parts of the country, as is exemplified by the delta area, transportation and communications will remain far from adequate for some years. It has also been noted that Nigeria has no urban sewerage system: The manufacturer has to dispose of his factory's effluents.

For an underdeveloped country, Nigeria is relatively well advanced in the provision of a comprehensive and partially integrated infrastructure. Even so, the external economies this implies cannot be taken for granted.

Human Resources

A rapidly growing population, a hallmark of so many underdeveloped nations, is a significant part of the Nigerian scene. Aside from the Nile Valley in Egypt, the Eastern Region's Iboland is now probably the most densely populated area in Africa. The complete 1963 census, when released, should produce the most accurate tabulation of the composition of the population yet made in Nigeria. Until then, it is estimated that 91 per cent of the 40 million or more Nigerians are less than 50 years of age.[6] The implications that arise from the growth of the large and young population range from the need for heavy expenditures on health and welfare to the demands of large numbers seeking education and work.

Nigerian leaders have often expressed the hope that the advent of modern industry would alleviate the mounting unemployment problem. Yet, as was stated above, only 0.5 per cent of the male labor force was recently employed in manufacturing and processing. And in the coming years there may well be disillusion regarding the absorption of urban dwellers into industrial jobs. Nigerians seek all the trappings of modernity from jet airliners to television stations. In the industrial sector, the most up-to-date technology is sought. However, since these advanced techniques from Europe and North America are often labor extensive and capital intensive,[7] new, large-scale industries employ only minimum numbers: for example, 350 in the oil refinery being constructed near Port Harcourt, and 100 in the Apapa flour mill.

The youthful structure of the population and the unemployment situation are typified in the school-leaver problem. "There are already something like three hundred thousand school-leavers in our region looking for jobs in the towns."[8] This is a problem that is exacerbated by the inadequate capital available for high schools. Universal primary education has been introduced in the south. But there are places in the secondary schools, and teachers to staff them, for a maximum of only 10 per cent of the primary graduates. Therefore, hundreds of thousands of incompletely educated youths are now entering the urban labor markets each year. To be sure, we all agree, and Nigeria realizes, that education is necessary to increase the quality and capability of her human resources. Yet, the introduction of universal primary education in the south during the late 1950's at the expense of secondary schools may be termed an unwise use of limited resources.[9] At least until more secondary spaces are available, it may be advisable for the other regions to follow the East's lead in raising, or instituting as the case may be, the fees paid by the primary students.

As with education outlays, regional expenditures on health and welfare compete with the more directly productive agriculture and industry for funds. Some of these overheads, especially preventive medicine, cannot be deferred. Others, in the category of social benefits, are of less urgency. Nigerian political leaders have not yet stressed that the economy's ability to pay for the gamut of social overheads is limited.

Government is not the only source of funds for expenditures on health and education. Many of the large companies provide medical services for their employees. More notably, the major business corporations have joined the Nigerian governments in embarking on a comprehensive, nation-wide training program that includes technical schools and on-the-job training. This investment in technical education will slowly but steadily improve the state of Nigeria's manpower. The program that commenced in the late 1950's should begin to bear fruit in the latter part of this decade. Yet, not until the 1970's will Nigeria be able to provide the engineers and administrators to manage the industry now being established.

It is true there may be a scarcity of qualified African managers and the labor force may not be adequately trained for most industrial jobs, especially with respect to maintenance and repair. Still, it is the consensus of many expatriate managers that Nigerians are willing to work in their plants, that the workers' absenteeism and turn-over rates are low, and, with good supervision and extensive training on the job, they are capable of adapting to the industrial milieu. Thus, it may be said, though Nigerian labor is not cheap, it need not be an imposing barrier to industrial development.

Markets

An examination of the extent and composition of effective demand for manufactured products will reveal a major limitation on industrial development in Nigeria. For there is an inadequate domestic market for a great number of products, notably consumer durables. A low per capita share of the national income and typically low personal incomes are indicative of the poverty in which the mass of the Nigerians live. At present growth rates for population and national income, the per capita share of national income will not reach $100 a year for many years. The small size of the domestic market was cited as one of the prime causes of the difficulties the Lafia Canning Factory has been encountering. In addition, the oil-seed mills may not be economically feasible because there is an insufficient demand for their by-products.

Were a major distributor of consumer goods to follow the example of Sears, Roebuck de Mexico, S.A., the market for Nigerian industry might be appreciably enlarged. By 1955, Sears purchased 80 per cent of its volume from more than 1,300 Mexican producers. Moreover, "Sears had played a major part in the development of many of its suppliers by giving them financial aid, lending them technical advisors, and sending them on trips to Europe and the United States to learn production and styling methods."[10] But to date, UAC, Leventis, and the other large expatriate trading firms have not shown much initiative in this direction.

It was noted above that industry has spurred economic development by taking advantage of regional rivalry in all fields, especially in industrial development. But this competition can work both ways. To date, there have not been many cases, a la the Eastern Region glass plant, of uneconomic industrial emulation on the part of a region. Yet the North proclaimed it would have a cement mill before the project had been proved feasible and justifiable. Also, in this vein, the rapid introduction of integrated textile facilities threatens to be too much of a good thing.

Regional me-tooism may be a threat to industrial development because it could excessively fragment the existing small market. Nigeria's large population is often cited as exerting an attractive pull on industry. But this presupposes the existence of a national market. If the nation becomes economically subdivided into regional components, prospective investors would rightly fear that their industrial projects may run into market difficulties and even eventually fail. Besides, invidious comparisons by the regions can lead to unwise government pressures on the entrepreneur. This was exemplified in the textile case study. Under the best of circumstances, some projects that are termed feasible will encounter serious troubles. Manifestly, government must be careful to assess the suitability of specific industries for the evolving Nigerian scene. Stimulating the introduction of inappropriate manufacturing will only invite failure, which may, in turn, discourage further investment and waste resources.

It may not be overly optimistic to state that responsible Nigerian officials at the federal level are aware of these pitfalls. The regions, too, are gradually gaining a greater realization of the possibility of industrial failures. Economic development plans were drawn up during the 1950's by the regions, as well as by the federal government. But the 1962-68 plan is the first exercise an interregional coordination with the federal government in the field of economic planning. Moreover, the regularly scheduled quarterly meetings of the National Economic Council, which includes four ministerial representatives from each of the governments, is fostering regional-federal cooperation. Nevertheless, awareness may not be enough. Political pressures and exigencies have led one region after another to resort to supplier credits and contractor financing. Industries that cannot now attract private investment are thus being established. Besides causing an inefficiency in the use of resources, the nation's short-term debt burden is increased and borrowing capacity decreased. Therefore, IBRD loans, for instance, will be harder to obtain.

Even though manufactures have never represented 1 per cent of Nigeria's total annual exports, foreign markets should also be considered because (1) many exports undergo some processing prior to shipment, and (2) export earnings play so important a part in the balance-of-payments picture. The decreasing prices recently received for her exports and Nigeria's view of the Common Market highlight a problem she has lived with since 1955. This is the steady depletion of Nigeria's reserves of foreign exchange. In each succeeding year, consumption plus investment have exceeded GDP; and, in 1960 only 39 per cent of the gap was filled by foreign investment. In addition, the Common Market timetable will aggravate this predicament. More than one-third of Nigeria's 1963 exports were sold to the six nations of the European Economic Community. But Nigeria is soon to face a tariff wall for some of her produce, a handicap with which eighteen other tropical African nations will not be burdened. How can Nigeria arrange a satisfactory accommodation with the EEC without "perpetuating unequal relationships, [and] making economic mockery of new-found political independence and frustrating the great pan-African dream"?[11] As in so many other matters, politics cannot be divorced from economics.

Both domestic and foreign markets present obstacles to the growth of the manufacturing sector. But it is the small size of the home market that may well limit the number of plants producing a specific product. Indeed, were Nigeria's national market to become subdivided, the scale of industry would have to be correspondingly decreased. An already small market should not be reduced by regional me-tooism.

Capital

As a result of the low per capita share of GDP, private domestic savings cannot be counted upon to provide much of the capital required for Nigeria's growing industrial sector. With their large expenditures on education and infrastructure, the governments will not be able to contribute most of the difference. Thus, it falls upon foreign capital to finance the continued establishment of modern industry in Nigeria.

In 1960, Nigeria received £28 million in overseas investment. This figure dropped to £23 million and £10.4 million in the succeeding two years. Complementing the public sector expenditure of £676.5 million, the 1962-68 economic development plan calls for £200 million of foreign investment in the private sector. For the sake of comparison, it would be well to bear in mind that overseas investment in Brazil in the six years from 1955 through 1960 yielded £292.5 million, including reinvested, undistributed earnings.[12] This was during a period generally considered to be one of great investment in an expanding industrial sector. Furthermore, Brazil has almost double the population of Nigeria, employs more than thirty times as many workers in industry, probably has many more trained and educated people, and is better known in the world investment community. Thus, it is far from certain that Nigeria will reach the foreign private investment target her economic advisers have set for her.

Assuming this to be the case, there are steps Nigeria can take to maximize her receipts and obtain a better utilization of the financial resources that will be at her disposal. Such steps might encompass a sale of government investments in industry (and plantation agriculture), a more impartial treatment of foreign investors, and a willingness to postpone some of the investments to which she appears to have committed herself.

The Nigerian agencies most concerned with industry are the regional development corporations. To varying degrees they have invested in manufacturing enterprises. Herein a problem develops. The majority opinion in the regional governments appears to be that a successful venture is one in which the government garners a profit. But an increase in the number of new productive enterprises is not usually commensurate with restricted sources of funds. So would not capital freed from old successes and transferred to new ventures--especially ones that would not otherwise be established[13]--extend these funds? In other words, limited financial resources of the governments would appear to have more strategic value if they were not permanently tied up in a relatively few (wholly owned, particularly) ventures.

Government participates in the development of industry in many other ways. Nigerian businessmen are aided by the extension of credit, by the supply of technical-extension services, and by the guaranty of loans. So far, though, these activities are relatively unimportant.

Of great interest to prospective private investors are the tax incentives proferred to a limited number of new ventures. Both indigenous and expatriate entrepreneurs are affected by the granting of exclusive privileges to some industries, and then to some units within these industries. This is exemplified by the tax holiday--up to five years--given to designated units within "Pioneer" industries such as textiles. Pioneer status, though, presents a problem because it often discriminates between similar units within the same industry. It "substitutes competition in bargaining power and negotiating skills for competition in productivity and economic efficiency."[14] Since a tax sacrifice is involved, the decision must be approved by the federal cabinet, and so delays are added to uncertainty. Evidently, government feels that too many plants may spring up in a Pioneer industry. Yet in certain areas such as Puerto Rico--where all enterprises within a sought-after industry are given tax forgiveness--the forces of supply and demand have tended to regulate the industrial growth. Furthermore, if tax rebates are proportional to the profits that are ploughed back, all foreign (and domestic) investors receive what amounts to both an impartial welcome and a special incentive.

Nigeria's scarce financial resources are also tapped for major, often nonindustrial, investments. Since independence, she has undertaken a series of investments from the nationalization of the air and shipping lines to the extension of the internal and external broadcasting services to the take-over of the communications services of the British Cable and Wireless Company.[15] Each of these may be listed as a fait accompli. Additionally, the commitment to the Niger Dam is irrevocable. The proposed steel mill is of a somewhat different nature. Its nonpublic-utility character lends itself less to doctrinaire slogans. However, the National Economic Council is presumably now committed to a mill per se. Political forces and economic interests have achieved an affirmative decision. The planners have still to consider the specifics, including the relatively small market, the absence of coking coal, the medium grade of ore, and the untried process that has been recommended by an American consortium.[16]

Nigeria may expect technical assistance in stretching out her available funds. For example, in the field of industrial credit she has received World Bank help. With the aid of IFC personnel, until such time as a sufficient number of Nigerians have been adequately trained, it is probable that better use of available loan capital for industrial ventures is being made. Further, it is possible that greater intranational cooperation will thus be affected in the development of industry.

All the gains foreseen, especially from technical assistance, government incentives, and foreign investment could be vitiated by inflation. For some years, inflationary pressures have been mounting. From December 31, 1961, to December 31, 1963, the money supply increased by more than 10 per cent. Moreover, wages have gone up, and foreign exchange reserves have fallen rapidly, from £216.5 million on December 31, 1959, to £87 million in mid-1964. Inflation could lead, as it has elsewhere, to an increased allocation of resources to speculative real estate construction at the expense of productive ventures; to an impairment of the incentive to save; to an excessive importation of nonessential goods; and, of course, to worsening balance-of-payments deficits. In the absence of restrictive fiscal and monetary measures, Nigerians may soon face the dilemma of either devaluing her currency, now at par with the British pound, or imposing stringent foreign-exchange control measures.

Some control measures have already been adopted, which have been likened to a fire extinguisher by the Minister of Finance. Also Nigerians may no longer participate in overseas football (soccer) pools, and tariffs have been raised for the second time in three years. Unfortunately, the use of such measures does have its disadvantages. They could alarm international investors in addition to the overseas legislators who must approve the appropriations of development grants and loans. Moreover, tighter controls would be difficult to administer, given the scarcity of trained personnel. They could result in economic waste insofar as limited resources are directed from fields in which Nigeria has the greatest comparative advantage--that is, the most competitive--to those which are most highly protective.

To recapitulate, the Nigerian governments have insufficient capital to meet the ever-increasing demands for expenditures on health, education, welfare, and infrastructure, and to finance the majority of the manufacturing facilities desired during this decade. Since the people cannot be expected to supply the requisite savings, Nigeria is turning abroad.

At the same time, the Nigerian governments can do much to alleviate the shortage of capital. They can accept the assistance of the World Bank and other international agencies and foundations, they can offer appropriate fiscal incentives to attract overseas investment, they can institute measures with a view to containing inflationary pressures, and they can place a rein on misplaced national pride, which has led to some questionable allocations of available capital.

SUMMARY AND CONCLUSIONS

If we assume that the next decade will not see *coup d'état*, secession, or any other such drastic event that would basically affect the fabric of the Federation as it is seen today, then we can make a series of observations that should serve to clear away visions that are, at least in part, fanciful. Nigeria has a dearth of trained managers, a limited effective demand for most industrial products, and a shortage of development capital. Yet, Nigeria does possess many useful natural resources, a fairly adequate infrastructure, a willing labor force, and governments that are actively promoting industry. Nigeria is directing the energies of her people toward the modernization of their newly independent nation.[17] It is in this effort that industry will continue to have its principal role for some time.

A number of problems that affect the nation's economy as a whole have been pointed up. They contribute to the description of the business setting, and relate, if not always directly, to the establishment of industry. Although many of the problems delineated are of an all-pervasive nature, industry, in turn, has an expanding and countervailing role to play in the amelioration of these difficulties.

Looking to the future, there appears to be no substantial evidence that modern manufacturing industry will not continue its recent growth. But a general barrier to its acceleration is the higher cost of conducting operations in Nigeria in contradistinction with the more advanced countries. This differential is primarily due to the limited purchasing power of the Nigerians, which does not allow many plants of optimum capacity to be constructed; to the need for high-wage expatriate managers; and to the comparatively low productivity of Nigerian labor.[18] Industry will, thus, remain a minor contributor to the national product, at least into the next decade. Therefore, this sector's forthcoming annual percentage increases should be viewed in conjunction with its small base.

In sum, it is more than likely that the manufacture and assembly of many new products will commence in Nigeria during the 1960's. This will result from, among other factors, the nature of her resources, her disposition, and outside investment. But a standard of living comparable to the highly developed countries appears to be the basic goal of this newly emergent nation. And industrial development usually seems to exemplify the greatest progress toward this goal. However, as has been indicated, industry is not and cannot be a *deus ex machina*. Nigerians, and friends of Nigeria, anticipating many immediate results, should best, perhaps, remember Rome.

Footnotes to Chapter 8

1. Jackson and Okigbo, op. cit., and Stolper, et al., op. cit. GDP is given in market prices of 1957.

2. Figures were tabulated for 1,207 firms hiring less than ten employees and all firms employing more than ten persons.

3. Possibly based on kenaf (Hibiscus cannabinus), a fiber experimentally grown during 1961-62 by UAC, NNDC, and the Dutch firm of N. V. Klattensche Cultuur Maatschappij at Jema'a, south of the Jos Plateau in the Northern Region.

4. "Last week it was revealed that the [U.S.] Agency for International Development in Washington had cautioned its overseas missions in underdeveloped countries not to commit aid funds to natural rubber programs until the effects of synthetic rubber on world rubber prices had become clearer. . . . Stereo rubbers . . . are being promoted as the final replacement of natural rubber." (The New York Times, January 7, 1962, p. 1, Financial Section.) "Synthetic rubber . . . accounted for three-fourths of all consumption of new rubber in the U.S. last year." (The Economist [London], February 29, 1964, p. 808.)

5. A complete hydrological survey might require thirty years. "This is the North's number one economic priority." (Interview with Dr. K. D. S. Baldwin, Economic Adviser to the Northern Region Government, Kaduna, October 23, 1961.)

6. See, for example, West Africa (London), December 2, 1961, p. 1343.

7. "Modern industry does not in the short run match its heavy capital with any heavy increase in employment." (Barbara Ward Jackson, "Change Comes to Africa's Villages," New York Times Magazine, November 19, 1961, p. 50.)

8. A statement by Dr. A. N. Obonna, Eastern Region Minister of Trade and Industry in West Africa (London), March 10, 1962, p. 257.

9. "This then is the contradiction: the more that is spent on education from the regional budgets, the less there is left to spend on the recurrent costs of further capital outlays that could be employment providing." (Arch. C. Callaway, op. cit., p. 10.)

10. John Fayerweather, Management of International Operations (New York: McGraw-Hill, 1960), pp. 225-26. Sears commenced operations in Mexico in 1947. (See National Planning Association, The Case Study of Sears, Roebuck de Mexico, S.A. [Washington, D.C.: NPA, 1953], 64 pp.)

11. Barbara Ward Jackson, "Free Africa and the Common Market," Foreign Affairs, Vol. 40 (April, 1962), p. 426.

12. Chemical Bank New York Trust Company, "Brazil," International Economic Survey, No. 135 (March, 1962), p. 6.

13. The federal government's sale of its equity interest in the Nkalagu cement mill was negated by the purchase of the shares by the ENDC.

14. Moore, et al., op. cit., p. 70.

15. West Africa (London), February 10, 1962, p. 161.

16. "As a working rule, it is only prudent to avoid a new process or radically unusual equipment or manufacturing methods which have not been proven successful for at least one year in several commercial enterprises of normal size in countries where the industry is important and competitive." (Murray D. Bryce, Industrial Development [New York: McGraw-Hill, 1960], p. 108.)

17. In this effort, Nigeria has been demonstrating ambition and initiative. One measure of these characteristics is a comparison of the foreign countries from which the U.K.'s Tropical Products Institute has received enquiries. In 1960 the Institute received 595 from 60 overseas countries. Nigeria led the list with 72 enquiries. (U.K., Department of Scientific and Industrial Research, Report of the Tropical Products Institute: 1960 [London: Her Majesty's Stationery Office, 1961], p. 35.) Another measure is the record of her students on U.S. campuses. "Outstanding among them were the Nigerians, who comprise about half of all A.S.P.A.U. [African Scholarship Program of American Universities] students." (Time, December 21, 1962, p. 55.)

18. Another factor that might be cited is Nigeria's tropical location. Deterministic arguments aside, the rate of depreciation is often increased by machinery deteriorating rapidly in the hot, humid climate.

APPENDIX

INVENTORY OF MAJOR NIGERIAN MODERN MANUFACTURING INDUSTRY: IN OPERATION, UNDER CONSTRUCTION, OR PROPOSED--SEPTEMBER, 1964 (EXCLUDING POWER GENERATION, MAINTENANCE AND REPAIR FACILITIES, AND STORAGE FACILITIES)*

A. MARKET-ORIENTED

1. appliances, miscellaneous electric

a. air-conditioner assembly--project in exploratory stage

b. toasters, fans, and irons--project planned for Port Harcourt by Eastern Region (ER) and G.B. Birla of India

2. asbestos cement

a. Ikeja--Asbestos Cement Products (Nigeria), Ltd. (Western Region, near Lagos)
In production since March, 1961.
£600,000 initial capital investment + £350,000 expansion
35% WNDC, 57% Italian (Eternit)-Belg. group, 4% John Holt Investment Co., 4% Paterson, Zochonis [Johns-Manville International has since acquired an interest.]
200 direct labor; 18,000 tons/yr "Nigerite" sheets (and, in 1964, pressure pipes) in 3 shifts

*Based on published materials, interviews, and news releases.

b. Emene--Turner's Asbestos Cement (Nigeria) Ltd. (Eastern Region, near Enugu)
In production since April, 1963.
£1.5 million investment
Turner and Newall Group of Manchester 80%, ER 20%
less than 250 direct labor; eventually 17-20,000 tons/yr of sheets and pipe

c. Northern Region--project proposed

3. bakery products

a. bread--over 100 with ten or more workers; the largest being "De Facto" Works Ltd. in Surulere (Lagos) with 190 employees and in production since 1954.

b. biscuits

(1) Ikeja--Biscuit Manufacturing Co. of Nigeria, Ltd.
In production since last quarter, 1961.
£225,000 investment
ICON, Western Region (WR), Wright and Co. (Liverpool) Ltd., and John Holt Investment Co.
70 or less direct labor; 2,000-2,500 tons/yr cabin biscuits

(2) Apapa (Lagos)--Narakat, Ltd.
In production during 1962.
£150,000 investment
100% Nassar Group
150 employees; "Pioneer" sweet biscuits

(3) Apapa--Niger Biscuit Company Ltd.
In production in late 1962.
£200,000 investment
67% Nassar Group, 16 2/3% WNDC, 16 1/3% Nigerian private
150 employees; 15 t/day capacity Oxford cabin biscuits

c. doughnuts

Lagos--Nidoco Ltd.
In production since September, 1961.
£10,000 investment
U.S. private--managed by African Research and Development Co. of NYC
less than 30 direct labor; 12,000/day

4. bedding and blankets

a. blankets

(1) Kano--Northern Textile Manufacturers Ltd.
In production since mid-1962.
£1 million investment
Nishizawa Co. (Japan), Raccah Co., Abculafia Co. (and probably NNIL)
300 employees; 800,000 cotton, woolen, and rayon blankets/yr production

(2) Kano--project proposed

b. mattresses

(1) Mushin--Vono (West Africa) Ltd. (Western Region, near Lagos)
In production since 1961.
£20,000 investment
55% Vono Ltd. (UK), 30% UAC, 15% WNDC
over 50 employees; mattresses with inner springs (plus some metal furniture)

(2) Ibadan--Nigerian Foam Rubber Company, Ltd.
In production since 1958.
Subsidiary of Odutola Tyre Retreading & Co., Ltd.
30 direct labor; 500 mattresses/month plus cushions

(3) Ikeja--Vitafoam (Nigeria) Ltd.
In production since mid-1963.
£125,000 investment
G.B. Ollivant (Unilever) and Vitafoam Ltd. (UK)
more than 50 employees; cushions, etc. too

(4) Ibadan--Nigerian Polyelastic Foam Co., Ltd. (now J.A. Odutola Plastic Foam Co. Ltd.)
Nigerian private
Polyurethane foam

(5) Yaba (Lagos)--Niger Upholstery Company Ltd.
In production since 1956.
Being expanded in 1964. Beds too

5. <u>bicycle assembly</u>

a. Port Harcourt--Raleigh Industries of Nigeria Ltd.
In production since late 1960.
$75,000 investment
UAC (and possibly INDAG and other private interests)
Assembles frames, forks, and backstays; some manufacture anticipated

b. Zaria--Raleigh Industries of Nigeria Ltd.
In production since 1958.

c. Mushin--Raleigh Industries of Nigeria Ltd.
In production since 1958.
The three plants produce more than 100,000 units/year

d. Warri--Raleigh Industries of Nigeria Ltd.
Small plant (under 25 employees) in prod. since 1960.

6. brewing

a. Apapa--Nigerian Breweries Ltd.
In production since 1949.
UAC, Heineken (technical partner), John Holt Investment Co. and other private interests
900 employees; $3\frac{1}{2}$ mn gal/yr capacity
Star Beer and Sampson Stout

b. Aba--Nigerian Breweries Ltd.
In production since 1957.
500 employees; about 2 mn gal/yr capacity

c. Kaduna--Nigerian Breweries Ltd.
In production since first quarter, 1963.
£1 million investment
about 300 employees; 3/4 mn gal/yr capacity

d. Ikeja--Guinness (Nigeria) Ltd.
In production since late 1962.
£1.8 million investment
UAC and Arthur Guinness Son and Co.
450 employees; 3 to $3\frac{1}{2}$ mn gal/yr capacity of stout

e. Umuahia (ER)--Independence Brewery Ltd.
In production since November, 1963.
£950,000 investment
100% ENDC
about 200 employees; $1\frac{1}{2}$ mn gal/yr of "Golden Guinea" capacity

f. Abeokuta (WR)--West African Brewery Co., Ltd.
In production since April, 1964.
£1 million investment
30% WNDC, 30% Nigerian private, 20% Dizengoff (Israel), 10% Leventis, 10% Henninger Int'l A.G. (German) (Tech. partner)
over 200 employees; about $1\frac{1}{2}$ mn gal "Top Beer"/yr capacity

7. candy

a. Kano--Chattalas Brothers, Ltd.
In production since 1959.
£20,000 investment
This plant and the following make toffee, sugar-coated nuts, and boiled sweets. Over 100 employees

b. Kano--Nigerian Sweets and Confectionary Co., Ltd.
In production since March, 1960.
£45,000 investment
90% NNDC, 10% Nigerian private
240 employees; 12 tons/day capacity

c. Apapa--Trebor (Nigeria) Ltd.
In production since early 1963.
£60,000 investment
Robertson and Woodcock, Ltd. (UK)
24 employees

d. Kano--Geka Trading Co., Ltd.
(also manufactures cosmetics)

e. Mushin--Jabr Brothers Industrial Co. (Nigeria) Ltd.
Into production during 1963.
£150,000 investment
25 employees

f. Kano--Kano Sweets and Confectionary
Overseas private

8. cement, Portland

a. Nkalagu--Nigerian Cement Company Ltd. (Eastern Region, east of Enugu)
In production since December, 1957.
£4.2 mn investment
controlled by ER, ENDC, and ERMB; 10% CDC, Tunnel Portland Cement Co., Fed. Govt (about 20%), F.L. Smidth and Co. (Denmark), and Nigerian private
550 employees (3 shifts) plus 250 on contract
In 1964 reached 500,000 tons "Nigercem"/yr capacity

b. Ewekoro--West African Portland Cement Co., Ltd. (WR, between Lagos and Abeokuta)
   In production since December, 1960.
   £5 million investment
   39% WNDC, 10% UAC, 51% Associated Portland Cement Manufacturers (UK) Ltd.
   500 employees; in mid-1964 reached 450,000 tons "Elephant" brand cement/yr capacity

c. Port Harcourt--Port Harcourt Portland Cement Co. Ltd.
   With its predecessor, NEMCO Ltd., in prod. since Dec., 1959.
   £300,000 investment
   25% NEMCO (Nigerian private), 25% ENDC, 50% European private
   110 employees (2 shifts); 35-40,000 tons/yr from clinker

d. Kalambaina--Cement Company of Northern Nigeria Ltd. (NR, near Sokoto)
   Under construction; production scheduled for 1965.
   $8 mn loan by Ferrostaal A.G. (German) over 10 yrs, plus £3 mn capital (80% NNDC, 20% Ferrostaal)
   350 employees; 100,000 tons/yr capacity planned

e. Apapa--Anglo-Canadian Cement Co., Ltd.
   In production since September, 1963.
   £500,000 investment
   49% Dr. W.K. Wallersteiner (Canadian), 51% Hartley Baird Ltd. (UK)
   over 200 employees; eventually 200,000 tons "Palm-Brand"/yr from clinker. (Also since 1955 has produced pipes, and other precast products to order.) Possibly will use local limestone.

f. Apapa--Lagos Cement Works Ltd.
   Under construction.
   £450,000 investment
   Nigerian and Israeli private plus 10% Coutinho, Caro and Co. (German)
   Scheduled capacity: 100,000 tons/yr from clinker

g. Koko--Mid-West Cement Co., Ltd.
Under construction; production planned for late 1964.
£300,000 investment
Nigerian private plus 10% Coutinho, Caro and Co.
60 employees; 70,000 tons/yr capacity from clinker

h. Calabar--project proposed based on German financing
Eventually would produce 70,000 tons clinker/yr for c. above, plus 100,000 tons/yr cement

i. Ukpilla--project planned at capital cost of £4.6 mn based on German financing
90% Mid-West Gov't (MW), 10% Coutinho, Caro and Co.
Initially would produce clinker for Koko plant

9. <u>ceramics, clays, and pottery</u>

a. Ikorodu (WR)--Ikorodu Ceramics Industries
In production since 1948.
£300,000 investment
Nigerian and British private interests
150 direct labor; 350,000 units/yr pots, mugs, plates, pans, etc.

b. Umuahia--Modern Ceramics Industry Ltd.
Under construction.
£600,000 investment
100% ENDC
400 employees; scheduled capacity: 300 tons/yr table ware and 600 t/yr vitreous sanitary ware

c. Ikeja--Clay Industries (Nigeria) Ltd.
In production since mid-1963.
£25,000 investment
Lebanese private and Italian private
62 employees; 33,000 t/yr capacity hollow clay building blocks and partitions

d. Isieke Iheku (near Enugu)--Denchukwu Ltd.
In production since 1961.
£30,000 investment
Nigerian private, Shell-BP, and J. Holt subsidiary; INDAG loan
over 50 employees; 3,000 bags/day powdered drilling clays (primarily for Shell-BP) (and paints)

e. Ekulu (near Enugu)--Ekulu Pottery Industry
In production since 1958.
£40,000 investment
100% ER
over 50 employees; 1962 prod.: 75,000 pieces

10. <u>concrete, tile, and other building products</u>

a. Abeokuta--Nigerian Pre-Stressed Concrete Co. Ltd.
In production since 1954.
£50,000 investment
20% WNDC, 40% CFAO, 40% Taylor Woodrow (UK)
over 200 employees; electric poles, culverts, etc.

b. Ibadan--Nigeria Industrial Products Ltd.
In production since 1953.
Lebanese private
25 employees; cement blocks and floor tiles

c. Kaduna--A-Concrete Ltd.
In production since 1st quarter, 1963.
£500,000 investment
Swedish Rail System and Conart Holding A.G., Nigerian private
139 employees; initially 145,000 railway sleepers/yr, also pre-stressed concrete ties, pipes, culverts, etc.

d. Mushin--Nigerian Concrete Industries Ltd.
In production since early 1963.
£50,000 investment (successor to M.M. Sadipe and Sons)
50% German private, 50% Nigerian private
over 100 employees; 12,000 blocks/day capacity

e. Ikeja--Nigeria Concrete Ltd.
Project in proposal stage.
Stanley Engineering (US), IBEC, and Nigerian private
pre-cast concrete products

f. Ebute-Metta (Lagos)--Nigerian Marble Industries Ltd.
In production since early 1964.
Nigerian and Italian private
Working marble mined in Kabba Province.

g. Abeokuta--Aro Quarry Ltd.
100% Costain (West Africa) Ltd. (UK firm)
100,000 t/yr crushed gneiss stone

h. Ikeja--Nigerian Mosaic and Glass Mfg. Co. Ltd.
In production since August, 1961.
£64,500 investment
26.6% WNDC plus Nigerian private
over 50 employees; 10,000 cement, glass mosaic, and terrazzo tiles/day

i. Kano--a number of other firms, including Dabian (West Africa) Tile Factory, here and elsewhere produce terrazzo tiles, work marble, crush stone, make concrete poles, etc., etc.

11. <u>cork products</u>

Ikeja--Crown Cork and Seal Co. of Nigeria Ltd.
Under construction.
£100,000 investment
Subsidiary of Crown Cork Co. of UK
soft drink bottle caps

12. <u>dairy products</u>

a. Mushin--Foremost Dairies (Nigeria) Ltd.
In production in 1960 as Swedish-African Milk Co. Ltd.
During first quarter, 1963, purchased by US firm (plus Nigerian private)

over 50 employees; "SAMCO" reconstituted imported powdered milk, and other dairy products, e.g., ice cream

b. Vom--Nigerian Creameries Ltd.
£170,000 investment
Unigate Ltd. (UK), and £35,000 NNDC (Now NNIL)
less than 50 employees; butter, cheese, and baby food

c. Apapa--Walls (Nigeria) Ltd.
In production since late 1961.
£90,000 investment
T. Wall and Sons Ice Cream Ltd. (UK) (Unilever)
34 direct labor; 1962 prod.: 150,000 gal. pasteurized ice cream. Higher in 1963. Second plant at Port Harcourt under consideration

d. Ibadan--Fan Milk Co. Ltd.
In production since late 1962.
£100,000 investment
Nigerian, British, and Scandinavian private (including UAC and Emborg)
about 75 employees; reconstituted dairy products

13. enamelware, and brass and aluminum holloware

a. Ikeja--Nigerian Enamelware Co. Ltd.
In production since July, 1961.
£200,000 investment
John Holt Investment Co., Kowloon Enamelware Co., and other private. Former acquired controlling interest in 1963
130 direct labor (including workers from Hong Kong); porcelain basins, curry dishes, bowls, and mugs

b. Ikeja--West African Household Utensils Mfg. Co. Ltd.
Under construction; prod. scheduled for late 1964.
£50,000 investment
Hong Kong private interests
about 100 employees

c. Kano--Northern Enamelware Co. Ltd.
Started production at end of 1959; not in full prod. until later due to financial problems
£25,000 NNDC investment plus NNIL and Abboud Bros. (Lebanese)

d. Port Harcourt--Eastern Enamelware Factory Ltd.
In production since spring, 1964.
£100,000 investment
20% ENDC and Hwa Chong Enamelware Factory Ltd. (H.K.)
over 200 employees; eventually, 1,500 tons/yr basins, kettles, pails, etc.

e. Ikeja--Tower Aluminium (Nigeria) Ltd.
In production since 1961.
£125,000 investment
25% Alcan, 23.2% WNDC, 51% Midland Metal Spinning Co. Ltd. (UK), Nigerian private
130 direct labor; 2,000 pots, kettles, and pans/day
Aluminum from Port Harcourt Alcan mill.

f. Kano--S. Raccah Ltd.
In production since 1961.
£30,000 investment
Lisbon pans (Northern wedding gift); over 100 employees

g. Kano--Nigerian Metal Fabricating Co. Ltd.
In production since August, 1960.
£45,000 investment
100% George Calil (a Lebanese businessman)
125 direct labor (3 shifts); foundry, platings, and aluminum holloware

h. Kano--Nigerian and Overseas Enamelware
In production since 1959.
over 50 employees; enamelware and Lisbon pans

14. flour and feed milling, and misc. products

a. Apapa--Flour Mills of Nigeria, Ltd.
In production since May, 1962.
£1.5 million investment
Southern Star Shipping Co. of NY (Mr. George P. Coumantaros), 12% Fed. Gov't. Export-Import Bank loan (Chase-Manhattan also has lien on Allis-Chalmers equipment)
over 100 direct labor; 90,000 tons "Golden Penny" flour produced in 1963 (about 50% capacity) from imported US and Canadian hard wheat. Also bran (30,000 tons/yr capacity) and semolina

b. Port Harcourt--Sunray Flour Mills proposed by ER and Italian interests

c. Ikeja--Livestock Feeds Ltd.
In production since February, 1964.
£60,000 investment
80% Pfizer (US) and 20% Nigerian private
Replaced WR mixing plants at Agege and Ibadan
61 employees; 100 tons/week production

d. Aba--Livestock Feeds Ltd.
In production since late 1963.
Pfizer plant replaced ER mixing plant at Enugu

e. Kaduna--third Pfizer plant proposed for this location

f. Kano--proposed macaroni plant

15. furniture and fixtures (wooden)

a. Mushin--Harmony House Furniture Co. Ltd.
In production since 1961. Over 100 employees.

b. Ebute-Metta--Costain (West Africa) Ltd.
In production since 1956. Over 200 employees.

c. Port Harcourt--Costain (West Africa) Ltd.
In production since 1956. Over 100 employees.

d. Ebute-Metta--Nigerian Joinery Company Ltd.
In production since 1958. Over 200 employees.
Taylor Woodrow (UK)
(Also at Kaduna)

e. Mushin--Construction and Furniture Co. (W. Afr.) Ltd.
In production since 1955.
Harris Lebus (UK) subsidiary
over 100 employees

f. Port Harcourt--C.F.C. Furniture Co. (E.N.) Ltd.
In production since 1960.
£50,000 investment
Harris Lebus subsidiary

g. Kaduna--Construction Furniture Co. Ltd.
In production during March, 1962. Now closed down.

h. Port Harcourt--Dolcino & Co. (Nigeria) Ltd.
In production since 1953.
£56,000 investment
over 200 employees

i. Ekulu--Eastern Nigeria Construction and Furniture Company Ltd.
In production since mid-1961.
£100,000 investment
51% ENDC and 49% Solel Boneh (Israeli)
150 employees

j. Port Harcourt--Micheletti & D'Alberto Ltd.
In production since 1958.
£10,000 investment
130 employees

k. Kano--Chakers Factory Ltd.
In production since 1952.
£20,000 investment
over 200 employees; also tubular furniture

l. Kano--A number of other firms, including G. Cappa Ltd., here and elsewhere employ over 100 workers each.

16. <u>industrial gases</u>

a. Apapa--Apapa Chemical Industries Ltd.
In production of CO_2 and dry ice since 1959.
under 50 employees

b. Apapa--Industrial Gases of Nigeria Ltd.
In production since 1961.
British Oxygen Co. Ltd.
over 50 employees; O_2 and C_2H_2

c. Apapa--Nigerian Industrial Domestic Gas Supply Co. Ltd.
Repackaging of liquefied petroleum gas since 1957.
£150,000 investment (including sales depots)
30% WNDC, 60% Liquigas of Milan Sp.a., 10% private

d. Emene--Niger Gas Ltd.
In production since 1962.
£111,000 investment
70% ER, 30% Siad Macchine Impianti (Italian)
under 25 employees; 2,000 bottles O_2/mo and 500 bottles C_2H_2/mo

e. Port Harcourt--P.H. Gas Producers Ltd.
In production since 1960.
£50,000 investment (foreign private)
prod. 2.4 mn cu ft O_2 and 400,000 cu ft C_2H_2/yr

f. Kano--Nigerian Carbon Dioxide Co., Ltd.
In production since 1958.
£24,000 investment
27% NNDC and private interests
Dry ice also manufactured.

g. Onitsha--Pepsi-Cola Bottling plant produces CO_2 as does Nigerian Breweries at its plants.

h. Mid-Western site--under consideration by Shell-BP

17. ink

Yaba--A UK firm will produce 3 mn bottles/yr as of 1965.

18. insecticides

Ikeja--I.C.I. Nigeria Ltd.
In production since 1962 (see "paints" below).

19. jewelry

a. Onitsha--Ottibros (Jewelry) Manufacturing
In production since 1962.
over 50 employees; dog chains and key chains too
proposed expansion of capital with Brandes of West Germany taking up new equity

b. Ikeja--Fimecon Ltd.
£100,000 plant proposed by US and Belgian private interests.

20. lens, optical--planned Arclex Optical Co. Ltd. plant

21. light bulbs

Apapa--Philips (Nigeria) Ltd. (see "radio ass'y" below)

22. matches

a. Ilorin--United Match Company (Nigeria) Ltd.
In production since early 1963.
£500,000 investment
Lebanese private
350 employees; 300,000 "Crown" boxes/day capacity

b. Ikeja--proposed plant
80% Hong Kong private and 20% Nigerian private

23. metal fabrication

a. Port Harcourt--Nigerian Aluminium Products Ltd.
In production since July, 1960.
£55,000 investment
60% Alcan, 40% ER (including possibly INDAG)
45 direct labor; 1-shift capacity of 9,000 t/yr aluminum corrugated building sheets and accessories, e.g., guttering

b. Port Harcourt--Alcan Aluminium of Nigeria Ltd.
In production since second quarter, 1963.
£1.25 million investment
Alcan, ICON, and INDAG
100 direct labor (3 shifts); mill will have capacity to roll 5-6,000 t/yr of imported aluminum ingots into coil, flat sheets, and circles by 1965; initially producing at 1,600 tons/yr

c. Apapa--Aluminium Manufacturing Co. of Nigeria Ltd.
In production since 1960.
Swiss controlling interest plus Nigerian private
roofing sheets, pots, pans, lorry bodies, etc.

d. Yaba--Lagos Metal Industries (Nigeria) Ltd.
In production since 1960.
Austrian and Nigerian private interests
600 tons/yr of roofing sheets for "bush" market

e. Port Harcourt--Williams and Williams (Nigeria) Ltd.
In production since 1960.
£80,000 investment
49% ER, 51% Williams and Williams (UK) Ltd.
75 direct labor (1 shift); 12½ tons/wk production of casement windows and doors. Addition of venetian blinds and sheet metal shelves planned.

f. Kaduna--Reliance Metal Products (Nigeria) Ltd.
In production since mid-1963.
£162,000 investment
50% (57% total cap.) Williams and Williams, 50% NNIL
52 employees; metal doors and windows from imported sheet metal and steel strips

g. Mushin--Crittall-Hope (Nigeria) Ltd.
In production since October, 1958.
£160,000 investment
51% Crittall Mfg. Co. Ltd. (UK), 22½% WNDC, 14% John Holt Investment Co., 12½% Henry Hope and Sons Ltd.
100 direct labor; about 1,700 tons of metal window frames and rolled steel doors/yr

h. Emene--Nigersteel Co. Ltd.
In production since July, 1962.
£300,000 investment
49% ER, 17% Italian private, 34% Mandilas & Karaberis
200 employees; mill has capacity to roll 10,000 tons/yr of steel scrap into rods

i. Ibadan--Western Nigeria Trading Company Ltd.
In production since 1958.
£25,000 investment
private European interests
over 100 employees; fences, windows, etc.

j. Kano--Steel Construction Company Ltd.
In production since 1957.
£30,000 investment by private interests
over 50 employees; fittings, light structures

k. Idi-Oro (Lagos)--Dorman Long & Amalgamated Eng. Ltd.
In production since 1948.
UK subsidiary; £70,000 CDC loan outstanding
over 200 employees; fabrication of bulk storage tanks, lorry bodies, rail wagons, and tank cars

l. Apapa--Metal Containers of West Africa Ltd.
In production since 1939.
Dutch subsidiary (branch factory at Port Harcourt in 1961)
over 200 employees; steel drums and containers

m. Apapa--Pressed Metal Works Co. Ltd.
In production since March, 1962.
£100,000 investment
UK subsidiary
under 100 employees; tanks, bulk liquid containers, and steel structures

n. Apapa--Metal Box Company of Nigeria Ltd.
In production since January, 1963.
£750,000 investment
Controlled by parent UK firm; also £100,000 CDFC investment
106 employees; metal drums and cans

o. Ikeja--Galvanising Industries (Nigeria) Ltd.
In production since May, 1964.
£300,000 investment
C. Itoh and Co. Ltd. and Yodogawa Steel Works Ltd. (Japanese), CFAO, and WNDC
250 employees; corrugated iron roofing sheets--eventually window sashes, water pipes, buckets, etc.

p. Port Harcourt--Whessoe Engineering Ltd.
In production since 1962.
£115,000 investment
100% Whessoe Ltd. (UK)
150 employees; steel structures, storage tanks, etc. 20,000 tons/yr

q. Apapa--Jammal Steel Structures Ltd.
Under construction; prod. scheduled for late 1964.
£500,000 investment
expansion of wrought iron works est. in 1958

r. Port Harcourt--Nigerian Galvanising Works Ltd.
In production since first quarter, 1963.
£485,000 investment
20% ER, 80% private (including Richard Thomas & Baldwin Ltd. of UK)
280 employees; galvanized iron sheets

s. Ikeja--Pioneer Metal Products (Nigeria) Ltd.
Under construction; prod. by late 1964
£300,000 investment
Nippon-Kokan Steel Industries (Japanese), Paterson, Zochonis and other private
galvanized roofing; as with o. above, about 20-25,000 tons/yr capacity

t. Kano--Northern Steelworks Ltd.
In production since February, 1964.
£40,000 investment
NNDC and private interests
under 100 employees; 50,000 steel doors and window frames/yr capacity

u. Isheri (WR)--Weissblum Ltd.
In production in 1964.
£34,000 investment
Israeli subsidiary
poultry equipment fabrication

v. Jos--Berry Hill (Nigeria) Ltd.
In production since early 1964.
£250,000 investment
Subsidiary of Berry Hill (Engineering) Ltd. (UK); parent bankrupt in mid-64 so now run by NR
over 200 employees; ferrous and non-ferrous castings

w. Apapa--Nigerial Ltd.
In production since 1963.
£40,000 investment
97 employees; corrugated aluminum sheets

x. Port Harcourt--United Eastern Metal Industries
In production since 1963. (Branch at Onitsha)
£50,000 investment
Nigerian private
100 employees; roofing and metal products

y. Port Harcourt--Wimpey Conder (Nigeria) Ltd.
In production since 1963.
£120,000 investment
50 employees; structural steel products

z. Apapa--Construction Industries Co. Ltd.
In production since 1958.
over 200 employees; metal furniture

aa. Ikeja--Nigerian Steel Products Ltd.

bb. Ikeja--Nigerian Glass Containers and Metal Manufacturing Co.
Under construction.
Private interests including Kowloon Enamelware Co. of Hong Kong

24. motor vehicle assembly

a. Apapa--Niger Motors Ltd.
In production since June, 1959.
£400,000 investment
100% UAC
270 direct labor (1 shift); assembly of 1,800 C.K.D. Bedford trucks and hundreds of jeeps and station wagons/yr plus buses--automobiles planned

b. Port Harcourt--BEWAC Automotive Products Ltd.
£200,000 proposed investment by BEWAC Ltd. (UK), INDAG, and ER
Land Rovers, Leyland trucks, and Massey-Ferguson tractors

c. Lagos (vicinity)--Ford Motor Co. proposing to establish assembly plant.

d. Apapa--others such as Leventis Motors Ltd. assemble vehicles on a S.K.D. basis--in this case, Mercedes

25. ordnance

Kaduna--Defense Industries Corporation
Under construction.
£3.7 million investment; £1.75 million Fed. Gov't. loan
100% Federal Government; Fritz Werner A.G. (German) supplier credit
300 employees; will produce small arms and ammunition

26. paints and varnishes

a. Ikeja--I.C.I. Paints (Nigeria) Ltd.
In production since October, 1962.
£135,000 investment
UK subsidiary
30 employees; 200,000 gal/yr capacity decorative paints

b. Ikeja--British Paints (West Africa) Ltd.
In production since January, 1962.
£300,000 investment
100 employees; 250,000 gal produced in first year

c. Ikeja--International Paints (West Africa) Ltd.
In production since January, 1962.
£150,000 investment
International Paints (UK) Ltd., and ICON
35 direct labor; building and marine paints

d. Port Harcourt--Permacem (Nigeria) Ltd.
In production since mid-1962.
£35,000 investment
G.B. Ollivant (Unilever) and Permacem (UK)
under 25 employees; waterproof cement paints

e. Port Harcourt--Pinchin Johnson and Associates Ltd.
£100,000 investment proposed for 1965 by UK parent (Courtoulds subsidiary);
50 employees

f. Lagos--Regency (Overseas) Co., Ltd.
In production since 1963.
£100,000 investment
37 employees; 200,000 gal/yr capacity vinol paints

g. Ibadan--Askar of Nigeria Ltd.
   In production since 1962.
   under 25 employees; 10,000 gal/mo capacity (prod. at 20%)

h. Port Harcourt--B.J.N. Paints (Nigeria) Ltd.
   Proposed by Berger, Jenson, and Nicholson (UK)

27. paper conversion and products

a. Apapa--Nigerian Paper Converters
   In production since late 1962.
   50 employees; toilet paper, drinking straws, index cards, folder files, etc.

b. Apapa--Bordpak Ltd.
   Construction due to start in late 1964.
   £1 million investment
   UAC and Thames Board Mills
   over 200 employees; corrugated cartons and printing

c. Ikeja--Paper Conversion Co. (Nigeria) Ltd.
   Under construction.
   less than 50 employees; paper bags, boxes

d. Apapa--Nigerpak Ltd.
   In production since March, 1962.
   £150,000 investment plus proposed £100,000 expansion
   51% Times Press Ltd. (of Nigeria) and 49% Marina Investments Ltd. (Nigerian Tobacco Co. subsidiary)
   50 employees; manufacture and print light packaging materials, including cigarette packets and shoe boxes

e. Lagos (vicinity)--Bemis Bag Co. (US)
   cardboard carton and packaging factory proposed.

f. Port Harcourt--Paper Products (Nigeria) Ltd.
   proposed paper bag factory

28. perfumes, cosmetics, and toilet preparations

a. Kano--Haco Ltd.
In production since 1954.
£100,000 investment
In 1963 J. Holt acquired controlling interest
over 200 employees; cosmetics and perfume bottling

b. Zaria--A.J. Seward (Nigeria) Ltd.
In production since February, 1964 (moved from Lagos).
£300,000 investment
100% UAC
about 100 employees; perfumes, powders, pomades, etc.

c. Kano--Geka Trading Co. Ltd.
In production since 1952.
Controlled by Albright and Wilson Ltd. (UK)
over 100 employees; perfumes and face powders

29. pharmaceuticals

a. Aba--Pfizer Products, Ltd.
In production since July, 1961.
$100,000 investment
100% Chas. Pfizer and Co., Inc. (US)
50 employees; formulation and packaging of antibiotics; capsuling and tableting foreseen

b. Apapa--Pharco Production Ltd.
In production since 1960.
Controlled by K. Chelleram and Co. (Indian)
over 100 employees; drugs, cosmetics, and candles

c. Apapa--Glaxo Laboratories (Nigeria) Ltd.
In production since 1960.
£150,000 expansion in 1963
UK subsidiary
under 50 employees; compounding sulfonamides, etc.

d. Ikeja--Major & Co. Manufacturing (Nigeria) Ltd.
Under construction. Proposed for Kaduna too.
UK subsidiary

e. Aba--Major & Co. Manufacturing (Nigeria) Ltd.
In production since mid-1964.
57 employees; pharmaceutical products

f. Kano--Pharmaceutical Co. of Nigeria Ltd.
Under construction.
£50,000 investment
40 employees; pharmaceutical products

30. phonograph records

a. Jos--E.M.I. (Nigeria) Ltd.
In production since late 1962.
£70,000 investment
51% UK parent and 49% NNIL
55 employees; 50,000 records/yr capacity

b. Onitsha--Nigerian Records Company Ltd.
In production since early 1963. Merged with Nigerphone Company Ltd., which had been in production in 1961.
£90,000 investment
Philips (Nigeria) Ltd. (Dutch subsidiary) and Nigerian private
about 50 employees; 3,000 records/day capacity

31. plastics

a. Ibadan--The Nigerian Plastics Co. Ltd. (NIPOL)
In production since August, 1957.
£105,000 investment
50% WNDC, 35% UAC, and 15% Yorkshire Imperial Metals, Ltd.
150 employees; 200 tons/yr water piping, polythene film, and housewares

b. Aba--Pfizer Products Ltd.
In production since March, 1963.
£100,000 investment
100 employees; teacups, saucers, etc.

d. Apapa--Metalloplastica (Nigeria) Ltd.
In production since 1961 (and Kano in 1964).
300 employees; plastic products

32. <u>printing and stationery</u>

a. Aba--International Press and Bookshop Co.
In production since 1951.
£50,000 investment
about 100 employees; printed products

b. Zaria--Gaskiya Corporation
In production since 1945.
NR statutory corporation
over 200 employees

c. Ebute-Metta--Thos. Wyatt and Sons (West Africa) Ltd.
In production since 1949.
Substantial stockholders include J. Holt and ICON
over 200 employees. Involved in Apex Paper Products, Ltd. in Ibadan, successor to £190,000 Western Nigeria Printing Corp. 1 yr later, in 1963, closed.
Also plants at Port Harcourt in 1962 with 50% ER; and Kaduna in 1963 with NNIL (£20,000 share)

d. Ibadan--Caxton Press (West Africa) Ltd.
about 50 employees; many other firms of this size throughout Federation

e. Victoria Island (Lagos)--Nigerian Security Printing and Minting Company
Under construction; partial prod. by 1966.
£1.3 million investment, including £½ mn CDC loan

55% Federal Gov't., 40% Thos. De La Rue Ltd. (UK), 5% Central Bank of Nigeria
Will operate federal mint.

33. radio and television set assembly

a. Apapa--Nigerian Electronics Ltd.
In production since 1962.
£25,000 investment
20% Ad. Auriema, Inc. (US), 20% WNDC, and Nigerian private
under 50 employees; radio ass'y (Westinghouse license)

b. Apapa--Philips (Nigeria) Ltd.
In production since late 1963.
£100,000 investment
100% Dutch subsidiary
over 100 employees; radio ass'y and elec. light bulbs

c. Apapa--Pye (Nigeria) Ltd.
In production since 1963.
£40,000 investment
Pye (UK) Ltd. and G.B. Ollivant (Unilever)
over 50 employees; transistor radios

34. sewing machine assembly

Apapa--Nigerian Sewing Machinery Mfg. Co. Ltd.
In production since late 1961.
Singer Manufacturing Co. (US) subsidiary
40 employees; 12,000 machines/yr (capacity higher) plus cabinets for the machines

35. shoes

a. Ikeja--Bata Shoe Co. (Nigeria) Ltd.
Under construction.
£500,000 investment
Subsidiary of Bata Co. of Canada
over 500 employees; leather footwear

b. Apapa--Bata Shoe Co. (Nigeria) Ltd.
   In production since November, 1960.
   £100,000 investment
   over 200 employees; plastic and rubber shoes

c. Kano--Rubber Industries, Ltd. (Nigerian Shoe Factory Ltd.)
   In production since 1959.
   £60,000 investment
   over 200 employees; plastic, canvas, and rubber shoes

d. Mushin--Nigerian Perfect Shoes Ltd.
   Under construction.
   £25,000 investment
   Italian and Nigerian private interests
   150 employees; initially 500 pairs/day, rubber and leather

e. Owerri (ER)--Modern Shoe Industry Ltd.
   Under construction.
   £120,000 investment
   ENDC and Svenska Skolastfabriken (Swedish)

f. Apapa--Salvi (Nigeria) Ltd.
   In production since March, 1964.
   £70,000 investment
   Mauro Shoe Co. (Italian) controlling interest
   60 employees; 500 pairs/day, eventually 1,000

g. Mushin--Polymera Industries (Nigeria) Ltd.
   In production since 1963.
   £100,000 investment
   150 employees; this and next entry produce about 1 million pairs/yr together; plastic shoes

h. Kano--Nigerian Leather Works Co. Ltd.
   In production since 1963.
   £200,000 investment
   Originally £100,000 NNDC loan; evidently converted and now 50% NNDC
   over 50 employees; shoes plus gloves, handbags, and suitcases

i. Sapele--Omimi Shoes Co. Ltd.
In production since 1963.
£100,000 investment
S.C.O.A. (French), Diezengoff (Israeli), and Nigerian private
165 employees; rubber and canvas shoes

j. Apapa--Utrilon Industries (Nigeria) Ltd.
In production since 1960.
over 50 employees; plastic shoes (as does Metalloplastica--see "plastics" above)

36. <u>singlets (men's undershirts) and knitted goods</u>

a. Ikorodu (WR)--Ikorodu Trading Co.
In production since 1956.
over 100 workers; singlets, underwear, and other knitwear

b. Enugu--Nigerian Clothing Co., Ltd.
Under construction.
£100,000 investment
British private plus ER
250 employees; 100 looms; skirts, shirts, blouses, dresses, and trousers

c. Jos--hosiery proposal abandoned

d. Kano--Gazal Industrial Enterprises proposed

e. Kano--Northern Knitting Works Ltd.
In production since 1963.
£90,000 investment
over 50 employees; socks and singlets

f. Mushin--Intra Garment Factory (Nigeria) Ltd.
In production since 1961.
over 50 employees

g. Yaba--Nigerian Tailoring Co. here since 1958--with over 100 employees--and many other small mills and tailoring establishments elsewhere manufacture these goods.

h. Apapa--Sunflag Knitting Mills (Nigeria) Ltd.
In production since 1961.
£25,000 investment
Nigerian private
over 50 employees; knitted cloth

37. <u>soft drink bottling</u>

a. Ibadan--Pepsi-Cola Bottling Plant
In production since late 1960.
£200,000 investment
100% WNDC

b. Mushin--Pepsi-Cola Bottling Plant
(same as above) (Mirinda orange & club too)

c. Apapa--Seven-Up Bottling Co. Ltd.
In production since 1960.
about 50 employees; Howdy orange too

d. Aba, Kaduna, and Apapa--Nigerian Breweries Ltd. (See "brewing" above.)
Kaduna plant produces 300,000 gal/yr
Tango orange, Krola, lemonade, tonic and soda water, and Schweppes products

e. Onitsha--Pepsi-Cola Bottling Plant
In production since March, 1961.
£346,000 investment by ENDC (100%)
100 direct labor; orange soda too

f. Ibadan--Nigerian Bottling Co., Ltd.
In production since April, 1962.
£250,000 investment
A.G. Leventis
Fanta orange, Sprite, and Coca-Cola

g. Apapa--Nigerian Bottling Co., Ltd.
In production since 1963.
Same as "f" (and now at Port Harcourt too)

h. Kano--Nigerian Bottling Co., Ltd.
In production since 1956.
Same as "f"

i. Apapa--London & Kano Trading Co.
In production since 1938. Bankrupt in 1964; probably will be liquidated.
Sword Brand soft drinks

j. Kano--Sword Brand Bottling Co. Ltd.
Closed down at present.
Merger of Bottling Corp. of Nigeria Ltd. and London & Kano's bottling plant
NNDC (£60,000 investment) plus L & K (to liquidate), Lebanese interests, and Jos mining interests
Sword Brand, Pepsi-Cola, and Mirinda

38. storage batteries, lead-acid

Ikeja--Associated Battery Manufacturers (Nigeria) Ltd.
In production since mid-1964.
UAC and Lucas-C.A.V.-Girling (UK)
motor vehicle wet-cell batteries

39. surgical and medical products

Yaba--Niger Sanitary Industry
In production since 1963.
under 50 employees; sanitary pads

40. tarpaulins

a. Apapa--Tarpaulin Industries (West Africa) Ltd.
In production since 1956.
British parent is Low and Bonar Ltd.
tents and awnings too

b. Yaba--Nigerian Tarpaulin Industry
under 50 employees

c. Kano--Nigerian Tarpaulin Manufacturing Co. Ltd.
£25,000 investment
under 50 employees

41. <u>tea and coffee blending and packing</u>

Apapa--Lipton of Nigeria Ltd.
In production since 1959.
UK subsidiary
130 employees; capacity: 1 mn lb. tea and .75 mn. lb coffee (Nigerian)/yr

42. <u>textiles</u>

a. Ikeja--Nigerian Textile Mills Ltd.
In production since September, 1962.
£2.6 million investment
loan capital of £350,000 from machinery suppliers and £1.8 mn from bank and shareholders, plus equity of £455,000
30% Arcturus (Chase Manhattan), 33% WNDC, and 37% Amenital Registered Trust (Ital.-Swiss)
1,300 employees; 15,000 spindles, 500 looms
18 mn sq yds/yr baft to printed piece goods plus 1 mn lb knitted goods for singlet manufacture

b. Aba--Aba Textile Mills Ltd.
Under construction.
$8.6 million investment
loan capital: $2 mn Export-Import Bank, $2.25 mn Taylor Woodrow (UK construction firm), $1.4 mn Barclays Bank
$3 million equity: 30% ER, 70% Indian Head Mills, Inc. (US)
1,200 employees; 15,000 spindles, 380 looms
30 mn sq yds/yr capacity; bleaching, finishing (including imported baft), dyeing, and printing

c. Mushin--Nigerian Spinning Company Ltd.
In production since 1948.
£30,000 investment
Private Nigerian interests
over 50 employees; 1,600 spindles, 50 looms
up to ½ mn sq yds/yr drills; bleaching and dyeing

d. Kano--Kano Citizens Trading Company Ltd.
In production since 1952 (at first a pilot scheme).
£108,000 investment
£35,100 NNDC loan plus £73,000 equity 41% NNDC and 59% Nigerian private interests
300 employees; 80 looms; 1.5 mn sq yds/yr of drills and Bedford cords; bleaching and dyeing
New spinning mill planned.
weaving capacity planned (and a "captive" supplier of yarn proposed for Kano)

e. Onitsha--Textile Printers of Nigeria Ltd.
Under construction.
£5 million investment, half of which loan capital
10% ER, plus UAC, Calico Printers' Assn (UK), Ankersmits (Dutch), and van Vlissingens (Dutch)
over 2,000 employees; 30 mn sq yds/yr including finishing as well as bleaching and printing

f. Kaduna--Kaduna Textiles Ltd.
In production since November, 1957.
£2½ million investment plus expansion, including NNDC loan of £300,000 and NRMB loan of £800,000
equity: 70% NNDC, 22.4% NNMB, and 7.6% David Whitehead and Sons (UK) (NNDC voting shares to NNIL)
2,800 employees (3 shifts); 40,000 spindles, 1,100 looms; over 40 mn sq yds/yr spinning and weaving baft plus bleached shirting

g. Kaduna--Nortex (Nigeria) Ltd.
   In production since October, 1962.
   £1.3 million investment
   loan capital from ICON and NNDC (£140,000) plus £400,000 equity: 55% E.A. Seroussi, 17.5% NNDC, 20% NNIL, 7.5% Nigerian private
   1,200 employees; 13,000 spindles, 300 looms; 12 mn sq yds/yr spinning, weaving, bleaching, finishing, and printing

h. Kaduna--Norspin Ltd. of Nigeria
   In production since early 1964.
   £2 million investment, including £400,000 CDFC loan and NNIL loan; UAC (managing agent), Dunlop Rubber Co., and English Sewing Cotton Company
   800 direct labor (1,200 employees); 26,000 spindles; 5.25 mn lb yarn/yr (to West African Thread Co. of Lagos with yarn for knitted fabric, and for tire cords and canvas to Dunlop's Ikeja tire factory)

i. Asaba--planned textile mill
   £4.4 million investment
   90% Mid-West Gov't, 10% Coutinho, Caro and Co.
   about 20 mn sq yds/yr

j. Kaduna--Arewa Textiles Ltd.
   Under construction; full prod. by March, 1966.
   £1.55 million investment
   loans: Overseas Spinning Investment Co. of Japan (10 firms) £480,000 machinery credit; NNDC £84,000; IFC £87,000 plus £46,000 (convert.)
   equity: 60% OSICJ, 16.7% IFC, and 23.3% NNDC plus NNIL
   600 employees; 10,000 spindles, 400 looms; 8.5 mn sq yds/yr capacity; bleaching and dyeing too

k. Gusau--Zamfara Textile Industries Ltd.
Under construction.
£870,000 investment including £110,000 NNDC loan
E.A. Seroussi, NNDC, and NNIL
1,000 employees; 10,000 spindles, 256 looms; 10 mn sq yds/yr capacity

l. Kaduna--United Nigerian Textiles Ltd.
Under construction.
China Dyeing Works Ltd. (HK)
100,000 sq yds/day finishing capacity (printing and dyeing); eventually spinning and weaving too

m. Kaduna--West Punjab Textile Mills Ltd.
Under construction.
Mr. I.Y. Gardee of Pakistan
360 synthetic fiber looms plus cotton printing
initially head ties (for women)

n. Kano--Kano Dyeing Works Ltd. proposed
Lebanese and Nigerian private interests
spinning and weaving poplins

43. thread, sewing

Apapa--West African Thread Company Ltd.
In production since 2nd quarter, 1962.
£500,000 investment
ICON, English Sewing Cotton Co., and G.B. Ollivant
100 direct labor; 1.25 mn lb spun yarn/yr capacity; knitted cloth goods too

44. tire production and retreading

a. Ikeja--Dunlop Nigerian Industries Ltd.
In production since the end of 1962.
£3.5 million investment including £150,000 loan by CDFC and £50,000 (of £300,000 available) CDC loan
equity: 10% WR (£150,000), Dunlop (UK), CDC (£50,000), CDFC (£100,000)
550 direct labor; 2,500 t/yr rubber to tires and tubes

b. Port Harcourt--Michelin (Nigeria) Ltd.
In production since third quarter, 1962.
£3 million investment
40% ER, 60% Michelin Tyres Co. (UK) Ltd.
over 200 employees; up to 10 t/day of tires and accessories for vehicles and bicycles

c. Jos--Terco (Nigeria) Ltd.
In production since 1955.
over 50 employees; retreading

d. Benin City--Ribway Tyre Retreading Co.
In production since mid-1964.
£50,000 investment
Nigerian and European private interests

e. Ibadan--Odutola Tyre Retreading Co. Ltd.
In production since 1956.
£75,000 investment
100% Mr. J.A. Odutola (Nigerian)
2 shifts; 50 tires/day retreading and remolding

f. Aba--Odutola Tyre Retreading Co., Ltd.
(Was West African Tyre Retreading Co. Ltd.)
In production since 1960.
£50,000 investment
same as above
2 shifts; 25 tires/day

g. Ibadan, Onitsha, and Kano--Odutola Tyre and Rubber Co.
In production since 1951, 1956, and 1957 respectively
£50,000 investment in Onitsha plant
100% Chief T.A. Odutola (Nigerian)
150, 80, and 80 direct labor (3 shifts); 1960-61: 35,000, 4,800, and 12,000 tires, respectively
plan to produce bicycle tires and inner tubes

h. Lagos--J. & A. Zarpas (Tyres) Ltd.
In production since 1957.
under 50 employees; retreading

i. Onitsha--Ugochukwu Tyres Ltd.
In production since 1958.
£40,000 investment
100% Nigerian private
over 50 employees; retreading

45. <u>tobacco products</u>

a. <u>cigars</u>--exploratory stage by Nigerian Tobacco Co. (Hand made in Calabar, Yaba, Ebute-Metta, etc.)

b. <u>cigarettes</u>

1. Ibadan, Port Harcourt, and Zaria--Nigerian Tobacco Company Ltd.
In production since 1936, 1956, and 1958 resp. (The Ibadan plant replaced plant in Ogbomosho, which had been established in 1933.)
£5 million investment
majority interest by British-American Tobacco Co.
over £200,000 sold to public in recent years
350 mn cigarettes/mo prod; 7 brands all told, over 2,000 employees

2. Ilorin--Kwara Tobacco Co. Ltd.
In production since April, 1964.
$1.4 million investment
67% UAC and 33% NNIL
200 employees; 600 mn/yr initially

46. <u>towels</u>

a. Apapa--NITOL Ltd.
Under construction.
Lebanese private
terry towels

b. Ikeja--Millet (Nigeria) Ltd.
Under construction.
£150,000 investment
Lebanese private
170 employees

47. toys

Abeokuta--NEVAC Ltd.

48. umbrella assembly

a. Lagos--West African Umbrella Co. Ltd.
In production since 1957.
over 50 employees

b. Apapa--Brittind (Nigeria) Ltd.
In production since 1961.
British and Indian private interests
under 50 employees; plastic sandals too

c. Lagos--Assan Umbrella Factory (Nigeria) Ltd.
In production since 1957.
over 50 employees

d. Onitsha--Okwuba Commercial Syndicate
In production since 1959.
23 employees; sandals too

49. wire products

a. Apapa--Nigerian Ropes Ltd.
In production since 1960.
£20,000 investment
British Ropes Ltd. and West African Engin. Co.
20 employees; steel wire cargo slings, pre-stressed concrete wire, plus splicing and fitting of fiber ropes, cords, and twines

b. Ikeja--B.R.C. Weldmesh (Nigeria) Ltd.
In production since 1962.
British Reinforced Concrete Engineering Corp.
20 employees; welded wire mesh

c. Ikeja--West African Steel and Wire Ltd.
In production since 1961. WASCO merged with B.R.C. in 1964. Both now 100% German private
over 200 employees; wire fending and nails

d. Onitsha--Beejay Manufacturing Co. Ltd.
In production since 1958 (with some interruptions due to technical and financial difficulties.)
£27,000 investment
Nigerian private
under 50 employees; wire nails

e. Kano--Kano Nails & Wires Ltd.
In production since 1962.
NNDC secured loan of £10,000
Lebanese private interests

f. Ikorodu--Industrial Enterprises (Nigeria) Ltd.
In production since 1959.
under 50 employees; nails

B. POWER-ORIENTED

glass

a. Port Harcourt--Nigerian Glass Company Ltd.
In production since mid-1963.
£1.5 million investment
100% ENDC (Coutinho, Caro and Co. supplier finance)
225 direct labor; 12,000 tons/yr jars and bottles
temporarily closed down in 1964 (see text)

b. Ughelli (Mid-West)--planned Mid-West Glass Industry Ltd.
£1.2 million capital cost with £350,000 authorized capital
90% Mid-West R. and 10% Coutinho, Caro and Co.

C. MULTI-ORIENTED

steel mill

Idah (NR) and Onitsha announced as sites of (presumably divided) steel mill [see text]
process, financing, etc. not yet made public

D. RAW MATERIAL-ORIENTED

1. abattoirs and meat packing

a. Onitsha--abattoir at Onitsha market
In production since 1956.
£25,000 investment
ENDC loan to City Council
10 direct labor

b. Kano--Kano Abattoir Ltd.
In production since 1963.
£80,000 NNDC loan and £10,000 NNDC equity
over 50 employees

c. Sokoto--Sokoto Native Authority Abattoir

d. Lagos--Lagos City Council
In production since 1943.
over 50 employees; meat and slaughtering

e. Maiduguri--Bornu Native Authority Abattoir
In production since 1959 and expanded in 1963 (with help of NNDC loan).
over 50 employees

f. Nguru--Bornu Native Authority Abattoir
In production since 1961.
over 100 employees' 400 head/day capacity

g. Apapa and Kano--K. Maroun (Pork Products) Ltd.
In production since 1956 and 1952, resp.
Lebanese private interests sold company to NNDC in mid-1964.
200 employees in total; bacon, ham, and sausage mfg.

h. Apapa--West African Cold Storage Co. of Nigeria Ltd.
In production since late 1962.
£250,000 investment

100% UAC
over 200 employees; "Satis" sausages, pork pies, bacon, ham, etc.; bristles to foam rubber manufacturers; eventually 30,000 pigs/yr (from Minna farm) and 2,000 head cattle/yr

i. Ibadan--Ibadan City Council (Abattoir)

j. Agege (WR, near Lagos)--Food and Commodities Production Group Ltd. (Mitchell Farms)
In production since 1963.
£100,000 investment
American and Nigerian private interests
33 employees; dressed chickens

2. <u>bags and sacks</u>

a. Jema'a--a sack factory was planned in conjunction with the kenaf and roselle plantation (pilot stage in 1961-63) at this town, near Kafanchan in Zaria Province
£2 million investment then envisioned
The Northern Fibre Syndicate was operated by NNDC, UAC, and VKCM (Dutch)
ultimate capacity: 4 mn bags/yr (@ 189 lb ea) for groundnuts, etc.
In 1964 Northern Nigeria Fibre Products Ltd. proposed
£2.1 million investment
Italian private interests plus NRMB and NNDC

b. WR--£1.5 million jute bag factory planned by WR and overseas private interests

c. Port Harcourt--jute bag factory proposed
Swiss and Nigerian private plus ENDC

3. bitumen processing

   a. Apapa--Shell Company of Nigeria Ltd.
      In production since 1955.
      £210,000 expansion in 1963 to include lube oil blending
      over 50 employees; 1961, 35,000 t/bitumen; and up to 10,000 tons/yr of lubricants now

   b. Port Harcourt--Shell Company of Nigeria Ltd.
      In production since late 1961.
      over 50 employees

   c. Apapa--Esso West Africa, Inc.
      Under construction.
      £250,000 investment
      100% Standard Oil (N.J.)
      also insecticide blending

4. boat building

   a. Opobo--Federal experimental yard in ER
      In production since 1950.
      over 50 employees; wood launches, barges, etc.

   b. Epe (WR), Makurdi (NR), and Opobo--Regional production yards
      In production since 1958, 1957, and 1954, respectively.
      Each has over 100 employees.
      WR has invested £60,000, NNDC £10,000, and ENDC £96,000.
      ER yard scheduled to merge with "a".

   c. Lagos, Warri, and Burutu--private yards
      These also use metal in addition to wood.

5. bone crushing

   Ibadan, Kano, and Nguru--production of bone meal

6. canning

a. Ibadan--Lafia Canning Factory
In production since 1954.
£579,000 investment
100% WNDC
over 100 employees (seasonal); capacity: 20,000 tons/yr fruit juices, pieces, and slices--in recent past, production at 10% of capacity

b. Kano--Nigerian Canning Company Ltd.
In production since 1955.
£100,000 investment
Liebig's Extract of Meat Co. Ltd., J. Holt, and NNIL
300 employees at full capacity; 1960 prod.: 4.8 mn cans "Crescent" [now "Beefex" too] brand corned beef @ 6 oz. and 250,000 tins jollof rice, guinea fowl stew, etc.

7. cocoa processing

Ife (WR)--proposed
First step would be production of cocoa butter.

8. cotton ginning

a. Oshogbo--This ginnery in the WR and the 12 in the NR are operated (and were built) by the British Cotton Growing Association. B.C.G.A. headquarters are located at Zaria in NR.
1959-60 cotton intake: about 2,600 tons

b. Funtua--northwest of Zaria
For this, and the succeeding ginneries, production is given in terms of tons of seed cotton
intake during 1960-61: 18,179 tons

c. Gombe--13,327 tons

d. Gusau--13,584 tons

e. Kontagora--west of Kaduna
9,447 tons

f. Kumo--south of Gombe
12,678 tons

g. Lamurde--southeast of Kumo
8,646 tons

h. Kuru--south of Jos
12,267 tons

i. Mai-Inchi--northwest of Gusau
14,228 tons

j. Malumfashi--north of Zaria
14,633 tons

k. Misau--northeast of Bauchi
5,569 tons

l. Zaria--19,012 tons

m. Lokoja--9, 181 tons

n. Keffi--southwest of Kafanchan
under consideration as a site

9. <u>distillery</u>

Apapa--Nigerian Fermentation Industries Ltd.
In production since May, 1964.
£30,000 investment
40% Fed. Govt, 40% Nigerian private, and 20% Dutch and Swiss partners (Erven Lucas Bols, tech. manager)
50 employees; bottling imported dry gin, brandy, and schnapps--6,000 bottles/day capacity
In 1966 company expects to open 200,000 gal/yr alcohol distillery (including industrial), using molasses from sugar refinery at Bacita (see below).

10. kapok cleaning

a. Ibadan--United Development Trading Company
In production since 1933.
£80,000 investment
Nigerian private interests
In addition to the cleaning and processing of these silky fibers, the plant crushes bones.

b. Kano--A.J. Karouni, Ltd., Kano Kapok Company, and Balmore Trading Company

11. margarine

Apapa--Lever Brothers (Nigeria) Ltd.
In production since 1923 (see soap below).
1,500 tons/yr capacity; 1,200 tons production of Blue Band margarine. The plant also produces a cooking fat (from palm oil and palm kernel oil), a bakery oil, pomades, and toothpaste.

12. oil-seed milling

a. Kano--P.S. Mandrides and Co. Ltd.
This plant and the following three have been producing groundnut oil and cake since the late 1940's. All have expanded in the past decade.
£400,000 investment
As with the other three, foreign private capital, mostly Lebanese, has been tapped.
over 100 employees; recent production for the four has been 150,000 t/yr

b. Kano--K. Maroun Ltd.
£250,000 investment
several hundred employees

c. Kano--Kano Oil Millers Ltd.
£350,000 investment
over 100 employees; also branch at Gusau

d. Kano--Nigerian Oil Mills Ltd.
£350,000 investment
over 200 employees

e. WR--Vegetable Oils for Nigeria Ltd.
Proposed £2 million palm kernel milling facility by WR in conjunction with German interests

f. ER--proposed £1.3 million palm kernel milling facility with 200,000 t/yr capacity

g. Zaria--Northern Oil Seeds Processing Development
In production, largely on an experimental basis, since November, 1959.
£171,000 investment by NR
now operated by NNDC
over 100 employees; groundnut "flour" supplied to Vom dairy and Glaxo Laboratories for baby food; production of shea nut butter and processing of cotton seeds are future possibilities

h. Zaria--proposed cotton seed mill
50% NNDC and 50% Otto Wolff Ltd. (German)

i. Zaria or Funtua--planned cotton seed mill by Wiedemann of Germany

j. Maiduguri--Maiduguri Oil Mills Ltd.
In production in 1964.
£50,000 investment
P.S. Mandrides
307 employees; groundnut oil and cake

k. NR--palm oil mills at Ayongba, Alade, and Ola
Operated by NNDC

l. ER--96 "Pioneer" oil mills operated by ENDC. Established in 1951, these ER-owned palm oil mills vary in production from 20,000 to 180,000 tons/yr. Average direct labor: 20.

m. ER--20 or so private--including Pamol (Nigeria) Ltd. with over 500 employees in Calabar area--and cooperative mills similar to the preceding entry

n. Sapele--Pamol (Nigeria) Ltd.
In production since 1940.
Unilever
over 500 employees

o. WR--three WNDC palm oil mills including plant at Irele (Ondo Province) with £30,000 investment

p. Port Harcourt, etc.--Bulk Oil Plants of Nigeria Ltd.
UAC built these 7 plants which engage in bulking, and the removal of water and impurities. UAC still owns and operates the plant at Apapa, but in 1961 transferred ownership of the other six to BOPN, Ltd., which is owned by the Nigeria Produce Marketing Co., and which in turn is owned by the regional marketing boards.
£650,000 investment in the six
1959 tonnages processed:
Opobo--13,631
Koko (MW)--5,420
Calabar--31,151
Burutu (MW)--5,641
Abonnema (ER near Degema)--10,410
Port Harcourt--110,125
P.H. plant has 300 direct labor

13. ore processing

a. Enugu--Nigerian Coal Corporation

b. Jos Plateau--The tin companies engage in washing, dressing, sorting, and concentrating operations.

14. <u>paper milling</u>

Jebba (NR)--Nigerian Papers Mills, Ltd.
Under construction.
£3.3 million investment
30.6% Fed. Gov't, 59.4% by regions (principally, NR), and 10% Coutinho, Caro and Co. (German); £2.3 million loan from Kreditanstalt für Wiederaufbau over 7 yrs @ 6%
Management by Escher Wyss Gmbh.
capacity: 12,000 t/yr--imported pulp until sufficient bagasse from sugar mill (see below)

15. <u>petroleum refining</u>

Alesa-Eleme (near Port Harcourt)--Nigerian Petroleum Refining Co., Ltd. is under construction.
$22.4 million investment
50% Federal and Regional gov'ts., 50% B.P.-Shell
250 direct labor; fractional distillation will produce primarily motor gasoline--1.6 million t/yr capacity

16. <u>rice hulling and milling</u>

a. Port Harcourt vicinity--planned mill of Niger Delta Development Board (Federal entity)--3,600 t/yr
£35,000 investment

b. Abakaliki and surrounding area (ER)--about 100 diesel mills

c. WR--co-operatives

d. Bida (NR)--Badeggi Rice Mill Ltd.
   In production since 1954.
   less than 25 employees

17. rubber processing

a. Sapele--Pamol (Nigeria) Ltd.
   In production since 1936.
   Unilever subsidiary
   1,200 tons/yr of crepe etc. plus palm oil

b. Akpanka (Calabar Province)--Dunlop Nigerian Plantations Ltd.
   In production since 1962.
   £2 million over-all investment
   production of sheet rubber

c. Benin City--Ikpoba Rubber Factory
   In production since 1954.
   £260,000 investment
   100% MNDC (transferred to MW after region created)
   over 100 employees; 3½ tons/day of crepe

d. Benin City--John Edokpolo and Sons
   In production since 1955.
   £81,000 investment
   Nigerian private interests
   over 200 employees; sheet and crepe rubber

e. Benin City--Phoebus Economides Rubber Plant
   In production since 1959.
   £15,000 investment
   Greek private interests
   over 50 employees; about 35 t/wk crepe

f. Sapele--Uodubi Rubber Industrial Company
   In production since 1954.
   £75,000 investment
   Nigerian private interests
   over 50 employees; crepe

g. Sapele--J.A. Thomas Rubber Estates Ltd.
In production since 1939.
£110,000 investment
Nigerian private interests
over 200 employees; 2 t/day crepe plus 5½ t/mo sheet (also 50,000 cu ft of timber/yr)

h. Benin City--Bata Shoe Co. (Nigeria) Ltd.
In production since late 1961.
£50,000 investment
over 50 employees; crepe rubber

i. Sapele--S. Thomopulos and Co. Ltd.
In production since 1946.
£250,000 investment
Greek private interests
over 500 employees; 17 t/week sheet

j. Mid-West--John Holt Co. Ltd.
This UK trading company operates plants at Warri, Sapele, and Benin City. The last named has over 200 employees and has been in operation since 1962.

k. Ijebu-Ode (WR)--Ilushin Estates Ltd.
In production since 1963.
£693,000 investment
jointly held by CDC, WNDC, and West African Joint Agency Ltd.

l. Sapele--Afro-Nigerian Export and Import Co.
In production since 1959.
over 100 employees; sheet and crepe rubber

m. Sapele--Nigerian Rubber Co. Ltd.
In production since 1961.
over 100 employees; sheet and crepe rubber

n. Sapele--UAC of Nigeria Ltd.
In production since 1952.
over 100 employees; crepe

o. Benin City--United States African Corporation
   defunct

p. Sapele--The New Independent Rubber Co. Ltd. in production here since 1961 plus others elsewhere in the south produce sheet and/or crepe.

q. Calabar--Oban (Nigeria) Rubber Estates Ltd.
   Started in 1952; most of 6,500 acres now in production.
   British private plus ENDC

18. <u>salt refining and packaging</u>

An American company, among others, is considering the establishment of such a plant.

19. <u>soap and detergents</u>

a. Aba--Lever Brothers (Nigeria) Ltd.
   In production since April, 1958.
   270 direct labor; 5 brands--10,000 t/yr

b. Apapa--Lever Brothers (Nigeria) Ltd.
   In production since 1924. In 1962 at cost of £250,000 added Omo detergent and now in process of £150,000 overall expansion.
   over 600 direct labor; 8 brands--7,000 t/yr

c. Aba--International Equitable Association, Ltd.
   In production since 1952.
   £150,000 investment
   Owned and operated by Mr. P.B. Nicholas
   77 employees; 2,700 tons/yr

d. Aba--Associated Industries Ltd.
   In production since 1948 as Alagbon Industries, and under present name since 1961.

£500,000 investment
Paterson, Zochonis and Co., Ltd. subsidiary
300 direct labor; 2 brands--7,000 t/yr

e. Ibadan--Metropolitan Syndicate
In production since 1959.
£30,000 investment
under 50 employees

f. Kano--Raad and Fadoul Ltd.
In production since 1955.
£20,000 investment
over 100 employees

g. Lagos (vicinity)--Soap and detergent plant proposed by overseas interests.

20. starch

The Starch and Glucose Co. of Nigeria has been registered. Plans to use cassava as raw material.

21. sugar refining

a. Bacita (NR near Jebba)--The Nigerian Sugar Co. Ltd.
Under construction.
£5 million investment
NR (£310,000), Booker Brothers (UK; managing agent), NIDB, Fed. Gov't., NNIL, United Molasses Co., Barclays O.D.C., and CDFC (£75,000 equity plus £350,000 loan)
300 employees in 1964 (plantation); initial capacity of 30,000 tons of white sugar/yr, plus molasses to distillery and probably bagasse to paper mill

b. ER--sugar facility proposed at location northwest of Enugu; American private interests involved

c. NR--plant proposed to convert bulk sugar to cubes by Tate and Lyle (UK).

22. tanning and leather

a. Sokoto--small plant (skins, no hides) owned by Rupert Clark (UK) and Nigerian private interests

b. Kano--Holt's Nigerian Tannery Ltd.
Pickling since 1949; leather production since 1961.
£150,000 investment
majority share holder (£70,000) NNIL; J. Holt and Co. and other private interests
50 direct labor; 1.25 million hides and skins/yr (mostly goat)

c. Kano--Great Northern Tanning Co. Ltd.
In production since late 1962.
over 50 employees

d. Maiduguri--Bornu Tannery Ltd.
In production since 1960.
£30,000 investment
otherwise known as David Ani Tannery; US (Seroussi) and Syrian private interests

e. Kano--Darum Enterprises Ltd.
In production since 1961.
under 25 employees; skins and hides

f. Zaria--Bata Shoe Co. (Nigeria) Ltd.
(see shoes above)
leather finishing plant

23. timber processing

a. Benin City--ECN Hardwood Impregnating Plant
Under construction in 1963.

b. Sapele--African Timber and Plywood (Nigeria) Ltd.
   In production since 1935. Plywood operation added in 1950 and sawmill modernized.
   £1.25 million investment
   100% UAC
   3,200 direct labor; sawmill processes about 5 mn cu ft/yr (£3 mn sales) plus plywood and veneers as well as round logs; in future maybe chipboard

c. Sapele--British West African Timber Co. Ltd.
   In production since 1956.
   over 200 employees; 16,000 cu ft/mo

d. Calabar--Brandler and Rylkes Ltd.
   In production since 1948.
   UK private interests
   over 500 employees; sawn timber

e. Port Harcourt--J.C. Okeke & Bros. Sawmill Industry
   In production since 1952.
   £35,000 investment
   under 25 direct labor; 30,000 cu ft/yr

f. Enugu--J.C. Okeke and Co.
   In production since 1959.
   over 500 employees; sawn timber

g. Oron (ER)--Oron Sawmill
   In production since 1934.
   £25,000 investment
   over 50 employees

h. Ijebu-Ode (WR)--Omo Sawmills of Nigeria Ltd.
   In production since 1946.
   £300,000 investment
   British and Nigerian private interests
   200 direct labor; 300,000 cu ft/yr

i. Akure (vicinity; WR)--The Pilot Sawmill
In production since 1953 under present management; set up by Forestry Dep't. in 1951, then sold.
£35,000 investment
156 direct labor; 140,000 cu ft/yr

j. Sapele--J. Asaboro and Company
In production since 1958.
£268,000 investment
over 1,000 employees; 32,000 cu ft/mo (plus 400 cwt/wk rubber processed)

k. Owo (WR)--Finch and Co. (West Africa) Ltd.
In production since 1952.
£10,000 investment
over 200 employees; 250,000 cu ft/yr

l. Sapele--Nigerian Hardwoods Company Ltd.
In production since 1946; expanded in 1959.
£50,000 investment
James Latham (UK) Ltd. majority share, and Nigerian private interests
over 100 employees; 95,000 cu ft/yr

m. Ondo (WR)--African Industrial Timber Co.
In production since 1960.
over 100 employees

n. Ondo--Coast Timber Co. Ltd.
In production since 1950.
over 200 employees

o. Ibadan--Ibadan Sawmill & Timber Export Ltd.
over 200 employees

p. Ibadan--J.A.O. Obadeyi Ltd.
In production since 1942.
over 100 employees

q. Sapele--J.A. Thomas Rubber Estates Ltd.
In production since 1916.

r. Benin City--A.O. Obasuyi and Sons
In production since 1957.
over 100 employees

s. Iddo (Lagos)--G. Cappa Sawmills here since 1940 and others elsewhere, especially in the south, operate smaller and less modern sawmills.

t. Kabba (NR)--Northern Nigeria Timber Co. Ltd.
Coast Timber Co. and NNDC

24. <u>tin smelting</u>

a. Jos--Nigeria Embel Tin Smelting Co. Ltd.
In production from March, 1961, to January, 1963, when closed (and bankrupt).
£250,000 investment
Portuguese private interests plus Chase-Manhattan loan
scheduled capacity: 12,960 tons ore/yr

b. Jos--Makeri Smelting Co. Ltd.
In production since 1962.
£500,000 investment
Consolidated Tin Smelters (UK)
over 200 employees; 7,000 tons ore in 1962--eventual capacity: 21,600 tons ore/yr

BIBLIOGRAPHY

Government Publications

Adedeji, Adebayo. A Survey of Highway Development in the Western Region of Nigeria. Ibadan: Government Printer, 1960.

Ashby, E., et al. Investment in Education. The Report of the Commission on Post-School Certificate and Higher Education in Nigeria. Lagos: Federal Government Printer, 1960.

Blankenheimer, B., Fischer, R. V., and Lebois, J. L. Investment in Nigeria: Basic Information for United States Businessmen. (Bureau of Foreign Commerce, U.S. Department of Commerce.) Washington, D.C.: Government Printing Office, 1957.

Coleman, E. H. How Aviation Came to Nigeria. Lagos: Federal Ministry of Information, 1960.

De Swardt, A. M. J. and Casey, O. P. The Coal Resources of Nigeria. Geological Survey of Nigeria Bulletin No. 28. Lagos: Federal Government Printer, 1961.

Dike, K. O. 100 Years of British Rule in Nigeria: 1851-1951. 1956 Lugard Lectures, A Series of Six Radio Broadcasts. Lagos: Federal Ministry of Information, 1960.

Eastern Region. Approved Estimates of Eastern Nigeria: 1964-1965 (Official Document No. 13 of 1964). Enugu: Government Printer, 1964.

______. Development Corporation. Annual Reports: 1956-61. Enugu: 1957-62.

______. Development Programme: 1958-62 (Official Document No. 2 of 1959). Enugu: Government Printer, 1959.

______. Marketing Board. First-Eighth Annual Reports: 1st January, 1956-62 - 31st December, 1956-61. Port Harcourt: 1956-64.

______. Ministry of Agriculture. Annual Report: 1959-60 (Official Document No. 2 of 1961). Enugu: Government Printer, 1961.

______. Ministry of Commerce. Annual Reports: 1958-59 and 1959-60. Enugu: Government Printer, 1960-61.

______. Ministry of Economic Planning. First Progress Report: Eastern Nigeria Development Plan: 1962-68 (Official Document No. 15 of 1964). Enugu: Government Printer, 1964.

______. Ministry of Health. Annual Report: 1958 (Official Document No. 11 of 1961). Enugu: Government Printer, 1961.

______. Ministry of Works. Report on Roads, Drainage and Sewerage in Port Harcourt. Enugu: 1961.

______. Revised Development Programme: 1958-62 (Official Document No. 13 of 1960). Enugu: Government Printer, 1960.

______. University of Nigeria Progress Report (Official Document No. 7 of 1960). Enugu: Government Printer, 1960.

Lagos Executive Development Board. Annual Report and Accounts (1959-1960 and 1960-61). Lagos, 1960-61.

Loynes, J. B. Report on the Establishment of a Nigerian Central Bank, the Introduction of a Nigerian Currency, and Other Associated Matters. Lagos: Government Printer, 1957.

Mid-Western Region. Estimates: 1964-65. Benin City: Ministry of Internal Affairs Printing Division, 1964.

Nigeria. Advisory Committee on Education in the Colonies. Ten-Year Education Plan (Sessional Paper No. 6 of 1944). Lagos: Federal Government Printer, 1949.

______. Central Bank. Annual Report and Statement of Accounts for the Periods Ended 31st March, 1960, 31st December 1960 through 31st December 1963. Lagos: 1960-64.

______. Central Bank. Economic and Financial Review. Vols. 1 and 2. Lagos: 1963-64.

______. Coal Corporation. Ninth-Thirteenth Annual Reports for the Years 1958-63. Enugu: 1959-63.

______. Constitution of the Federation (Supplement to Official Gazette Extraordinary No. 71, Vol. 50). Lagos: 1963.

______. Education Development: 1961-70 (Sessional Paper No. 3 of 1961). Lagos: Federal Government Printer, 1961.

______. Electricity Corporation. Annual Reports: 1959-60 through 1962-63. Lagos: 1960, 1962, and 1963.

______. Establishment of Oil Refinery in Nigeria (Sessional Paper No. 5 of 1960). Lagos: Federal Government Printer, 1960.

______. Estimates of the Government of the Federal Republic of Nigeria: 1964-65. Lagos: Ministry of Information Printing Division, 1964.

______. Federal Department of Education. Annual Report: 1959. Lagos: Federal Government Printer, 1961.

______. Federal Department of Labour. Annual Reports: 1958-59 and 1960-61. Lagos: Federal Government Printer, 1961, and Federal Ministry of Information Printing Division, 1964.

______. Federal Institute of Industrial Research. Annual Report: 1963-64. Lagos: Ministry of Information Printing Division, 1964.

______. Federal Loans Board. 1st-6th Annual Reports: 1st July, 1956-61 - 30th June, 1957-62. Lagos: Federal Government Printer, 1957-63.

______. Federal Ministry of Commerce and Industry. Annual Reports: 1958-59 through 1960-61. Lagos: Federal Government Printer, 1960 and 1964.

______. Federal Ministry of Commerce and Industry. Industrial Directory: 1964. Lagos: 1964.

______. Federal Ministry of Communications. Annual Report of the Nigeria Post Office Savings Bank: 1959-60. Lagos: Ministry of Information Printing Division, 1963.

______. Federal Ministry of Economic Development. National Development Plan: 1962-68. Lagos: 1962.

______. Federal Ministry of Information. Our Communications: Highways and Bridges. Lagos: 1958.

______. Federal Ministry of Mines and Power. Mines Division. Annual Reports for the Years ended 31st March, 1960 and 1962. Lagos: Federal Government Printer, 1961 and 1963.

______. Federal Ministry of Mines and Power. Annual Reports of the Geological Survey for the Years 1955-59. Lagos: Federal Government Printer, 1957-61.

______. Federal Ministry of Lands, Mines and Power. Minerals and Industry in Nigeria. Lagos: Federal Government Printer, 1957.

______. Federal Ministry of Works and Surveys. Federal Public Works Department. Annual Reports: 1958-59 and 1959-60. Lagos: Federal Government Printer, 1960 and 1962.

______. Federal Office of Statistics. Annual Abstract of Statistics: 1963. Lagos: 1963.

______. Federal Office of Statistics. Digest of Statistics. Vol. 12, No. 4 and Vol. 13, No. 1. Lagos: 1963-64.

______. Federal Office of Statistics. Estimates of Capital Formation: 1958-59. Lagos: 1960. (Mimeographed.)

______. Federal Office of Statistics. Nigeria Trade Summary. Vols. 45 through 48. Lagos: 1960-63.

______. First-Fifth Progress Reports on the Economic Programme: 1955-60-62. Lagos: Federal Government Printer, 1957-61.

______. Handbook of Commerce and Industry in Nigeria. 5th ed. Lagos: Federal Ministry of Commerce and Industry, 1962.

______. Mines Department. Mining and Mineral Resources in Nigeria. Lagos: Federal Government Printer, 1957.

______. National Economic Council. Economic Survey of Nigeria: 1959. Lagos: Federal Government Printer, 1959.

______. National Manpower Board. Manpower Situation in Nigeria (Preliminary Report). Manpower Studies, No. 1. Lagos: Ministry of Information Printing Division, 1963.

______. Nigeria Magazine. Lagos: Federal Government Printer, 1960-62.

______. Nigeria Trade Journal. Lagos: Federal Ministry of Information, 1960-64.

______. Ports Authority. Annual Reports for the Years Ended 31st March, 1959, 1961, and 1963. Lagos: 1959, 1961, and 1963.

______. Posts and Telegraphs Department. Annual Report for the Year 1957-58. Lagos: Federal Government Printer, 1960.

______. Proposals for Dams on the Niger and Kaduna Rivers. Lagos: Federal Government Printer, 1960.

______. Railway Corporation. Bauchi-Bornu Railway Extension: Review of Revenue Potential. Ebute Metta: Railway Printer, 1960.

______. Railway Corporation. Report and Accounts for the Years Ended 31st March, 1960-63. Ebute Metta: Railway Printer, 1961-63.

______. Report of the Advisory Committee on Aids to African Businessmen. Lagos: Federal Government Printer, 1959.

______. Report of the Coker Commission of Inquiry into the affairs of Certain Statutory Corporations in Western Nigeria. Four volumes. Lagos: Ministry of Information Printing Division, 1962.

______. Report on Education Development in Lagos. Lagos: Federal Government Printer, 1957.

______. Report of the Elias Commission of Inquiry into the Administration, Economics, and Industrial Relations of the Nigeria Railway Corporation. Lagos: Federal Government Printer, 1960.

______. Report of the [Morgan] Commission in the Review of Wages, Salary and Conditions of Service of the Junior Employees of the Governments of the Federation and in Private Establishments. Lagos: Ministry of Information Printing Division, 1964.

______. The Economic Programme of the Government of the Federation of Nigeria: 1955-60 (Sessional Paper No. 2 of 1956). Lagos: Federal Government Printer, 1959.

______. The Role of the Federal Government in Promoting Industrial Development in Nigeria (Sessional Paper No. 3 of 1958). Lagos: Federal Government Printer, 1958.

______. The Sovereignty Budget (Budget Speech by Chief The Honourable Festus Sam Okotie-Eboh, Federal Minister of Finance, on 6th April, 1961). Lagos: Federal Ministry of Information, 1961.

______. Trade Reports: 1957-58. Lagos: Federal Government Printer, 1960.

Northern Region. A Statement of Policy on the Development Finance Programme: 1955-60. Kaduna: Government Printer, 1955.

______. Development Corporation. 1st-8th Annual Reports: 1955/56 - 1962/63. Kaduna: 1956-63.

______. Estimates of the Government of Northern Nigeria: 1964-65. Kaduna: Government Printer, 1964.

______. Industrialists' Guide to Northern Nigeria. Kaduna: 1960.

______. Marketing Board. First-Seventh Annual Reports: 1st November, 1954-59 - 31st October, 1955-61. Kano: 1956-62.

______. Ministry of Agriculture. Annual Reports: 1955-56 and 1957-58. Kaduna: Government Printer, 1959-60.

______. Ministry of Trade and Industry. The Industrial Potentialities of Northern Nigeria. Kaduna: 1963.

______. Ministry of Works. Annual Reports: 1958-60. Kaduna: Government Printer, 1960-61.

______. The Extension to the Development Finance Programme: 1955-1960, 1st April, 1960 to 31st March, 1962. Kaduna: Government Printer, 1961.

Oliver, E. I. Nigeria: Economic and Commercial Conditions. (Overseas Economic Survey, Board of Trade.) London: Her Majesty's Stationery Office, 1957.

Prest, A. R. and Stewart, I. G. The National Income of Nigeria, 1950-1. (Colonial Research Study No. 11.) London: Her Majesty's Stationery Office, 1953.

Rivkin, A., et al. Report of the Special U.S. Economic Mission to Nigeria. Washington, D.C.: Department of State, 1961.

Stewart, I. G., et al. Nigeria: Determinants of Projected Level of Demand, Supply, and Imports of Farm Products in 1965 and 1975. A report for the Economic Research Service; ERS-Foreign -32. Washington, D.C.: Department of Agriculture, August, 1962.

United Kingdom. Colonial Office. Report of the Fiscal Commission. A Report by Sir J. Raisman et al. Cmnd. 481. London: Her Majesty's Stationery Office, 1958.

______. Commonwealth Development Corporation. Report and Accounts: 1963 (House of Commons Paper No. 219). London: 1964.

______. Commonwealth Economic Committee. Commonwealth Development and its Financing. Vol. 5 (Nigeria). London: Her Majesty's Stationery Office, 1963.

______. Department of Scientific and Industrial Research. Reports of the Tropical Products Institute: 1959-60. London: Her Majesty's Stationery Office, 1960-61.

______. Nigeria: Report of the Commission appointed to enquire into the fears of Minorities and the means of allaying them. A Report to Parliament by the Secretary of State for the Colonies. Cmnd. 505. London: Her Majesty's Stationery Office, 1958.

United States. Congress, House, Committee on Foreign Affairs. Hearings, Activities of Private United States Organizations in Africa. 87th Cong., 1st Sess., 1961.

Western Region. A Directory of Industries and Allied Trades in the Western Region of Nigeria. Ibadan: Ministry of Information, 1960.

______. Department of Agriculture. Annual Report: 1953-54 (Sessional Paper No. 6 of 1959). Ibadan: Government Printer, 1959.

______. Development Corporation. Annual Reports: 1958-59, 1959-60, and 1961-62. Ibadan: 1960, 1961, and 1963.

______. Development of the Western Region of Nigeria: 1955-60 (Sessional Paper No. 4 of 1955). Ibadan: Government Printer, 1959.

______. Estimates: 1964-65. Ibadan: Government Printer, 1964.

______. Marketing Board. First-Seventh Annual Reports: 1st October, 1954-59 - 30th September, 1955-61. Ibadan: 1956-62.

______. Ministry of Economic Planning and Community Development. Statistics Division. Western Nigeria Statistical Bulletin: December 1960. Ibadan: Government Printer, 1961.

______. Ministry of Economic Planning. Statistics Division. Annual Abstract of Education Statistics: 1953-58. Ibadan: Government Printer, 1959.

______. Report of the Commission Appointed to Review the Educational System of Western Nigeria. Ibadan: Government Printer, 1961.

______. Western Region Development Plan: 1960-65 (Sessional Paper No. 17 of 1959.) Ibadan: Government Printer, 1959.

______. Western Region Finance Corporation. 1st-7th Annual Reports (1955/56 - 1961/62). Ibadan: Government Printer, 1957-63.

______. Western Region Housing Corporation. Annual Report and Accounts for the Years Ended 31st March, 1959 and 1962 (Sessional Paper No. 1 of 1960 and O.D. No. 4 of 1963). Ibadan: Government Printer, 1960 and 1963.

______. White Paper on the Establishment of a University in Western Nigeria (Sessional Paper No. 12 of 1960). Ibadan: Government Printer, 1960.

Williams, D. H. A Short Survey of Education in Northern Nigeria. Kaduna: Government Printer, 1960.

Wyatt, G. E. The Price of Electricity in Nigeria. Lagos: Electricity Corporation of Nigeria, 1961.

Books

Awolowo, Obafemi. AWO: The Autobiography of Chief Obafemi Awolowo. Cambridge: Cambridge University Press, 1960.

Bauer, Peter T. West African Trade: A Study of Competition, Oligopoly and Monopoly in a Changing Economy. Cambridge: Cambridge University Press, 1954.

Bello, Sir Ahmadu. My Life. Cambridge: Cambridge University Press, 1962.

Buchanan, K. M. and Pugh, J. C. Land and People in Nigeria: The Human Geography of Nigeria and Its Environmental Background. London: University of London Press, 1955.

Burns, Alan. History of Nigeria. 5th ed. London: George Allen and Unwin, Ltd., 1955.

Coleman, James S. Nigeria: Background to Nationalism. Berkeley: University of California Press, 1958.

Crowder, Michael. The Story of Nigeria. London: Faber and Faber, 1962.

Dike, K. O. Trade and Politics in the Niger Delta: 1830-1885. London: Oxford University Press, 1956.

Frankel, S. H. Capital Investment in Africa: Its Course and Effects. London: Oxford University Press, 1938.

Grant, J. A Geography of Western Nigeria. New York: Cambridge University Press, 1960.

Hawkins, E. K. Road Transport in Nigeria: A Study of African Enterprise. New York: Oxford University Press, 1958.

Inter-African Labour Institute. The Human Factors of Productivity in Africa: A Preliminary Survey. 2nd ed. London: Commission for Technical Co-operation in Africa South of the Sahara, 1960.

International Bank for Reconstruction and Development. The Economic Development of Nigeria. The Report of the Mission Organized by the IBRD at the Request of the Governments of Nigeria and the United Kingdom. Lagos: Federal Government Printer, 1954. Later published by Johns Hopkins Press, Baltimore, 1955.

Netherlands Engineering Consultants. River Studies and Recommendations on Improvement of Niger and Benue. Amsterdam: North-Holland Publishing Co., 1959.

Roper, J. I. Labour Problems in West Africa. London: Penguin Books, Ltd., 1958.

Royal Institute of International Affairs. Nigeria: The Political and Economic Background. London: Oxford University Press, 1960.

Sklar, Richard L. Nigerian Political Parties: Power in an Emergent African Nation. Princeton: Princeton University Press, 1963.

Smythe, Hugh H. and Smythe, Mabel M. The New Nigerian Elite. Stanford: Stanford University Press, 1960.

Stapleton, G. B. The Wealth of Nigeria. London: Oxford University Press, 1958.

Yesufu, T. M. An Introduction to Industrial Relations in Nigeria. London: Oxford University Press, 1962.

Articles and Periodicals

Africa Report (formerly African Special Report). Washington, D.C.: The African-American Institute, 1959-64.

Buckle, D. H. "Timber Operations in West Africa," Unasylva, Vol. 13, No. 1. Rome: Food and Agriculture Organ., 1959.

Daily Express. Lagos, July-November, 1961; January, 1963 - October, 1964.

Daily Times. Lagos, July-November, 1961. January, 1963 - October, 1964.

Economist. London, 1959-1964.

Frodin, Ruben. AUFS Reports Service. West African Series. Vol. IV, Nos. 1-6. New York: American Universities Fields Staff, Inc., 1961.

Hance, William A. "West African Industry: An Analysis of Locational Orientation," _Journal of International Affairs_, XV, No. 1 (Winter, 1961), 29-41.

International Financial News Survey (IMF). Washington, D.C., 1960-2.

Jucker-Fleetwood, Erin E. _Monetary and Financial Problems of Certain New Countries in Africa_ (Series A: No. 34). Basle: Centre for Economic and Financial Research, 1961.

______. _The Monetary and Financial Position in Ghana and Nigeria_ (Series A: No. 29). Basle: Centre for Economic and Financial Research, 1960.

Kilby, Peter. "African Labour Productivity Reconsidered," _The Economic Journal_, LXXI (June, 1961).

Morning Post. Lagos, July, 1963 - October, 1964.

New York Times. 1956-1964.

Overseas Review. London: Barclays Bank D.C.O., 1960-64.

Sinclair, W. E. "Tin Mining in Nigeria," _The South African Mining and Engineering Journal_, August 14, 1943.

Statistical and Economic Review. Issues 1-29. London: United Africa Company, Ltd., 1948-1964.

Times Review of Industry. London, 1959-1962.

Wall Street Journal. 1959-1962.

West Africa. London: West African Graphic Co., Ltd., 1961-64.

West African Pilot. Lagos (Yaba). July-November, 1961; January, 1963 - October, 1964.

Reports

Armour Research Foundation. Technological-Economic Evaluation of Opportunities for Establishment of a Textile Products Manufacturing Plant in Nigeria. A Report for the Empire Bloomer Company of New York. Chicago: 1961.

______. The Potential for Lead Utilizing Industries in Nigeria and Prospectus for the Establishment of a Lead-Acid Automotive Storage Battery Company in Nigeria. A Two-Part Report for the Rockefeller Bros. Fund. Chicago: 1960.

Auriema Development Associates. A Study of the Advisability of Building a Plant to Manufacture Electric Appliances in Nigeria. A Report for the Rockefeller Bros. Fund. New York: 1961.

Covey, John E. Economic Feasibility of a Meat Industry in Northern Nigeria. A Report for Rockefeller Bros. Fund. 1959.

Eadie, A. G. Report on the Establishment of a Glass Container Industry in Eastern Nigeria. A Report to the Eastern Nigeria Development Corporation by Industrial and Processing Engineering Consultants. London: 1961.

Economist Intelligence Unit, Ltd. Investment Opportunities in Eastern Nigeria. London: 1960.

Federation of British Industries. Nigeria: An Industrial Reconnaissance. The Report of the FBI Delegation to the Industrial Development Conference. Lagos: January, 1961. London: 1961.

______. Report on a Visit to Nigeria and the Gold Coast: 1955. A Report by Sir P. Griffiths and Mr. J. Watt. London: 1955.

Gardner, J. C. Oilseed Processing in Nigeria. A Report to the Government of Nigeria and the Nigerian Groundnut Marketing Board. 1952.

Industrial Development Company. Feasibility Study: Diversified Nigerian Wood Products Industries. A Report for Rockefeller Bros. Fund. Tacoma, Washington: 1960.

Industries Development Corporation, Ltd. Nails Plant for Eastern Nigeria. A Report for Rockefeller Bros. Fund. Jerusalem: 1960.

Massler, A. I., and Gershen, I. J. A Feasibility Report on the Establishment of a Phonograph Record and General Plastics Industry in Nigeria. A Report for Rockefeller Brothers Fund. Maplewood, N.J.: 1961.

Moore, Frank, et al. Prospects and Policies for Development of the Eastern Region of Nigeria. A Report Prepared by a Ford Foundation team. Enugu, 1960.

NEDECO and Balfour, Beatty & Co. Ltd. Niger Dams Project. A Report in Seven Volumes for the Federal Government of Nigeria and the Electricity Corporation of Nigeria. The Hague and London: April, 1961.

Production Engineering Management Group (Nigeria), Ltd. Compendium of Basic Information Relating to the Proposed Iron and Steel Industry and Market Survey of Iron and Steel Products. A Report Prepared for the National Economic Council of Nigeria. Lagos: 1961.

Robinson, H., et al. The Economic Co-ordination of Transport Development in Nigeria. A Report Prepared by the Stanford Research Institute for the Joint Planning Committee, National Economic Council, Federation of Nigeria. Menlo Park: 1961.

Scheur Textile Consultants, Inc. Feasibility Report on Integrated Textile Mill in the Eastern Region of the Federation of Nigeria. A Report Prepared for the Rockefeller Bros. Fund. New York: 1961.

Shell-BP Petroleum Development Company of Nigeria, Ltd. The Story of Oil in Nigeria. 1960.

Stanford Research Institute. Technical and Economic Feasibility of a Structural Clay Tile Plant for Western Nigeria. A Report Prepared for the Rockefeller Bros. Fund. Menlo Park: 1959.

Stanley Engineering (Nigeria), Ltd. Feasibility Report on Cement Manufacturing Industry in the Northern Region of the Federation of Nigeria. A Report Prepared for the Rockefeller Bros. Fund. Lagos: 1961.

______. Feasibility Report on Concrete Masonry Products Industry in Federation of Nigeria. A Report Prepared for the Rockefeller Bros. Fund. Lagos: 1960.

______. Feasibility Report on Plastics Industry in Federation of Nigeria. A Report Prepared for the Rockefeller Bros. Fund. Lagos: 1960.

Stephenson-Walsh and Associates, Inc. The Economic and Technical Feasibility of a Machete Manufacturing Plant for Nigeria. A Report Prepared for the Rockefeller Bros. Fund. York, Pennsylvania: 1960.

Westinghouse Electric International Co., et al. Report on the Feasibility of Establishing an Integrated Steel Mill in Nigeria. A Report Prepared for the Federation of Nigeria. New York: 1961.

Wood, R. C. Report on the Possibilities for Cigar Leaf and Cigar Production in Nigeria. A Report Prepared for the Rockefeller Bros. Fund. New York: 1961.

Unpublished Materials

Callaway, Arch C. School Leavers and the Developing Economy of Nigeria. Ibadan, 1961. (Mimeographed.)

Hoslett, Schuyler. Working Paper on the Proposed Nigerian Center of Management and Administration. A Report Prepared for the Ford Foundation. Lagos, 1961. (Mimeographed.)

Jackson, E. F., and Okigbo, P. N. C. National Income of Nigeria for the Period 1950-57. Lagos: Federal Ministry of Economic Development, 1960. (Mimeographed.)

Manderstan, L. H. and Partners. Enquiry Into the Economics of Cottonseed Crushing in Northern Nigeria. A Private Report Prepared for Mr. George Calil of Kano. London: 1956.

Nigeria. Federal Institute of Industrial Research. Annual Report: 1959-60. Oshodi, 1960. (Mimeographed.)

______. Federal Ministry of Commerce and Industry. Some Existing Industries in Nigeria. Lagos, 1961. (Mimeographed.)

Northern Region. Ministry of Trade and Industry. The Industrial Development of Northern Nigeria. Kaduna, 1961. (Mimeographed.)

Stolper, W., Hansen, L., and Iwuagwu, E. O. Government Expenditures on Goods and Services. Lagos: Federal Ministry of Economic Development, 1961. (Mimeographed.)

Summary of News from Nigerian Daily Newspapers. New York: Nigerian Consulate-General, 1961. (Mimeographed.)

Terrel, Charles L. Private Enterprise Program for Nigeria. A Report Prepared for the ICA by the Chief of the Industrial Development Division, USOM/Nigeria. Lagos: 1961. (Mimeographed.)

Western Region. Ministry of Trade and Industry. Schedule of Industries Operating in Western Nigeria. Ibadan: 1960. (Mimeographed.)

Wood, C. W., and Alderman, L. Production of Metallurgical Coke Using Pitch Blending (Large Scale Tests). A Report to the Nigerian Coal Corporation (CWD Ref. No. R/45/3/2). 1961. (Mimeographed.)

INDEX